The Hebrew God

The Hebrew God

Portrait of an Ancient Deity

Bernhard Lang

Yale University Press
New Haven and London

For information about this and other Yale University Press publications, please contact:
U.S. Office: sales.press@yale.edu   yalebooks.com
Europe Office: sales@yaleup.co.uk   www.yaleup.co.uk

Set in Ehrhardt by SNP Best-set Typesetter Ltd, Hong Kong
Printed in Great Britain by The Bath Press

Library of Congress Control Number: 2001098607

A catalogue record for this book is available from the British Library.

10 9 8 7 6 5 4 3 2 1

Contents

Preface

The Hebrew God ranks as the most distinguished deity on record in human history. Although beginning his career in the worship of a small and politically insignificant people on the eastern shore of the Mediterranean, he became the God first of Jewish and then also of Christian monotheism. Originally known by the name of Yahweh, he belonged with Zeus, Marduk, Mars, and Venus to the deities of the ancient world. Later, his devotees no longer used his name, for he had become, quite simply, God—the only god, the one who holds the universe in his hands and controls the course of history as well as the fate of the individual.

The present book deals with the character of this god as it was seen when he still had a name but was already acknowledged as the deity of monotheism—at a time when the other gods had begun to fade, at least in the eyes of his believers. The basis of our research is a collection of ancient Hebrew writings which, traditionally entitled the Old Testament, is still treated in church and synagogue as sacred scripture. Today, Jews and Christians see their religion in continuity, however defined and debated, with the Old Testament, and they consider the deity of that book as the God they worship, celebrate, trust, pray to, and believe in. It is he whom they call "the Lord" and "the Almighty." It is of him that they sing "Holy, holy, holy is the Lord of hosts; the whole earth is full of his glory." It is of him that they profess with confidence: "The Lord is my shepherd, I shall not want." It is his commandment that they respect: "You shall have no other gods besides me." When reciting the Christian creed, believers affirm: "I believe in God the Father almighty, creator of heaven and earth." No other deity can boast a biography comparable to that of the Hebrew God.

Strangely, this unprecedented and truly divine career in the hearts and minds of the believers—and unbelievers, who as atheists reject the monotheistic, Hebrew God—has not been matched by an equal amount of scholarly interest. In recent decades, historians of religion have typically studied this deity's names, mythology (or lack thereof), female companion (for whom there is no solid, conclusive evidence), ancient Near Eastern background, and monolatric worship. Their contributions are often innovative and impressive, but generally stay on the level of unstructured, unclassified details. Scholars have failed to produce a comprehensive and convincing account of the Hebrew God, one that sums up and completes previous research. The present book is meant to fill this gap.

Two basic assumptions underlie and inspire my presentation: the indebtedness of the Hebrew God—and indeed of all of biblical culture—to the ancient Near Eastern civilizations, especially to those of Mesopotamia and Egypt; and the value of anthropological theory as an aid in interpreting religious history.

When nineteenth-century scholars began to translate the newly discovered and deciphered hieroglyphic and cuneiform texts, they were far from encountering a vanished world. Many of the texts translated from the ancient sources and a great variety of objects displayed in museums did not appear foreign and incomprehensible, but were instead "strangely familiar," "déjà vu," and immediately understood, for they were rightly recognized as belonging to the culture in which the Bible had originated. As Morton Smith has suggested, we should think of Israel's religion "as one form of the common religion of the ancient Near East."[1] To the cultural historian, it no longer makes sense to discuss things biblical without reference to their ancient context; it is therefore imperative to represent this context by quoting ancient writings and tapping the rich resources of the art of Egypt and Western Asia. These venerable civilizations had their last period of efflorescence during the first millennium B.C.E. When Alexander the Great established his universal empire toward the end of the fourth century B.C.E., they were in rapid decline. Their legacy was best preserved by the biblical people. Between the seventh and the second centuries B.C.E., Israel's religion metamorphosed into a book religion that conserved much of the ancient Near Eastern culture and placed it as a legacy into the hands of both Jews and Christians. Despite its narrow, monotheistic, partisan outlook, biblical literature nevertheless shares fundamental notions with those surrounding civilizations. It often echoes Bronze Age poetry, seeks to solve problems of Bronze Age theology, and lends the mask of its one deity to a multitude of ancient gods. As Othmar Keel has observed, Israel not only inherited much light from its surrounding cultures, it also served as a lens that collected straying rays of light, concentrating them into one single, powerful ray.[2]

Just as Judaism and Christianity have their roots in biblical Israel, so ancient Hebrew culture has its basis in the antecedent high cultures. In considering these striking continuities we get a broad perspective on Western history. In religion, as in other areas of life and thought, we still have strong links to the Bronze Age civilizations of the ancient East, for it was there and at that time (ca. 3400–1200 B.C.E.) that the scribal arts were invented, the state first united large groups of people, and spiritual ideas and institutions were first and fundamentally shaped. Just as our Latin alphabet goes back to the ancient scribes, so our concept of God is owed to the priests, sages, and prophets. In examining these early cultural forms, we study our own beginnings. As Barry Kemp aptly puts it: "We still live in the shadow of the Bronze Age."[3]

Understanding depends on theory. The cultural and anthropological theory used in the present study is a simplified and adapted version of Georges Dumézil's view of the "three functions." With rare exceptions among scholars—Jean Lambert in France, Nicolas Wyatt in Scotland, Hans Lundager Jensen in Denmark, and the late Geo Widengren in Sweden, for instance—this theory has not been applied to the Bible and its cultural world. When I taught at the Sorbonne and the Ecole des Hautes Etudes en Sciences Sociales in the early 1990s, I came across Dumézil's *La religion romaine archaïque*. No sooner had I begun to read, than I became totally immersed in this great work, and the more I read, the more I came to realize its potential as an analytical guide in dealing with ancient Semitic religions. The unexpected encounter with the oeuvre of Dumézil gave me the idea of describing the Hebrew God as the lord of the three gifts of wisdom, victory, and life. From the notion of the three gifts it was only a small step to developing the structure for the present work: a portrait of the Hebrew God in five images, with each image sketched in a section of its own. The first image presents God as the giver of wisdom, the second as the lord of war, and the remaining three as the creator and sustainer of the life of animals, humans, and plants. Each of the chapters may be read and appreciated independently of the others, just as one may look at an isolated canvas in a series of paintings portraying the same person. Nevertheless, the five images are meant to be part of a single, comprehensive portrait.

In applying trifunctional analysis to biblical religion, we depart from Dumézil's notion that in its pronounced form the tripartite ideology is unique to Indo-European civilizations. Freed from such exclusivity, the theory of functional tripartition may help us achieve a better understanding of biblical literature, religion, and culture. A simple yet powerful tool, it renders us more sensitive to the material at hand, and develops our capacity for analysis and synthesis in interpretation. It helps us see many features that we have previously missed, overlooked, or understood imperfectly. It improves our insight into ancient civilizations. Tripartite theory, moreover, with its conceptual economy, can usefully simplify the complexity typical of social and religious realities of the biblical world. In applying tripartite theory we follow a well-known rule of historical and sociological research. In his *Gay Science*, Friedrich Nietzsche ironically defined the "thinker" as "one who knows how to make things simpler than they are."[4] Whatever Nietzsche may have meant to say, he gave a correct description of what historians do. Applying what has been called the method of "disciplined exaggeration in the service of knowledge," they simplify by reducing complex realities to elementary structures.[5] "Every discipline," explains Sir Ralf Dahrendorf, "if it is to make its statements precise and testable, must reduce its huge subject matter to certain elements from which may be systematically reconstructed, if not a portrait of the reality of experience, then a structure in whose tissue a segment of reality may be caught."[6] The recognition of basic patterns enables us to pose and answer crucial questions and to uncover important interconnections that would otherwise remain hidden and undetected. So while academic research involves a certain reductionism and fails to capture the fullness of reality, this disadvantage is genuinely compensated for in other respects. What we may lose in detail, we gain in clarity and understanding.

Armed with the insight of Dumézil and drawing, as will be evident, on sources from Egypt and the ancient Near East, I hope to paint a fresh and vivid portrait of the biblical God that is reasonably sophisticated in detail while at the same time sufficiently sharp in profile.

Biblical texts are generally quoted from the New Revised Standard Version, but I have occasionally deviated from this convention in the interests of style or accuracy. I depart from most biblical translations in retaining the divine name Yahweh, for this seems unavoidable in a historical study such as ours—with apologies to all who, for religious reasons, prefer to write YHWH and to read "the Lord."

The writing of *The Hebrew God* was made possible by teachers I have had in the past and facilitated by friends and colleagues on whose help I can rely in the present. Among my teachers, I have the pleasure to name the late Hellmut Brunner, who introduced me to the world of hieroglyphs and served as the ideal guide on a tour of Egypt, and the late Wolfram von Soden, under whom I had the privilege to study Assyriology. Other colleagues and friends who have helped me along the way include Bruce Chilton, Jean-Georges Heintz, Tim Ingold, Catherine Kerr-Dineen, Robert Murray SJ, Daniel Schwemer, Robert Shore, Solfrid Storøy, Denise Sokolowski, Gia Toussaint, John R. Williams (to whom I owe an English version of a few lines from Goethe's *Four Seasons*), and Nicolas Wyatt. Special mention must be made of Ronald Piper, who generously invited me to teach at the University of St. Andrews in Scotland. To all of them, I am very much indebted.

Introduction
Lord of Three Gifts: A New Approach to the Hebrew God

According to a well-known biblical story, King Solomon requested the gift of governmental wisdom from God, but Yahweh also granted him, in addition to a wise and discerning mind, victory and long life. This and other, related traditions not only highlight the three tasks of the king who must govern and secure peace and wealth for his people, but also reveal the nature of the Hebrew God as a deity owning the three gifts of wisdom, victory, and life. These gifts can be understood in terms of a theory developed by the French scholar Georges Dumézil (1898–1986), a specialist in Indo-European religion and folklore. Dumézil describes Indo-European culture as being based on the "tripartition" of society into priests, warriors, and food producers, echoed in a corresponding tripartition of the pantheon into sovereign gods, war deities, and divine providers of wealth. This chapter introduces Dumézil's theory, discusses its applicability to ancient Near Eastern cultures, and argues that the notion of the three divine gifts can be used as the basis for studying the character of the Hebrew God. Thus, five images of the Hebrew God may be constructed: Lord of Wisdom, Lord of War, and Lord of Life, with the last of these subdivided into the more particular ones of Lord of the Animals, Lord of the Individual, and Lord of the Harvest.

Most of the things they teach us are certainly quite right and true, but you can also look at them in a different way than the teachers do—and generally they make much better sense.

Hermann Hesse, *Demian*

1.   Dumézil, the Deluge, and the Dream of Solomon

A common Indo-European myth tells of the first man or king.[1] He was dismembered, and from the three parts of his body came the three social classes that make up society: from his head came the most noble, priestly class; from his upper torso the warrior class, characterized by courage and physical energy; finally, the commoners came from the lower torso of the primeval victim, i.e. from the part of the body that is reproductive and corresponds to sexuality and food production.[2]

For all its apparent simplicity, this mythical narrative conveys a manifold message. The image of the human body suggests that the various social classes belong together, forming an integrated whole, just as the various parts of the human body constitute an organic, functional unit. A complex cultural phenomenon—the distinction of social classes—is explained in terms of a natural symbol, the human body. The myth also says something about different positions within a hierarchical structure: priests and warriors occupy the higher, more respected ranks, whereas the commoners—peasants and artisans—form the lower classes. It is not accidental that the first man is often called the first king in this mythology. The identification of the king with the complete body implies a significant political philosophy: the king does not belong to a specific social class or group, but transcends and encompasses all social classes. Symbolizing their essential unity, he is responsible for and must promote their cooperation.

According to this view, social life is based on harmonious cooperation between three social classes: the intellectuals or sages, the warriors, and the peasants. Each of these groups satisfies certain basic needs of the society as a whole. The teachers provide leadership and education; they not only teach and perpetuate their own elite, but also provide teaching and leadership for the entire community. Moreover, they offer sacrifices and thereby fulfill the duties of priests. The warriors protect not only themselves, but the entire society, making life secure. Finally, the peasants produce food not only for themselves, but for the other two groups as well. If one of the three castes or estates does not perform its duty properly, social life—or life in general—suffers or simply becomes impossible. The harmonious interaction and cooperation of the various social groups lead to what may be termed "tripartite completeness." The tripartite social structure ranks as one of the most widespread political philosophies. Its archaic elegance and brilliant simplicity remain admirable.

The social theory of the three classes has often been noted, but in the twentieth century no one has spent more energy working out its implications than Georges Dumézil, who made an original and quite fruitful discovery. Analyzing the traditions of the Indians, Scandinavians, Germanic peoples, and Greeks and Romans, he realized that the tripartite system is not merely social, but also applied to other domains such as religion, mythology, medicine, folklore, narrative, and law. Thus Dumézil and his school explored the three kinds of punishment envisaged by certain legal traditions and the three kinds of medicine administered in certain medical systems. According to a common ancient medical idea, there are three ways of treating illness: with magic spells, with the surgeon's knife, and with herbal medicine. It is easy to see that the three remedies correspond to the priestly, the military, and the food-producing classes.

Dumézil's most significant discovery concerned religion, however. He realized that deities and spirits were often organized according to this trifunctional pattern, for the same tripartite system underlies both the divine world and human society. In human society, the three components are teachers, warriors, and peasants; in religion, there are wise deities, gods of war, and demons promoting fertility. Each of the three agents, human or divine, has a particular mandate or, in the language of Dumézil, a certain "function." Dumézil's descriptions of the three basic social mandates and the corresponding three divine "functions" or domains can be summarized as follows:

The First Function: sovereignty and the sacred. In society, ultimate leadership is in the hands of teachers, jurists, and priests; in the divine world, it is in the hands of a father of the gods—for the Greeks, Zeus, and for the Romans, Jupiter (whose name means, etymologically, "Zeus father"). In India, two gods occupy the supreme rank: Mitra and Varuna, representing the divine lawyer and the celestial magician.

The Second Function: war or, more generally, physical power and bravery in fighting. In human society, this duty or "function" is assigned to the military commander (often corresponding with the warrior king) and to the army. In the realm of the gods, a heavenly army or a Lord of War make fighting their business: the Roman god Mars and the Indian god Indra are good examples.

The Third Function: life, supported by fertility and food, and culminating in prosperity and wealth. In social life, the task of producing and supplying food falls to the peasants and the lower classes, for premodern societies derive their wealth primarily from farming and livestock husbandry—from their crops and the products of their flocks and herds. In the realm of the gods the Third Function is often represented by a plethora of deities—in Rome by Quirinus, who watched over the supply of grain, but also by Ceres, the grain goddess; Ops, the female personification of abundance; Flora, the goddess of flowering; Lucina and Diana, the goddesses of childbirth; and many others. These gods and goddesses maintain and promote plant and animal fertility, assure bountiful harvests, and generally preside over matters of human physical wellbeing and comfort. In India, the foremost Third Function deities are the Nâsatyas, divine twins whose twinhood suggests abundance.

An easy way to remember the three social functions—the basic concepts and spheres of human and divine action—is to name them wisdom, war, and wealth.

Dumézil was repeatedly asked two questions: Are the three functions, rather than being specific to a certain homogeneous cultural group like the Indo-Europeans, actually universal and are they therefore present in *all* societies? And: can tripartite analysis be applied to documents of Semitic provenance such as the Bible? The Bible was a kind of test case, and Dumézil acknowledged that there are a few scattered instances in it in which tripartite thought can be discerned.[3] But in ancient Israel tripartite thought never developed into a generalized, pervasive approach to reality. Dumézil insisted that only the Indo-Europeans formalized the three functions into a "tripartite ideology." The three needs as such "are in fact basic everywhere," he admitted; but "the majority of human groups have been content merely to satisfy" them, "without theorizing about them" and placing them at the center of their thought.[4] Nevertheless, Dumézil was not dogmatic about his interpretation. This is his final verdict on the subject: "We must continue to scrutinize the Bible, the Semitic texts of the Near East and consider even Egypt, looking for possible instances of the tripartite structure and determine whether they are indigenous and how they function within the ideology of a given people."[5]

The present writer assumes that there is indeed evidence of tripartite thought in the Bible. Can we account for its existence? It may be due to cultural borrowing from neighboring civilizations that had developed or adopted ideological tripartism. In historical times, there were many contacts between Indo-Europeans and other peoples. Horsemanship and chariot warfare, developed by Indo-Europeans, spread throughout the Near East; dragon-slaying mythology is shared by both groups; a significant number of Indo-Aryan personal names appear in ancient Semitic sources.[6] Conversely, Semitic words can be found in the languages of ancient India.[7] There must also have been contact in prehistoric times. It has been argued that the shared vocabulary of the proto-Semitic and the proto-Indo-European languages reflects a common culture in which the Indo-Europeans borrowed from the Semites. Accordingly, an area immediately to the north of Assyria has been suggested as the original homeland of the Indo-Europeans.[8] Borrowing may have taken place in both directions, and elements of ideological tripartism may have found their way from the Indo-Europeans to the Semites.

There could be a much simpler explanation, however, for the tripartite structure may be considered as somehow *universal*, reflecting an elementary mode of social organization. Dumézil described the three functions with great virtuosity, but, placing the emphasis on specific cultural traditions, he neglected their archetypal and universal character. The archetypal basis of the three functions is easy to understand. Imagine a simple society with only a small number of people, for example a horde of archaic hunters and gatherers living at an early stage of human history. In this group we can recognize the three functions and assign them to different individuals. The First Function is doubtlessly represented by the older members of the group: they provide leadership, set policy, and give advice, based on their experience in life. The young, vigorous lad stands for the Second Function: he and his peers are trained in the use of weapons and warfare and protect the group from enemies. Women, who bear children and at the same time collect food or, under advanced conditions, cultivate gardens, are responsible for the Third Function. Only as long as each element performs its duty and the members harmonize can the group as a whole survive and prosper. At this stage, social life can be analyzed in terms of the division of labor, and the labor is assigned to three different functional groups. In those cases where a counsel of elders or a chief or, at a later stage, a king emerged, this central institution transcended the functional division of labor, controlled its proper management, and embodied in itself the three mandates of wisdom, victory, and wealth.[9]

While we depart from Dumézil in claiming the universality of the tripartite system, we join him in emphasizing its *implicit* rather than explicit character. The worldview of a particular culture, called its "ideology" by Dumézil and defined as "an idea and an appreciation of the great forces that sustain and shape the world and society, and their connections," is often "only implicit and must be drawn out by an analysis of what is plainly said about the gods and especially their activities in the theology and mythology associated with them."[10] Here Dumézil is alluding to the well-known insight that the rules and patterns that anthropologists seek to discern in social institutions, ritual, and mythology are analytical devices constructed by the modern observers rather than theories known to the people they study.[11] In other words: it is the interpreter's task, with the help of modern theory, to discover and describe the hidden philosophy, theology, and spiritual universe that underlie the relevant documents. In what follows, we will discuss several instances in which it makes sense to read certain ancient Semitic sources or institutions in the light of tripartite notions.

The Babylonian Deluge: A Tripartite Reading

The Babylonian version of the myth of the deluge, the great flood sent by the gods to destroy humankind, shows the gods in dramatic interaction, conflict, and eventual reconciliation.[12] The principal divine characters in this story—Enki, Enlil, Nintu—are three in number, and they can be understood as standing for the three functions. The account begins with the creation of humankind. Advised by the wise god Enki, the goddess Nintu fashions men and women from clay, mixed with the flesh and blood of a god who has been specially slaughtered for the purpose. Nintu also establishes the marriage bond, endows humans with the power to procreate, and fixes a ten-month period for pregnancy. Once created, men and women multiply at a tremendous rate, and the gods begin to feel that their creatures make too much noise, which prevents them from sleeping. So one of the gods, the fierce Enlil, persuades the divine assembly that humankind should be destroyed. After various attempted methods of destruction—such as drought and the plague—have failed to produce the desired result, a terrible thunderstorm is sent and a flood ensues, covering the entire surface of the earth. But the flood is not entirely successful in its goal, for Enki has forewarned a man named Atrahasis of the divine plan. Atrahasis has therefore built a huge boat in which he and a certain number of animals might survive the deluge. While the goddess Nintu laments the death of her creatures, Enlil becomes angry with Enki, whom he accuses of obstructing the divine assembly's resolution. Eventually, however, the two gods are reconciled, and Enki tells Nintu to limit the success of female pregnancy and to let demons snatch a baby from its mother's lap.

The god Enlil, who is explicitly called a "warrior," represents the Second Function; with his insistence on the destruction of humanity, he reflects the excesses characteristic of the military mind. Nintu, called the "womb goddess," must be seen as a Third Function figure, for she is ultimately responsible for the ongoing existence of human life through marriage, procreation, pregnancy, and birth. As life-giving and life-destroying forces, Nintu and Enlil are set against each other. The god Enki mediates between the two by imposing limits on both the creation and the destruction of human life. At the beginning of the myth, as a concession to Nintu, he finds a way of preventing Enlil's flood from destroying all of humankind; at the end, as a concession to Enlil, he imposes limits on Nintu's creation of new life. Just as Enlil must renounce his destructive ambitions, so Nintu must forsake her wish to create babies who are immune to demonic attack. It is not difficult to see that Enki is here depicted as a wise and friendly being, as a god who obstructs the other gods' plans so as to determine the final outcome of the story. Often called "lord of wisdom"[13] in cuneiform texts, Enki represents the First Function, that of sovereign god and creator. The cooperation, conflict, and final reconciliation of the three deities

Enki, Enlil, and Nintu form the plot of one of Mesopotamia's central myths, a myth clearly amenable to tripartite analysis. As will be argued presently, the same is true of the biblical story of Solomon's dream.

The Dream of King Solomon: A Tripartite Reading

Favored by Israel's national God, Yahweh, Solomon was the wisest and wealthiest of all kings. God appeared to King Solomon in a dream and promised him the granting of a wish. Solomon's wish was as follows: "Give your servant an understanding mind to govern your people, able to discern between good and evil." God answered:

> Because you have asked this, and have not asked for yourself long life or riches, or for the life of your enemies, but have asked for yourself understanding to discern what is right, I now do according to your word. Indeed I give you a wise and discerning mind; no one like you has been before you and no one like you shall arise after you. (1 Kgs 3:9, 11–12)

God's granting of a wish apparently implies a test: without knowing what is at stake, Solomon must ask for the highest-ranking divine gift, wisdom, and not for health and wealth or the death of his enemies. The king's wish must be for intellectual goods that facilitate the peaceful administration of his country; any other wish would mean that he fails the test. But in fact Solomon's wish was the proper one, to God's satisfaction: "It pleased Yahweh that Solomon had asked this" (1 Kgs 3:10). By requesting wisdom—the one thing he might legitimately and successfully ask for—Solomon transcended what someone like Job, the private citizen, would want: health and wealth. He also stood above the wish of the revengeful warrior, the desire to kill his enemies. Yet at the same time, God granted Solomon more gifts than he had wished for: "I give you also what you have not asked, wealth and glory all your life; no other king shall compare with you" (1 Kgs 3:13). While the Hebrew expression "wealth and glory" presumably refers only to wealth, the dream story as a whole clearly implies that God grants all three gifts: wisdom, wealth, and victory. While wisdom is here extolled as God's foremost gift, victory and wealth are not devalued. The king needs all three gifts to govern his people properly and to guide them in all situations, for the life of the nation depends on all of them.

The story of King Solomon transports us into a dream-like world, one that we normally associate with fairy tales or stories from *The Arabian Nights*. Solomon's superior wisdom is highlighted not only in the dream, but also throughout the account—he appears as the wise judge, the famous compiler of books, the organizer of the national administration, the builder of the temple. We are also told how Solomon had his personal enemies killed, and that he boasted a standing army of numerous chariots and horsemen. His wealth is evident from his sumptuous palace, his many wives, and his lavish entertainment of guests, some, like the queen of Sheba, traveling from foreign lands. The palace was flooded with riches that came from his own country as well as with presents from other kingdoms. Even his drinking vessels (normally made of earthenware) were of pure gold.[14] King Solomon's reign lasted a very long time—forty years—and he appears to have died in old age, in peace. Both King Solomon's dream and the story of his reign convey a sense of tripartite completeness—the harmony achieved through the use of God's three gifts: wisdom, military strength, and wealth.

If we wish to enter the intellectual world in which Solomon's dream originated, we have to consider parts of the Bible that are deemed difficult, that are not understood as easily as the lively narrative passages. In the Bible two kinds of language can be distinguished. The first, represented by the story of Solomon's dream, is vivid, almost always immediately understandable, elaborate in its description and narrative development. The second can be found in some of the psalms and in the prophetic and apocalyptic writings. Here poetry or theological argument dominates, narrative is either in short supply and allusive or altogether absent, and the modern reader more often than not has a hard time penetrating the density of its religious, esoteric-sounding vocabulary and making sense of its fragmentary nature. Borrowing notions developed from the discipline of socio-linguistics, we may call the first type of language the "elaborated style" and the second, with its density and heaviness, the "restricted style," or style of the priests. If we want to find out about the character and nature of the Hebrew God, we should not be content merely to study the Bible's "elaborated" texts, for the "restricted" ones, properly understood, occasionally provide invaluable insights into the basic ideas presupposed by and underlying the elaborated literature.

Using scattered biblical texts of the "restricted," priestly type, we can recognize and in part reconstruct the ritual performance that inspired the story of King Solomon's dream. That performance is the ritual of the royal induction, practiced at the Jerusalem temple during the period of the Judean monarchy each time a new ruler was to assume office. It was possibly practiced more often, as the Judeans may well have imitated the Babylonians in annually renewing the royal induction at every New Year celebration in the fall.[15] The most vivid, though brief and elliptic, description of the royal induction can be found in the book of Daniel. Here a man is led before God and given three gifts:

> I saw one like a human being coming with the clouds of heaven. And he came to the Ancient One and was presented before him. To him was given dominion and glory and kingship, that all peoples, nations, and languages should serve him. His dominion is an everlasting dominion that shall not pass away, and his kingship is one that shall never be destroyed. (Dan 7:13–14)

The scene echoed here must have taken place in the temple of Jerusalem: accompanied by clouds of incense,[16] the candidate was led before a statue or symbol representing the deity.[17] There he was given the power to be active in the three spheres of royal rule: dominion, glory, and kingship. "Dominion" seems to refer to the power to administrate (Aramaic *shaltân*, sultanship), "glory" to wealth (*yeqâr*, actually "precious objects"), and "kingship" (*malkû*) to royal warfare. These three realms of royal rule correspond to the divine gifts of Solomon's dream in the following way:

Royal induction (Dan 7)	Solomon's dream (1 Kgs 3)
dominion	wise and understanding mind
kingship	life of the enemies
glory	long life and riches

Evidence from Egypt and Mesopotamia suggests that at this moment the king also received his regalia, perhaps three objects representing the three divine gifts. Of these, we can recognize one: a weapon, standing for the divine gift of victory.[18] It seems to have been handed to the king with the words "Rule in the midst of your foes" (Ps 110:2). In the sacred and often exaggerated courtly rhetoric (the so-called *Hofstil*) of the book of Daniel, the sovereignty of the king is over *all* nations, and not just over his own people, and the rule is forever, i.e. it will be passed on to the king's successors. One of the royal psalms uses similar language when a prophet addresses the new king in the following manner: "Ask of me [God], and I will make the nations your heritage, and the ends of the earth your possession. You shall break them with a rod of iron, and dash them in pieces like a potter's vessel" (Ps 2:8–9). This poem implies a reference to the king's request for victory, subsequent to prophetic exhortation. From other, scattered passages we can reconstruct two more requests: one for "life" (meaning long life) and one for "wisdom," so that we have three requests corresponding to the three spheres of royal rule.[19] As part of the royal enthronement ritual, the king was asked three times what he requested, and his answer had to be: wisdom, victory, and long life.

During the royal induction, the king is also given special honorific titles that reflect the duties implied in his office. The New Revised Standard Version renders the four throne names mentioned by the prophet Isaiah of Jerusalem as follows: "Wonderful Counselor, Mighty God, Everlasting Father, Prince of Peace" (Isa 9:6/Hebr. 9:5).[20] The first title, "Wonderful Counselor," suggests the divine gift of wise leadership. The Hebrew term *yo'ez* refers to the wise counselor working at the royal court, but here it is the king himself who is the foremost of the sages. The second title, "Mighty God," corresponds to the gift of victory. In the Hebrew Bible, "might" (*geburah*) is the regular attribute of the warrior, who is often designated by the same term—"the mighty one" (*gibbor*). We may also translate the title as "Divine Warrior." The third title,

"Everlasting Father," suggests the king's endowment with wealth, and we may think of a rich patron who cares for his clients, the latter being somehow co-extensive with the entire society. He is the one who provides and on festive occasions distributes food among the population, giving to both men and women.[21] The last title on the list, the one generally, though somewhat color-lessly, rendered as "Prince of Peace" (*sar shalom*), may alternatively be trans-lated as "Prince of Prosperity," "Prince of Abundance," "Prince of Plenty," or "Prince of Wellbeing." *Shalom* serves to express not the opposite of war but a comprehensive state of wellbeing, associated specifically with the ideas of wealth, abundance of food, and fertility. The "Prince of Plenty" is clearly a king endowed with another special divine gift.

It is easy to see how the royal names relate to the three divine gifts given to the king, and we can now complete the table offered above:

	Royal induction (Dan 7)	Royal induction (Isa 9)	Solomon's dream (1 Kgs 3)
First gift: wisdom	dominion	Wonderful Counselor	wise and discerning mind
Second gift: victory	kingship	Mighty God	life of the enemies (also Ps 2:8)
Third gift: wealth	glory	Everlasting Father, Prince of Peace	long life and riches (also Ps 21:4/Hebr. 21:5)

The duplication of the royal title referring to the divine gifts of wealth and wellbeing—"Everlasting Father, Prince of Peace"—highlights the fact that the nation's wellbeing ranks as the king's foremost responsibility.

Although Israel's tradition makes the nation's efficient functioning depen-dent upon the monarch, the king is not alone in performing these mandates. He is helped by the three classes that, in theory at least, make up society. The prophet Jeremiah calls them the "wise," the "mighty," and the "wealthy" (Jer 9:23/Hebr. 9:22). The "wise one" or "sage" represents the educated elite—the scribal class of bureaucrats, administrators, and priests. The "mighty one" is the soldier, and the "wealthy one" must be the rich landowner and farmer who stands for the third of the divine gifts: the one granting the production of food and, ultimately, wealth.

2. The Thesis of the Present Book

Once we have gained an insight into the nature of Israel's God as the Lord of Three Gifts, we can review the biblical record and related traditions and study in detail how Yahweh dispenses these gifts, bestowing them upon his people and perhaps upon humankind as a whole (for he eventually came to be considered the deity of monotheism, the creator and sustainer of all life). This review of the biblical tradition, the subject of the present book, leads to the following five images of the Hebrew God:

— As dispenser of the First Gift, wisdom, Israel's God is a benign, wise ruler, who owns and directs the universe. We may call him the Lord of Wisdom (1). The Lord of Wisdom rules, promulgates the law, and judges; the Hebrew verb *shafat*, "to judge, to rule," can be used as a representative term to designate divine leadership. In this sense, the psalmist says, "God is a righteous judge [*shofet*]" (Ps 7:12), and Isaiah, "Yahweh is our judge [*shofet*], Yahweh is our ruler" (Isa 33:22).

— As the one who assists on the battlefield and grants the Second Gift, victory in war, he shows himself a bellicose deity, prone to anger and destruction, most often helping the Israelites in their wars against their enemies. He can be called the Lord of War (2). The Divine Warrior conquers and rescues his followers from the hands of the foes; as Isaiah says, in the passage just quoted, "Yahweh is our king; he will save us [*yashaʿ*]." Acting as the Divine Warrior, Yahweh rescues or delivers (*yashaʿ*) people from the hands of the enemy, or comes to their help (*yashaʿ*) when they are in difficult situations.

— As the ultimate source of the Third Gift, life in all its positive meanings, the Hebrew God cares for animals and human beings alike. As Lord of the Animals (3), he acts as a spirit of nature who cares for the wild beasts, blessing both animals and people with the power to reproduce. As Lord of the Individual (4), or "personal god," as historians of religion have come to call him, he protects and blesses individuals even prior to birth, and throughout the course of their lives is responsible for the health and general well-being of each person. Finally, as Lord of the Harvest (5), he unceasingly provides for the local or territorial community and grants general prosperity; he does this primarily by sending rain and thereby blessing the peasants' fields with abundance. When looking for a Hebrew term to denote the central activity of the Lord of the Animals, the Personal God, and the Lord of the Harvest, there is only one word that suggests itself: he "blesses" (*berekh*).

In order to speak meaningfully about the Hebrew God and to make sense of the ancient sources, we will use a specific cultural theory as an analytical and interpretive tool: the "trifunctional theory" associated with the name of Georges Dumézil. This theory not only enables us to interpret the Hebrew experience of God in terms of the three divine gifts of sovereignty (First Function), victory (Second Function), and life (productivity, wellbeing, wealth—Third Function); it also helps us to understand that the Third Function is represented by three divine roles, not just one. For this point we rely on comparative evidence provided by Dumézil. In studying the leading divine triad of the earliest religion of Rome—Jupiter, Mars, and Quirinus—he notes that Quirinus, the god who watches over the supply of grain, did not cover all aspects of the Third Function, and lists other Third Function deities: Ops, the goddess of abundance and opulence; Flora, the goddess of flowering; and Lucina and Diana, the goddesses of childbirth. Due to their involvement in the concrete matters of life, Third Function deities are more numerous, more varied, and more specialized than First and Second Function ones. This can be explained in terms of the relatively simple definition of intellectual and military activities as compared with "the innumerable particular patterns of behavior demanded by the exploitation of different soils, the raising of various kinds of animals, and the administration of increasingly differentiated riches, as well as the supervision of health and fertility, and the enjoyment of the pleasure of the senses."[22] "One result of this parceling out of the Third Function, at Rome and elsewhere, is that none of the gods who patronize it partially can represent it completely."[23] Moreover, Third Function deities tend to be distinguished from those of the higher functions by the fact that "they may willingly live like humans, and among them."[24] Both this variety within the image of the Third Function deity and its radical closeness to human life are also to be found in the biblical texts. In the Bible, God's Third Function roles—which we term Lord of the Animals, Lord of the Individual, and Lord of the Harvest—are clearly more varied than the roles of Lord of Wisdom or Lord of War.

Just as a portrait painter's brush moves from palette to canvas and shapes a face, so the historian's words must travel from his collected evidence to the contours of the text. In the present text each of the five images of the Hebrew God will be painted in words, but in such a way that it can ultimately be visualized. Each of the names given to the divine roles—Lord of Wisdom, Lord of War, and so on—is designed to evoke an image that may be absorbed instantaneously like a painting that can be "read" at a glance; for an image, in Ezra Pound's definition, "is that which presents an intellectual and emotional complex in an instant of time."[25] From the collocation of the five images of the Hebrew God, a composite portrait of this ancient deity will finally emerge.

The First Image: Lord of Wisdom

Toward the end of the fourth millennium B.C.E.*, high cultures developed in Mesopotamia and Egypt. One of the pillars on which they rested was wisdom, understood as the esoteric wisdom of the scholars and the pragmatic, political knowledge of the rulers and administrators. During the Bronze Age (ca. 3400–1200* B.C.E.*) literature flourished for the first time in human history, and huge, uniformly governed states emerged. The governing class of these early high cultures understood intellectual ability as a divine gift associated with wise deities, holders of ultimate authority over the universe. The influence of Bronze Age sapiential culture is evident in many parts of the Bible. Ancient Israelite civilization emerged during the Iron Age (ca. 1200–500* B.C.E.*), but, like that of all its neighbors, was profoundly indebted to Bronze Age traditions.*

Israelite notions of the deity, in particular, show clear evidence of Bronze Age influence as mediated through Canaanite city-states and Mesopotamian scribal traditions. Certain parts of the Bible reflect an archaic, polytheistic worldview. The creator and divine judge who is surrounded by numerous other deities, including his daughter, Wisdom, can be compared to the Ugaritic god El, wise owner of the universe. The elite's close association with this Lord of Wisdom can be seen in the initiation of priest, prophet, and king, which was either ritually staged or mystically experienced as a heavenly journey to the throne of God, who gave them their legitimacy. Strictly monotheistic notions such as dominate the book of Deuteronomy form a stark contrast to archaic polytheism, but still echo the world of the ancient scribes. The biblical ideas of divine legislation and bookkeeping reflect Babylonian scribal culture. Moreover, the notion of a covenant between God and his people, devised by Israelite theologians during the seventh century B.C.E.*, echoes the diplomatic wisdom of Mesopotamia in general and the Assyrian model in particular.*

3. The Lord of Esoteric Wisdom

The Bronze Age (3400–1200 B.C.E.) marks the beginning of significant urbanization and the leap from "primitive culture" to the more sophisticated and advanced forms of "high culture," characterized by an astonishing amount of creative energy. Three basic developments embody its achievements: writing, large-scale social management, and scholarship. While writing as such was considered important, the skills of social management and the accumulation of scholarly knowledge—in ancient times generally referred to by terms denoting intellectual capacities such as "wisdom" and "knowledge"—were acquired by a small class who came to control social, cultural, and political life at least until the end of the Iron Age (1200–500 B.C.E.), if not longer. To this class belonged a group that cultivated what may be termed esoteric wisdom.

According to the ancient Mesopotamians, the gods met each new year to decree what would happen in the coming year, inscribing their decisions on the tablets of fate. While humans had no direct knowledge of the latter, they were given signs in the form of omens that allowed trained experts to divine the fated events before they happened. The group cultivating the esoteric art of divination was a board of scholars attached to the court; regularly consulted, it formed a kind of state department. A list dating from the time of Ashurbanipal (669–630 B.C.E.) enumerates forty-five individuals by name—seven astrologers, nine exorcists, five diviners, nine physicians, six lamentation chanters, three augurs, three Egyptian magicians, and three Egyptian scribes.[1] Kept secret and controlled by the king, the scholars' wisdom served as a distinguishing body of knowledge for the ruling elite.[2] Ashurbanipal has left an account in which he boasts of his ability to converse with his board of experts (such boasting belongs to the traditional courtly rhetoric in Mesopotamia): "I am familiar with the secret storehouse of all scribal learning, including celestial and terrestrial portents. I can debate in an assembly of scholars and discuss with the clever oil diviners the treatise *If the Liver Is a Replica of the Sky*."[3] Mesopotamian evidence for this kind of esoteric lore abounds, and it is not foreign to the biblical tradition. Babylonian court diviners are mentioned by Deutero-Isaiah, and the story of Daniel makes its Judean hero "the chief of the magicians, enchanters, Chaldeans, and diviners" at the court of Babylon and extolls his ability to "interpret dreams, explain riddles, and solve problems."[4] The association of Daniel with the Babylonian diviners echoes the desire of the ancient

Mesopotamian courts to employ foreign magicians and thereby to enhance their magical expertise.

In Israel, things were similar. In the seventh century B.C.E., King Manasseh seems to have surrounded himself with practitioners of soothsaying and augury, with mediums and wizards, presumably attaching them to his court in Jerusalem, and King Zedekiah believed in the advice of his prophets, diviners, dreamers, soothsayers, and sorcerers.[5] The concentration of diviners at the royal court meant that the state claimed an exclusive right to practice divination, i.e. research the future by magical means. Divination at the court enjoyed royal patronage, but private magic was outlawed, and its practitioners feared for their lives.[6] While very little evidence for the royal board of magicians survives, tradition credits King Solomon with the writing of sayings and songs relating to trees and animals, as well as with much knowledge in esoteric matters such as the constellations of the stars and the virtues of roots.[7] According to the ancient Jewish historian Josephus, "God granted him knowledge of the art used against demons for the benefit and healing of humans. He also composed incantations by which illnesses are relieved, and left behind forms of exorcisms with which the experts drive the demons out, never to return."[8] Azariah, the "priest" attached to Solomon's court, no doubt contributed to Solomon's esoteric expertise.[9] In postbiblical tradition, Solomon came to epitomize royal patronage over the esoteric side of higher learning as it was cultivated at the courts of Western Asia.

At the heart of ancient esoteric lore was the belief that certain deities of high rank not only held supreme authority and owned all knowledge, but also granted the gift of wisdom to some men and (presumably more rarely) women, endowing them with superior intelligence and making them their earthly representatives. To this favored group of humans belonged, in addition to the king and his scholarly entourage already mentioned, priests and prophets.

The wisdom claimed by priests, magicians, and kings was derived from or acquired through certain initiatory experiences which involved an encounter with the Lord of Wisdom. Although no comprehensive accounts of Israelite initiation events and rituals have been included in the Bible, there are enough hints to enable us to understand their spiritual side. Perhaps the best way to approach the subject is to look at shamanism, for all rituals and ideas connected with religious roles ultimately derive from and echo those of the archaic shaman. Whereas scribal wisdom originated with Bronze Age culture, esoteric wisdom has much older roots.

Shamanism appears to be humanity's oldest religious culture. In the world of the early hunters and gatherers, as well as among pastoralists, shamans acted as the religious specialists in their tribe, village, or camp community. They mediated between this world and the other world, the realm of humans and the realm of the gods, ancestors, and spirits. Sickness could not be cured nor disputes settled without their intervention. Two intimately related notions form the core of shamanistic cults: transformation and heavenly journey. In their initiation the young persons destined for the shamanic role undergo a transformation that typically involves their symbolic death. Upon completion of the initiation, shamans no longer count as normal human persons; instead, they are beings endowed with extraordinary skills and powers that are useful, if not essential, for the community's wellbeing and survival. During sleep or in a state of trance, they can immobilize their bodies and send their souls to the other world in order to negotiate with superior beings, collect information, or find help.

Especially in northern Asia shamanism has survived down to our generation and, although marginal to modern culture, can be studied as a living institution. However, the advanced cultures of the Near East are no longer based on the hunting-and-gathering or pastoralist economies, and their religions—including biblical religion—can no longer be identified with shamanism. Civilizations based on agriculture tend to have more than just one religious authority: biblical Israel is a good example. Among the Hebrews, a new and different set of mediators emerged within the class of the scribes and the learned elite and replaced the archaic shamans. These new mediators included the prophet, who communicates with the gods either in ecstatic trance or intuitively; the priest, who uses various technical means to examine the will of the deities; and the king, who is seen as standing especially close to the divine world. Nevertheless, the shamanistic heritage still lingered, and the two essential features of the shaman are not in fact missing from the picture of his successors: the heavenly journey and the office-holder's transformation into a figure with special and sometimes divine qualities. A review of the biblical traditions reveals a peculiar phenomenon that no doubt reflects the development of social and political hierarchies: the splitting of the shamanistic heritage into a "major" and a "minor" charisma. Priests and prophets generally own the "minor" divine gift, while the "major" variety is reserved for the king and eminent religious leaders. In what follows this distinction will be demonstrated in relation to the heavenly journey. The celestial ascent brings a human being into the presence of the Lord of Wisdom, who then confers the minor or major charisma.

The Royal Ascent to Heaven

An impressive prophetic poem tells the story of a king who loses his place in the paradise on the mountain of the gods. Sitting on the earth having lost his splendor, he must suffer the scornful glances of others.[10] Another king, who had his throne above the stars, shares this unfortunate fate.[11] These two prophetic passages are fraught with interpretive problems, not all of which can be solved.[12] Both are polemical and therefore say little about a normal king's heavenly abode. Nevertheless, the two texts, along with evidence about the ritual of the royal candidate's induction to office, permit us to see how the king's relationship to heaven and the sovereign God of heaven was understood.

The king's ascent to heaven happened on the day of his induction to office: he was transformed into a divine being and, ascending to heaven, took his place on the mountain of the gods. Divinized, he appeared as "the signet of perfection, full of wisdom and beauty" (Ezek 28:12). In the words of Isaiah:

> The spirit of Yahweh rests on him:
> the spirit of wisdom and understanding,
> the spirit of counsel and might,
> the spirit of knowledge and the fear of Yahweh. (Isa 11:2)

On the mountain of God the ruler was accompanied by "an anointed cherub" or, in another interpretation, was himself transformed into an angelic being (Ezek 28:14). He was declared "son of God," and one of his titles translates as "Mighty God" (Ps 2:7; Isa 9:6/Hebr. 9:5). Apparently, this heavenly ascent was—at least to modern eyes—a rather unspectacular ritual event, but one dense in symbolism. When the royal candidate sat down on the throne placed in the temple, this meant nothing less than his ascent to the sacred mountain and his adoption among the gods. The scene may be visualized as follows: accompanied by priests and prophets, the royal candidate entered the temple. In front of the statue of the deity the procession came to a halt.[13] Now a priest, who spoke on behalf of the deity, addressed the king with the following oracle: "Sit at my right hand" (Ps 110:1). Apparently the divine image represented a sitting deity, and the royal candidate sat down on the throne placed next to it. The fact that this was "merely" a ritual event in no way minimizes its significance, for it was understood that the enthronement would transform the candidate into a different, new kind of being—a god. In society he had no equal. Neither priest nor prophet could claim a similar status.

If we are looking for a more elaborate description of a leader's transformation into a divine being, we have to consider the figure of Moses, for Israel's sacred legend gives him a quasi-royal status. The heavenly ascent of Moses is a common theme in early Jewish literature. The old biblical legend describes Moses' meeting with God on Mount Sinai in a discreet manner, but even there traces of the deification of Israel's leader can be detected. When Moses came back into the camp of the Israelites, he had horns (like the gods of the ancient Near East) or, according to another interpretation of the same biblical text, his face shone with light.[14] In the second century B.C.E., Ezekiel the Tragedian imagined the scene of Moses' meeting with God as follows:

> On Sinai's peak I [Moses] saw what seemed a throne
> so great in size it touched the clouds of heaven.
> Upon it sat a man of noble mien,
> becrowned, and with a scepter in one hand . . .
> I made approach and stood before the throne.

> He handed o'er the scepter and he bade
> me mount the throne, and gave to me a crown;
> then he himself withdrew from off the throne.
> I gazed upon the whole earth round about;
> things under it and high above the skies.
> Then at my feet a multitude of stars
> fell down, and I their number reckoned up.[15]

Here God cedes throne and scepter to Moses, which is tantamount to a deification. Jesus Sirach, a contemporary of Ezekiel the Tragedian, shares the poet's belief in the divinity of Moses. In the Greek version of the book of Jesus Sirach, this conviction is summed up as follows: God "made him [Moses] equal in glory to the holy ones"; Moses, in other words, is transformed into an angelic being (Sir 45:2). In the original Hebrew text, the passage survives as a fragment that states, quite simply: "he called him a god."

The notion of the divine king who has access to heaven was not confined to the Hebrews. In Mesopotamia, the idea assumes a vivid quality in the myth of King Etana, whom an eagle carries up to the gods in heaven. There he receives the plant of birth, which renders him able to procreate a son.[16] Another myth tells of King Enmeduranki's entry into the divine council, his heavenly enthronement, and how the gods instructed him in divination.[17] Ugaritic mythology permits the reconstruction of important features of the royal enthronement and the king's ideological status.[18] When at his royal installation the candidate took his seat on the throne, this was understood as a heavenly enthronement which transformed a mere human being into a god. As the king then left the throne, he descended to earth to rule his people. The king enjoyed privileged access to the celestial gods, whom he could approach by going through a complex ritual that involved his entering the sanctuary, ascending the temple tower, and raising his hands to heaven in a gesture affirming the contact achieved.

Prophetic and Priestly Ascent to Heaven

If the king's ceremonial induction to office was understood as his ascension to heaven, then the same must be said of the induction of prophet and priest. In this case, however, the biblical sources say nothing about induction rituals that would symbolize a heavenly ascent (although such rituals may have been practiced). The relevant biblical texts seem to echo mystical and visionary experiences rather than ritual events celebrated in the temple. Two passages merit attention. The first tells of the prophet Isaiah's inaugural vision. Standing before the divine throne, he listened in awed silence to the angelic song.[19] According to the second passage, the high priest Joshua (or Jeshua) "stood before the angel of Yahweh" to receive precious vestments.[20] These mark his induction into office. As a matter of fact, these prophetic passages are loaded with interpretive difficulties. Thus it remains unclear whether Isaiah had his inaugural vision in the Jerusalem temple's holy of holies. Another possibility is that the prophet had to undertake some kind of heavenly ascent to the divine throne chamber before experiencing his call. In the case of the high priest we cannot decide whether he stood before Yahweh himself or before an angel.

A close reading of the biblical passages and a comparison between the royal heavenly ascent and that of the priest and prophet reveal a clear distinction between two kinds of heavenly journey: we may call them the "minor" and the "major" ascents. The "major" variety is the king's privilege, whereas the "minor" type features prophets and priests. In either case, the ascent leads right into heaven and before the very throne of God, but a world of difference separates what the king and the prophet (or priest) experience in God's throne chamber. An angel touches Isaiah's mouth with a burning coal in order to prepare him for his mission: "One of the seraphs flew to me, holding a live coal that he had taken from the altar with a pair of tongs. The seraph touched my mouth with it and said: Now that this has touched your lips, your guilt has departed and your sin is blotted out" (Isa 6:6–7). Thus prepared, Isaiah can begin his prophetic activity among his contemporaries. The story of the high priest is similar. Wearing filthy clothes, the priest stands before the divine throne. After an accuser (in Hebrew, *satan*) has been silenced, heavenly servants are told to dress him in costly vestments:

> The angel said to those who were standing before him, "Take off his filthy clothes." And to him he said, "See, I have taken your guilt away from you, and I will clothe you with festal apparel." And he said: "Let them put on a clean turban on his head." So they put a clean turban on his head and clothed him with the apparel. (Zech 3:4–5)

Both prophet and priest are cleansed of the stain of human guilt and thereby made fit for their office. They leave heaven as new, transformed beings, characterized by extraordinary, celestial purity.

As in the case of the king, we can again refer to legendary and mythical prototypes of the priestly heavenly journey. For Levi, the ancestor of a priestly tribe, there can be only a "minor" heavenly ascent. In his testament, Levi tells his sons of his visionary journey: "The angel opened for me the gates of heaven and I saw the Holy Most High sitting on the throne. And he said to me: Levi, to you I have given the blessing of the priesthood until I shall come and dwell in the midst of Israel."[21] Then the angel guides him back to earth. Merely endowed with a priestly office, Levi ranks far below the divine Moses or the king. The Mesopotamian myth of Adapa, of which the earliest fragments date from the fifteenth century B.C.E., deals with the heavenly journey of the sage and priest in an exemplary manner.[22] Adapa, the priestly counselor of the first king, ranks as the model and archetype of all sages. Arriving in heaven, Adapa is welcomed by the gods. He refuses to touch divine food and objects to being anointed, but he accepts the gift of wisdom and has his mourning garment exchanged for festal apparel. Thus transformed and equipped for his courtly office, he returns to earth. So again, we have a non-royal figure whom the gods endow with a "minor," though very impressive, charisma.

4. Mythology Associated with the Lord of Wisdom

Before they developed a monotheistic book religion, ancient Israel's intellectual and religious leaders were committed to a polytheistic worldview, some of the mythology and ritual of which can be tentatively reconstructed from scattered biblical texts and traditions. This mythology features an account of creation, while the ritual consists of heavenly ascensions whereby human individuals— political and religious leaders—were brought before the gods (or God) and endowed with special wisdom. When we dare to offer some thoughts on this difficult and only recently discovered subject, we do so knowing that the fascinating world of the "Older Testament" (as it has been called by Margaret Barker)[23] is full of riddles and that frequently we depend on educated guesses. We feel that the project is valuable nevertheless, not least because of the survival of some of the "Older Testament" notions in postbiblical Judaism and in early Christianity. Reconstructing ancient Israel's earliest religion is not only worthwhile, but also possible, for Ugarit provides comparative evidence.

Unearthed in 1929 (and later), the cuneiform tablets of the city of Ugarit, situated on the Mediterranean coast of northern Syria, supply basic information about the religion of the Western Semites. Since the Ugaritic pantheon functions like an extended family, only one person, a patriarch, can be the head of the pantheon. This is El, a god whose name means "deity," the foremost of the gods.

El owns the entire universe.[24] He does not govern his realm all by himself, but delegates certain responsibilities to his sons and daughters, the gods and goddesses, whom he has begotten with his spouse, the goddess Asherah. When conflict arises, the divine assembly can discuss the issue, but it is El as president who decides. El is never partial; he stands above all conflict. He wants to stay in the background, interfering only when order is severely challenged. El's authority is acknowledged by everyone: "Your word, El, is wise: you are everlastingly wise; a life of good fortune is your word."[25] Pronouncing these phrases, the gods of Ugarit accept the decisions of their lord, who thus determines their fate.

In works of art, the Ugaritic El is represented as a benign male figure who sits enthroned and wears a crown (fig. 1, p. 25). Looking friendly, he raises his hand in a gesture of blessing and greeting. El has a beard, an attribute of old age and wisdom. In the second century C.E., Semitic priests still understood the

1. *El, the Ugaritic god of wisdom.* Although this small bronze figurine covered with gold (13.8 cm high) is not identified by an inscription, specialists feel that it must represent El, head of the pantheon of the ancient city of Ugarit in Syria. The bearded figure wears an Egyptian-style crown, a long garment with padded or rolled hem, and sandals. He raises his right hand in a benign gesture of blessing.—Two views of the same Ugaritic statuette, ca. 1400 B.C.E.

concept behind this piece of symbolism. When asked why their statue of Apollo portrayed him as an old man rather than a youth in his prime, they gave this answer: As a perfect god, Apollo must be represented with a beard; youth is an imperfect state.[26]

Several Old Testament passages reflect a mythology related to the religion of Ugarit. Fragmentary biblical passages depict Israel's God as a wise character similar to El.

The Wise God's Establishment of Cosmic Order

The mythology of ancient Syria can be recognized in those parts of the Bible in which Israel's mythology has not been eliminated by monotheistic revisers. Two divine figures dominate this tradition: a wise creator deity who is sometimes called Yahweh but whose original name seems to have been El (as in Ugarit) or Elohim; and a patroness of the scribes and administrators by the name of Hokhmah, whose name our Bible translations render as "Wisdom." Since the wisdom goddess is clearly subordinate to the creator god,

2. *Wisdom god and wisdom goddess.* Hebrew polytheism has left substantial traces in the Old Testament, and with the help of ancient iconography some of its features can be visualized. The wise Creator and the scribal goddess Wisdom, in the book of Proverbs presented as father and daughter, seem to resemble the bearded Ugaritic deity El and the Egyptian goddess Seshat, whose Bronze Age iconography is used in the illustration. The Hebrews recognized the importance and the comprehensive nature of wisdom—it is both young and old, male and female, and merits embodiment in two deities.—The author's attempt to visualize ancient Hebrew polytheism.

she survived the otherwise merciless activity of the later monotheistic revisers (fig. 2).

   The most relevant evidence for a wise god and a wisdom goddess in the Bible comes from Proverbs. This book may qualify as the oldest extant piece of Hebrew literature. Some sections seem to be older than the book of Amos, the oldest explicitly dated body of writing in the Old Testament. By the period of Amos's activity, ca. 750 B.C.E., part of the book of Proverbs may already have been of venerable antiquity. The most important section for our purposes comprises chapters 1–9, which I take to be an independent piece of writing rather than a mere preface. Here the goddess of scribes and administrators figures prominently; although in later times she was considered a mere poetic personification, her divine character can easily be discerned.[27]

Chapter 8 includes a detailed self-introduction by the goddess. All translations of the passage have their problems; hence, the following rendering draws upon both the New Revised Standard Version and the Revised English Bible:

I am Wisdom, I bestow shrewdness
and show the way to knowledge and discretion.
[*possibly added to the original text:* The fear of Yahweh is hatred of evil.]
Pride and arrogance and the way of evil
and perverted speech I hate.
I have good advice and sound wisdom;
I have insight, I have strength.
By me kings reign,
and rulers decree what is just;
by me rulers rule,
and nobles, all who govern rightly . . .
I walk in the way of righteousness,
along the paths of justice,
endowing with wealth those who love me,
and filling their treasuries. (Prov 8:12–16, 20–21)

Some of the language used in this poetic text merits attention. First of all, there is the concentration of words denoting intellectual capacities: wisdom, shrewdness, knowledge, insight. These are special virtues of administrators. "Strength" or "might" figures only marginally, for the scribes generally rely more on their wisdom than on physical force. They aim at establishing the proper order, as indicated by "righteousness" and "justice." Administrators and kings can become fairly rich, but they would always attribute worldly success to their devotion to the goddess.

This little self-portrait of the goddess of scribes and administrators is supplemented by a mythological passage. There the goddess speaks about her origins and her presence at the act of creation. The traditional form of the text printed in our Bibles gives the name of the creator god as Yahweh, but it may well be that this appellation has supplanted another, more original designation—El or Elohim. This speculation is based on the fact that old West-Semitic documents call their creator deity El; moreover, there is evidence that in ancient times the book of Proverbs received a revision in which originally used divine names such as Elohim were replaced by "Yahweh."[28] It is with wisdom that Elohim establishes the cosmic order: "Elohim [*the traditional Hebrew text has:* Yahweh] by wisdom founded the earth; by understanding he established the heavens; by his knowledge the deeps broke open, and the clouds drop down the dew" (Prov 3:19–20). During his activity as creator, the wise god is accompanied by the wisdom goddess. She is presented as his little daughter. These are her words:

> When he established the heavens, I was there . . .
> when he marked out the foundations of the earth,
> then I was beside him, like a little child;
> and I was daily his delight,
> rejoicing before him always,
> rejoicing in his inhabited world
> and delighting in the human race. (Prov 8:27, 29–31)[29]

The presence of Wisdom as a playing child should not be mistaken for an idyllic scene meant to enliven the poem. The little wisdom goddess watches the creator's activity and, looking into the heart of creation, learns the cosmic secrets. Those who witness the making or creating of something can understand it in a way that mere observers of the final product cannot. Accordingly, she is the one who knows the world better than all others, and her superior knowledge is the basis of all wisdom. We may here discern an echo of "nature wisdom" as it was developed among the teachers of the scribal schools. We meet this kind of wisdom in the legend of King Solomon, who is said to have compiled a manual of nature wisdom—a book with sayings on all the animals and plants of the world.[30] As part of their training the scribes had to study all domains of creation, for only a truly comprehensive knowledge, including esoteric lore, counts as wisdom. Before the scribes are given duties and responsibilities in the administration, they have to be thoroughly familiar with the cosmic order. Their professional activities must be in tune with that order, for only then can righteousness and justice be established in society.

The Sovereign God Allots the Nations to the Gods

The process of creation does not end with the establishment of sky, sea, and earth. Humans must be created and divided into various nations which must then be given territories and tutelary deities. This scene is half-present and half-absent in the Bible, for in the traditional Hebrew text the relevant passage exists only in a revised, demythologized form. With the help of the Septuagint, the pre-Christian Greek translation of the Bible, we can reconstruct the original wording. As is sometimes the case, the Septuagint seems to presuppose a Hebrew text that shows less monotheistic revision than the traditional Hebrew one. The passage reads:

> Remember the days of old,
> consider the years for past ages.
> Ask your father, and he shall relate to you,
> your elders, and they shall tell you:
> When the Most High divided the nations,
> when he separated the sons of Adam,

he set the bounds of the nations
according to the numbers of the angels of God.
And his people Jacob became the portion of the Lord [*kyrios*],
Israel was the line of his inheritance. (Deut 32:7–9, Septuagint)

The elders were familiar with the ancient mythology, which now, at the time of writing, was no longer generally known. After these short prefatory remarks, the poet recounts the entire sacred story. The most interesting part is the beginning, which surprises through its polytheistic character. The poet refers to the "Most High" and the "angels of God." The Most High is of course El Elyon, the creator god—the same deity who, according to our reading of Proverbs 8, established the cosmic order. As the Hebrew text implies, the Septuagint's "angels of God" are the "sons of God," the sons and daughters of the creator deity. The wisdom goddess Hokhmah also belongs among the children of this god. The divine sovereign and owner of the universe allots the nations to his sons, so that each of them is responsible for one particular people. Israel is assigned to a deity called *kyrios*, "the Lord." This must be Yahweh, the God of Israel.

Only to the monotheistic mind is it difficult to accept that there should be a deity of a rank superior to the God of Israel. But this is exactly what the passage implies: ancient Israel's polytheistic mythology distinguishes between a wisdom god, who owns the universe, and Yahweh, who is one of this deity's sons (fig. 3, p. 30). In this context Yahweh may be seen as a warrior deity, for the main god of a Semitic nation is usually its Divine Warrior. For us, this subordinate war deity is irrelevant, as our focus is on the "Most High," the sovereign god who owns the universe. His rule can be described as consisting solely of acts of administration, such as allotting the government of the nations to his divine sons. Just like his daughter, the wisdom goddess, the wise god is an administrator rather than a warrior. The highest-ranking god is formed in the image of an administrator, and for this reason we are justified in calling him a "wise deity."

The most recent biblical report about someone who is granted contact with the "Older Testament's" polytheistic divine world comes from the second-century B.C.E. book of Daniel.

Daniel's Dream

The book of Daniel introduces its protagonist as a young Judean man who receives his education at the Babylonian court and is eventually promoted to a high-ranking administrative position. While living at the pagan court, Daniel stays true to his Jewish faith and has an intensely religious way of life. He spurns meat, because in the foreign king's kitchen it is not prepared in the Jewish way. Three times a day he opens his window to direct his prayers toward Jerusalem, to the God of Israel. Daniel's religious life culminates in a series of

3. *Hebrew polytheism visualized.* According to an ancient poem that survives in the Greek version of the Hebrew Bible, a high god assigns the Israelites to the care of Yahweh and other peoples to other deities. The scene, which involves a divine father and a divine son, seems to evoke the association of the Ugaritic deity El (right) with his son, the young warrior Baal (left).—The author's attempt to visualize ancient Hebrew polytheism.

dream visions of the divine world, visions that reveal the fate of the Babylonian Empire and the deliverance of the Jewish people. For our purposes, the most interesting dream is the first one, reported in Daniel 7. Here we are explicitly told that Daniel himself has recorded his dream in writing—as an administrator he is, of course, literate.

Daniel's dream consists of several scenes that follow each other in quick succession and that are puzzling to him. First, he sees a raging sea out of which emerge huge beasts. These take the forms of a lion, a bear, a leopard, and (presumably) an elephant, and rule over the earth. The elephant is described as "terrifying and dreadful and exceedingly strong. It had great iron teeth and was devouring, breaking in pieces, and stamping what was left with its feet" (Dan 7:7). The scene immediately following, which apparently takes place in heaven, is reported:

> Thrones were set in place, and an Ancient One took his throne, his clothing was white as snow, and the hair of his head like pure wool; his throne was fiery flames, and its wheels were burning fire. A stream of fire issued and

4. *King Hammurabi standing before the sun-god Shamash.* The enthroned sun-god is depicted as an old, bearded man who wears a cap of horns. The rays of light emanating from his shoulders define the sun-god's fiery nature. The artist took care to contrast the divine and the human figures: Hammurabi stands erect, his right hand raised in a stiff gesture of adoration, his left arm held tightly to his body—he is a man visibly frozen in awe. Shamash, by contrast, sits relaxed, his arms open and welcoming, and his right hand holding the divine attributes of rod and ring, extended toward the king. The long text of Hammurabi's law code is inscribed below this scene of his encounter with the deity.—Babylonian relief. Detail of Hammurabi's law stela, ca. 1750 B.C.E.

flowed out from his presence. A thousand thousands served him, and ten thousand times ten thousand stood attending him. The court sat in judgment, and the books were opened. I watched then because of the noise of the arrogant words that the horn was speaking. As I watched, the beast was put to death, and its body destroyed and given over to be burned with fire. As for the rest of the beasts, their dominion was taken away, but their lives were prolonged for a season and a time. (Dan 7:9–12)

The white-haired man enthroned on a fiery and therefore intimidating chariot is the Most High god. His fiery throne and the stream of fire issuing from him are reminiscent of the flames that radiate from the shoulders of the Mesopotamian god Shamash (fig. 4). Servants are in attendance. He presides over a meeting of the heavenly tribunal during which written records are consulted (again an echo of the scribal culture). The beasts are sentenced and one of them is immediately executed. The others are stripped of their power. What Daniel sees in his dream can be readily understood: the heavenly court passes judgment against the tutelary deities of the Babylonian kings and the Babylonian Empire. The deities of the Babylonians have metamorphosed into disgusting beasts. But the highest god, called the "Ancient One," has never lost control over them and now proceeds to punish them. As a wise god he does not wage war against the hostile powers; rather, like a high-ranking administrator, he sits in judgment and has them punished.

The raging sea out of which the beasts emerge may echo the conflict mythology according to which a Divine Warrior triumphs over the dragon of the sea (see below, chapter 8). In this case we would have here a reinterpretation of the ancient conflict mythology that sheds its original warlike features: the battle is replaced by a simple and calm administrative act. The unruly beasts are executed. Blood flows, but not as a result of fighting. Administrators tend to resolve the mythological conflict not by war, but by legal action.

The dream of Daniel does not end with the passing of the sentence by the judge. Another scene follows, and once more we witness an administrative act of the highest god. Daniel reports:

> I saw one like a human being coming with the clouds of heaven. And he came to the Ancient One and was presented before him. To him was given dominion and glory and kingship, that all peoples, nations, and languages should serve him. His dominion is an everlasting dominion that shall not pass away, and his kingship is one that shall never be destroyed. (Dan 7:13–14)

This is another administrative act: the appointment of a deity to high office. The highest god invests a younger, man-shaped spirit with sovereign rule over all the nations. The man-shaped deity receives the power to be active in the three spheres of royal rule: dominion, glory, and kingship. "Dominion" refers to the power to administrate, "glory" to wealth, and "kingship" to royal warfare (see above, chapter 1). The young god is not given a name; he is merely called "one like a human being" (NRSV), literally "a son of man" or "someone in human form." This anthropomorphic deity can be identified with an angel who is admitted into the presence of the highest god. The more precise identification remains controversial among specialists. In light of the tradition of the sovereign god's appointment of the gods,[31] it makes sense to equate the son of man with Yahweh, the God of Israel. Other suggestions include one of the archangels—Gabriel or Michael, or the high priest of Jerusalem who, when performing certain ritual tasks in the temple, assumes an angelic role.[32] We may leave this detail undecided. It is clear, however, that the deity is invested with trifunctional authority, evoked in the solemn phrase "dominion and glory and kingship." This comprehensive power is conferred on a being who up to the moment witnessed by Daniel lacked this authority. The highest god makes sure that Israel gets special attention from on high: this is the essential message implied in Daniel's dream. Normally, the place where decisions are made remains beyond human knowledge. Only as an exception can the visionary be granted a glimpse of heaven; overwhelmed by what he sees, he cannot bear more than a brief sight of it.

In addition to the announcement of divine favor granted to the Jewish nation, Daniel's dream has another, more indirect message. Admitted in his vision to the heavenly courtroom, Daniel visits the administrative center of the universe. Here the fate of the nations is decided. The author of the chapter establishes a striking contrast between the earthly court of the Babylonians and the corresponding heavenly institution. Daniel, a man "versed in every branch of wisdom, endowed with knowledge and insight, and competent to serve in the king's palace" (Dan 1:4), apparently served as a court scholar who interpreted dreams and omens and gave counsel to the ruler. From his courtroom in Babylon, King Belshazzar seemed to rule the world. His Jewish counselor, however, knew better. He had witnessed the proceedings at another court, that of heaven, a court that could open its books and pass judgment on the kingdoms of the earth.

5. An Alternative View: God as Lawgiver and Scribe

The members of the ancient Near Eastern states' intellectual elite not only cultivated the esoteric wisdom of divination and mythology; rulers and scholars also focused on pragmatic wisdom aiming at social management.

Social management was in the hands of the king and the bureaucrats who supported his wise rule. In order to be able to provide for the internal wellbeing and ordered life of the community, the king depends upon wisdom, and in the ancient sources royal wisdom is often extolled as the superior kind. The Babylonian king Hammurabi is called "the one who is steeped in wisdom," "the wise one, the organizer, he who has mastered all wisdom."[33] The wise king's proud self-assessment is particularly well expressed in the (Egyptian) Teaching for King Merikare, dating from after 1900 B.C.E.: "The Lord of the Two Banks [i.e., the king of Egypt] is a sage. The king, the lord of courtiers, cannot be foolish. When he came out of the womb he had understanding, and God has set him apart before a million other men."[34] In other words: royal wisdom is a divine gift.[35]

The divine gift of wisdom did not dispense anyone from being trained in the scribal arts, and it seems that among the urban bourgeoisie of Mesopotamia a certain degree of literacy was both popular and appreciated.[36] Like the king himself, the bureaucrats had to acquire their expertise through scholastic training, especially the study of law. Most important were the laws of contract. While general law was binding for everyone, contracts were binding only for the parties concerned. In Mesopotamian business and private life, contracts abounded. The marriage contract had to be in written form, as is explicitly stated in the Code of Hammurabi: "If a man marries a wife but does not draw up a formal contract for her, she is not a wife."[37] Taking a loan, adopting a child, selling landed property, renting a field or an animal, and many other transactions had to be formalized in writing and signed by witnesses. The cuneiform archives of Babylonia and Assyria include thousands of contracts, and their study has become a new discipline within the field of legal history.

Several of the Near Eastern states—the Hittite state, Assyria, and Babylonia—extended the use of contracts to the sphere of politics. Treaties were concluded between the overlord and the vassal states, and sometimes these were styled as pacts of friendship and mutual assistance, giving an almost equal footing to all partners. During the classical Neo-Assyrian period, i.e. between developed juridical culture of Mesopotamia. When Judaism is termed the "religion of the law"—as for instance by St. Paul in the New Testament—this also has to do with the same Mesopotamian culture. The following considerations focus on the image of God in the legal sections of the Old Testament.

The dominant Old Testament tradition defines God as the Lord who revealed himself at Mount Sinai and had a sacred law promulgated through and a covenant concluded by the Israelite leader Moses. The covenant unites God and people in an eternal partnership: whereas God promises his patronage, Israel acknowledges its duty to keep the revealed law. As long as Israel keeps the divine law and especially its main commandment—that of exclusive veneration of the one deity, Yahweh—God will guide the people and grant protection and all manner of blessings.

As we have seen, the Babylonian god Shamash was the guarantor of the law promulgated by the king and put into practice by the administrators. In Israel, the same role of divine guarantor was attributed to Yahweh. In making Yahweh the legislator, however, biblical tradition radicalized Mesopotamian Bronze Age theology. It considered *all* legal statements as the very words of the deity, and all legislation was written down in the first person singular. In Israel's law codes it is always God who speaks. According to biblical legend, God has revealed the law to a human mediator. Thus we read in the book of Exodus: "He [Moses] was there [on the mountain] with Yahweh forty days and forty nights; he neither ate bread nor drank water. And he wrote on the tablets the words of the covenant, the ten words" (Exod 34:28). According to another tradition, it was God himself who wrote down the laws. The book of Deuteronomy is quite explicit on this point: "Yahweh gave me the two stone tablets written with the finger of God; on them were all the words that Yahweh had spoken to you at the mountain out of the fire on the day of the assembly" (Deut 9:10).[43] Elsewhere we find the same idea: "The tablets were the work of God, and the writing was the writing of God, engraved upon the tablets" (Exod 32:16).

Tradition has not refrained from being specific and giving details: "Then Moses turned and went down from the mountain, carrying the two tablets of the covenant in his hands, tablets that were written on both sides, written on the front and on the back" (Exod 32:15). There is only one scribal culture in the biblical milieu that writes on both sides of a tablet—that of Mesopotamia. Babylonian and Assyrian scribes inscribed the cuneiform signs with the sharp, square end of a stylus into the surface of a lump of fine clay. They used both the obverse and the reverse of the clay. As it dried, the tablet hardened; but to make it more durable, it could be baked in the sun, or even better, in the kiln. Once baked, a tablet could easily travel or be placed in storage. The tradition that ascribes to God himself the writing of the laws depicts him in the image of a wise administrator of Mesopotamian provenance.

In the context of divine legislation the favorite vocabulary of the scribes and administrators is not lacking: "wisdom," "justice," and similar words figure prominently. In an exhortation addressing the people, Moses says: "You must observe them [the laws] diligently, for this will show your *wisdom* and *discernment* to the peoples, who, when they hear all these statutes, will say, 'Surely, this great nation is a *wise* and *discerning* people!' . . . What other great nation has statutes and ordinances as *just* as this entire law that I am setting before you today?" (Deut 4:6, 9, italics added).

The Covenant between Yahweh and his People

The ancient Israelite scribe, according to James George Frazer,

> was a lawyer as well as an ecclesiastic, and as such he took great pains to prove that the friendly relations of God to his people rested on a strictly legal basis, being authenticated by a series of contracts into which both parties entered with all due formality. He is never so much in his element as when he is expounding these covenants; he never wearies of recalling the long series of Israel's title-deeds. Nowhere does this dry-as-dust antiquary, this rigid ritualist, so sensibly relax his normal severity, nowhere does he so nearly unbend and thaw, as when he is expatiating on the congenial subject of contracts and conveyances.[44]

Frazer is right: the notion of covenant may count as one of the most significant contributions the scribes made to religion. The ancient scribes lived in a world in which contracts structured family life, the domain of business and trade, and the realm of international politics. So why not extend it also to the sphere of religion, making it a matter of a contractual relationship between the gods and their human partners? It was assumed that the gods were willing to cooperate in the diplomatic game and act as reliable partners in contractual relationships. Mesopotamian and West Semitic documents suggest that this idea may have been current in the seventh century B.C.E.[45] However, only the Judeans developed the notion fully, making it a leading concept of their theology. Their traditional idea of the ethnic group as a national community implied a patron–client relationship, with the tutelary deity taking the role of the patron and the nation that of the client;[46] the new theology simply described this relationship in legal, contractual terms.

The books of Exodus and Deuteronomy know of a contract between Israel and its God. Exodus describes a formal covenant ceremony:

> Moses came and told the people all the words of Yahweh and all the ordinances; and all the people answered with one voice, and said: "All the words that Yahweh has spoken we will do." And Moses wrote down all the words of Yahweh. He rose early in the morning, and built an altar at the foot of the mountain, and set up twelve pillars, corresponding to the twelve tribes of

Israel. He sent young men of the people of Israel, who offered burnt offerings and sacrificed oxen as offerings of well-being to Yahweh. Moses took half of the blood and put it in basins, and half of the blood he dashed against the altar. Then he took the book of the covenant, and read it in the hearing of the people; and they said, "All that Yahweh has spoken we will do, and we will be obedient." Moses took the blood and dashed it on the people, and said, "See the blood of the covenant that Yahweh has made with you in accordance with all these words." (Exod 24:3–11)

From the point of view of legal practice, the most important part of this ceremony is the public reading of a written document that states the covenant obligations to which the people assent. The accompanying ritual acts supply a sense of drama, but are otherwise irrelevant.

Scholars agree that the idea of a covenant or treaty between God and his people is not an ancient one within the history of biblical religion. Originating in the late seventh century within the Yahweh-alone movement, it figures most prominently in the book of Deuteronomy and in passages whose language and theology derive from this book. The idea of the covenant relationship between God and his people was presumably devised during the time of King Josiah, the king who is well known for his religious reform in 622 B.C.E. Deuteronomy includes a whole series of features characteristic of the Assyrian vassal treaties:

1) The identification of the speaker (Moses).[47]
2) A historical prologue describing previous relations between the two partners.[48]
3) Stipulations detailing the obligations of the vassal state.[49]
4) A document clause providing for the safekeeping and the regular reading of the agreement; the reading is to take place every seventh year.[50]
5) Naming the god or gods who act as witnesses to the treaty.[51]
6) Blessings and curses.[52]

Among the biblical stipulations are several that are either akin to or clearly patterned on passages in Assyrian treaties. The requirement for the exclusive worship of Yahweh corresponds to the exclusive loyalty demanded of the vassal. The similarity is striking: "You shall hearken to whatever he [the overlord] says and do whatever he commands, and you shall not seek any other king or any other lord against him . . . Do not place any other king or any other lord over you."[53] These passages date from 672 B.C.E. and are included in King Esarhaddon's so-called Succession Treaty. This elaborate document was designed to inculcate the vassals' loyalty not only to the Assyrian ruler himself, but also to his son and successor. It is possible, and even likely, that the Judeans knew this text. King Manasseh of Judah must have been just one among the many vassals bound by the Succession Treaty. Moreover, it was not the king alone who was responsible for loyalty to the overlord. The entire population, represented by the elders, had to listen when the vassal treaty was read in public, and everyone was considered responsible for its implementation. In the case of noncompliance, everyone was technically punishable. As is known from history, the Assyrians were capable of deporting entire populations to other parts of the Empire. Taking the Assyrian treaty of 672 B.C.E. or a similar text as their model, Judean scribes devised their covenantal theology. However, it was not a political contract with the Assyrian overlord that was to be the basis of life, but a religious covenant with their own national deity, Yahweh.

Divine Bookkeeping

The book serves not only as the inventory of laws; in the covenantal tradition, it is also the "book of life"—another echo of the scribal culture in which this tradition originated. According to legend, the angry Moses broke the tablets of the law because the people danced around the Golden Calf. Afterwards, Moses ascended the holy mountain again and interceded for the sinful people. If God was not willing to forgive their sin, Moses wanted his name to be expunged from the book of life: "They have made for themselves gods of gold. But now, if you will only forgive their sin—but if not, blot me out of the book that you have written. But Yahweh said to Moses, Whoever has sinned against me I will blot out of my book" (Exod 32:31–33).

God has a book into which he writes the names of individuals. The book of Psalms occasionally refers to this register. Thus we hear the voice of someone asking God to take steps against his enemies. He requests, in particular, that God blot their names out of the book of life: "Let them be blotted out of the book of the living; let them not be enrolled among the righteous" (Ps 69:28/Hebr. 69:29). Another passage from Psalms assumes that the all-knowing God has written down the entire biography of an individual even before his birth.[54] Moreover, "everyone who is found written in the book" will be saved from damnation (Dan 12:1). This mysterious "book of life" also figures in certain passages of the New Testament. St. Paul refers to his collaborators as people "whose names are in the book of life" (Phil 4:3). In the context of the Last Judgment, the book of Revelation also mentions the "book of life." John, the visionary of Patmos, describes the following scene: "I saw the dead, great and small, standing before the throne, and books were opened. Also another book was opened, the book of life. And the dead were judged according to their works, as recorded in the books" (Rev 20:12).

Ideas relating to heavenly books, heavenly bookkeeping, and heavenly tablets of fate abound, and there can be no doubt about their origin in the scribal culture of Bronze Age Mesopotamia.[55] God is seen as an administrator who, like his earthly counterparts, has extensive archives at his disposal. Even the future is already determined and written down in a book.[56] The Latin proverb *quod non est in actis, non est in mundo* echoes the same mentality: what is not in the official records does not exist in the world.[57] Administrators, including those residing in heaven, take their written records to be an adequate copy of—and even a model for—reality.

Words such as "covenant" and "law" have become key concepts of religion. It is accepted that religion uses codified law and that God keeps written records about human behavior: all of this reflects Near Eastern scribal culture. Judean scribes created an image of God in line with their own ideals of wisdom, diplomacy, law, and the culture of writing. Their God is Lord of the Covenant, the Law, and the Book. Later, the word "Torah" (Hebrew for "instruction, law") was to summarize the essence of Jewish religion, and piety came to be defined as "love of Torah."[58] Israel became the "people of the book," a textual community, and the highest wisdom and knowledge were to be obtained not by independent observation, not by the free investigation of nature and society, but by the interpretation of a written record. Terms such as "book religion," "religion of the law," and "religion of revelation," all used to characterize Jewish religion, point to the same fact: that the covenantal law, as revealed by God and codified in a book, forms the basis and center of biblical theology. Later, Christians adopted the idea and could state, quite simply, that "our religion is in a book."[59]

The Book of Deuteronomy's Opposition to Heavenly Ascents

The notion of the heavenly journey as we reconstructed it for Israel's monarchical period received a destructive blow in the sixth century B.C.E. The fall of Jerusalem and its temple in the year 586 meant the end of the kingship and, along with it, the end of the royal ideology. Not much later, the book of Deuteronomy suppressed the ritual and visionary reality of the heavenly journey. When the temple was restored during the late sixth century, it no longer included a divine image—the well-known Jewish ban on images had begun to take hold. The temple was considered either a "residential temple" or a "sanctuary of manifestation."[60] It no longer counted as God's permanent abode on the sacred mount of the temple, though some still understood it as a place where God's "name" resided (presumably accompanied by the divine "eyes" and "heart"), a kind of diminished, residual form of divine presence ("residential temple").[61] Others thought of the temple as a place where he would manifest his "glory" on certain ritual occasions ("sanctuary of manifestation").[62] And of course, as kingship no longer existed, the ritual staging of the royal ascent to heaven had become obsolete. The divine will and commission no longer had to be sought *ad hoc* on a heavenly journey, but were permanently available in a sacred book. In the canon of the Hebrew Bible, the Deuteronomic ideology succeeded in asserting itself—which explains the scarcity of evidence for the traditional heavenly ascent.

In a religion based on a legal code understood as divine revelation codified, there is no need for regular shamanistic contact with the other world; one such contact, located in the mythic, far-away past and hardly reminiscent of shamanism, suffices. This is the picture conveyed by the book of Deuteronomy, generally taken to explain the dominant view within the biblical tradition. While the Israelites stood at the foot of Mount Horeb (or Mount Sinai, according to another version), listening with awe to the thunder of an active, fire-spitting volcano, Moses received the divine law written on two stone tablets.[63] With this event, the foundational, one-time contact was completed, for a prophet like Moses would never arise again.[64]

The book of Deuteronomy advocates an uncompromisingly nonshamanistic view. God's law, it states,

> is not in heaven, that you should say, "Who will go up to heaven for us, and get it for us so that we may hear it and observe it?" Neither is it beyond the sea, that you should say, "Who will cross to the other side of the sea for us, and get it for us that we may hear it and observe it?" No, the word [of God] is very near to you; it is in your mouth and in your heart for you to observe. (Deut 30:12–14)

The reference to the divine word in the heart and in the mouth implies that God's commandments are known and can be memorized and recited. So much is Deuteronomy part of an "oral culture" that the passage refrains from making the written nature of the divine law explicit. No doubt the book of Deuteronomy itself was thought of as the actual source of the commandments that have to be learned by heart.

Deuteronomy juxtaposes and contrasts two opinions about heavenly journeys: an older one, which must be rejected, and a more recent, correct and orthodox one. The older view is indebted to a shamanistic view of revelation, according to which divine direction can only be obtained through a mediator who is able to establish contact with the divine realm. He must travel across the sea[65] to the end of the world or ascend to heaven. The view promoted by Deuteronomy renders prophetic journeys to heaven superfluous, for divine revelation has already reached its fullness, and, having the Torah of Moses, Israel owns it in written form. A one-time ascent to heaven in the remote past— Moses' ascent to Mount Sinai to receive the Torah—suffices for all time, making any further prophetic effort unnecessary. While the archaic religion needed constant access to the other world, Deuteronomy has outgrown this stage. Arguing that revelation has been completed, it represents a new type of religion—book religion.

Intellectuals have always been somewhat skeptical about new and surprising revelations. In book religion, which emerged in a scholarly milieu, these reservations became the very basis of a new kind of religious worldview. Even outside of the Bible, rationalist voices comparable to that of Deuteronomy can be heard. Thus we read in the Babylonian Epic of Gilgamesh: "Who is there, my friend, who can climb to the sky? Only the gods dwell forever in sunlight."[66] The distance between the divine and the human realms cannot be bridged, either by shamanistic or prophetic ascents (as mentioned in Deuteronomy), or by a journey that ends with someone's adoption among the immortal gods in heaven (as referred to elsewhere in the Epic of Gilgamesh).

The contrast between shamanistic and Deuteronomic religion is sharp and does not allow for any compromises. No doubt we have here a conscious policy which seeks to erase all surviving traces of shamanism in order to give biblical theology its own, postarchaic profile. Reading Deuteronomy, we witness how a new type of religion—book religion—emerges. As a matter of fact, the book of Deuteronomy's influence on subsequent Jewish history can hardly be over-estimated. Even in modern discussions of Israelite religion, this book shapes the scholarly perception. It is not without reason that Deuteronomy counts as "the center of biblical theology" or as "the essence of Old Testament thought."[67] "Theology of the Old Testament, however differentiated, will in the final analysis be a theology which takes Deuteronomy as its point of orientation," asserts a leading biblical scholar.[68]

Having concluded our description of the two images of the Lord of Wisdom—archaic and Deuteronomic—we may ask how they fit in with Dumézil's theory of social and supernatural organization. As a matter of fact, Dumézil has pointed out that the First Function—sovereignty—often takes the form of joint or dual rulership. The most characteristic example comes from early Indic literature. The two deities Mitra and Varuna act as the original creators and share in the rule over the universe. Frequently, they act in tandem, but they are also ascribed differing, complementary roles and characteristics.[69] Personifying the idea of the contract, Mitra is defined as pursuing rational and legal aims. He settles disputes and generally behaves in a fashion immediately beneficial to humankind. Concerned with the maintenance of order among both gods and humans, he can be compared to a friendly, reassuring scribe, lawyer, or bureaucrat of the state. Varuna, by contrast, endowed with personal and magical charisma, often acts violently and not always in a manner entirely beneficial to his devotees, achieving his ends through the exercise of occult powers. The awe-inspiring Varuna stands for religion and the incalculable, uncontrollable forces associated with the divine, with night, the other world, and water. Concerned with the enforcement of proper magico-religious belief and practice, he behaves like an oriental despot whose will remains inscrutable.

In the Bible's monotheistic religion, the First Function place is not held by two deities, but by the one God. The character of the biblical Lord of Wisdom can nevertheless take different forms. Viewed from the perspective of Dumézil's theory of dual sovereignty, the Deuteronomic Lord of Wisdom appears to be of the Mitra type, whereas the archaic image of God seems to represent the Varuna pattern. In ancient Israel, the Mitra type of wisdom has led to the creation of book religion based on a contract or covenant between the deity and the people. The archaic Varuna aspect of the deity, though increasingly relegated to the background, remains visible and powerful. Yet it is Yahweh's Mitra side that prevails in much of biblical literature.

The Second Image: Lord of War

The major civilizations of the Bronze and Iron Ages not only depended on wisdom, institutionalized in the scribal administration and in political leadership (the subject of the previous section); they also relied on physical power, visibly present in armies, weapons, and warfare. Throughout the ancient Near East, including Israel, warfare was supported by an ideology that featured a Divine Warrior. Two different ideologies of sacred warfare can be distinguished: an archaic one that believed in divine support on the battlefield, and a postarchaic one that expected the deity to do all the fighting.

The Israelite legends of the conquest of Canaan by General Joshua echo many ideas connected with archaic warfare, for Israel's national deity, Yahweh, was believed to provide assistance on the battlefield. This belief forms part of a more comprehensive ideology. At the royal investiture, the king was given a divine weapon, symbol of the task of divine warfare, for king and Divine Warrior fought against the same enemy. In ancient mythological lore, the theme of war also figures prominently, especially in tales about cosmic conflicts, which in scholarship are often referred to as "chaos battles." The Divine Warrior's enemy, represented by a sea monster or a huge serpent (also associated with the sea), was for the first time subdued at the dawn of creation; yet it is only during the rainy season that the Divine Warrior celebrates his victory, for the long, dry summers demonstrate his enemy's temporary success.

According to the postarchaic tradition, the deity, rather than giving support on the battlefield, does all the fighting and defeats the enemy without any human participation at all. The same tradition refers to the involvement of the Divine Judge in warfare and God's complete annihilation of the foe. These features characterize the emerging apocalyptic ideology in which hitherto opposing approaches to dealing with evil—juridical and bellicose—combine.

6. God as Lord of War

In the ancient world, the king is often represented as a deity's human war leader. Waging "holy war," he prays to his god for help and, where victory ensues, ascribes the triumph to the support of the *deus militans*. The exemplary source for this ideology is the so-called "Stela of the Vultures," a Mesopotamian commemorative stela dating from around 2500 B.C.E. In southern Mesopotamia two neighboring states were involved in armed conflict over land and water rights, for both claimed ownership of a fertile piece of land. Eventually, the city-state of Lagash prevailed over the city-state of Umma and recovered the disputed territory. After victory, the triumphant party set up a monument with a long text[1] illustrated by several reliefs. The stela, now reconstructed from substantial fragments, can be seen in the Louvre in Paris.

The main scene on the front of the stela shows the god Ningirsu, the tutelary deity of Lagash, the triumphant city (fig. 5, p. 48). There can be no doubt about its meaning: the city of Lagash owes its victory to its tutelary deity. Marching in front of the soldiers and forming the royal army's divine vanguard, Ningirsu was present on the battlefield.[2] Here we are becoming acquainted with the great doctrine of Bronze Age theology: God is a triumphant warrior—*deus militans* and *deus victor*. Presumably the victory stela had its original place in one of the temples of Ningirsu,[3] possibly in the city of Girsu, where it was found by the French excavators. On the reverse of the stela the Sumerian artist has depicted several "real" battle scenes, i.e. scenes that involve fighting soldiers and not the fighting deity (fig. 6, p. 49). Characteristically, the king does not stay in the background but is conspicuously present. The message conveyed by this political iconography cannot be missed: the king is a warrior. More precisely: it is in the service of his god that he wages war. Accordingly, the inscription placed near King Eanatum says: "Eanatum, who subjugates foreign lands for [the god] Ningirsu."[4] The idea implied seems to be: the deity helps the king in his military exploits, and, conversely, the king serves as the god's helper on the battlefield—he fights in the service of and for his divine patron.

The images on the Stela of the Vultures are accompanied by an inscription in Sumerian. The text begins with a detailed account of the border conflict between the city-states of Lagash and Umma, starting from ancient times. Embedded in this is the story of the creation of King Eanatum as the superhuman champion of the god Ningirsu. This god is reported to have fathered

5. *Caught in the war-god's net.* In his left hand the Sumerian god Ningirsu, bearded
and bare-chested, holds a large net densely packed with captives, most of them
apparently dead. One captive is trying to climb free, but to no avail, for the god
pushes him back with his mace. The net is fixed to a pole and crowned with an
ornament representing an eagle with a lion's head—the city of Lagash's sacred
emblem. The net serves as a weapon in face-to-face fighting between infantry soldiers
on the battlefield: the warrior throws the net over an enemy so that he gets entangled
and can be overwhelmed.—Fragment of a Sumerian stone relief. Stela of the
Vultures, obverse, ca. 2500 B.C.E.

the king and lavished his blessings upon him. One night Eanatum has a dream
in which his divine father appears to him, giving him the order to wage war
against Umma and promising him victory. Then follows a brief account of the
actual battle in which Eanatum himself participates. Much space is given to the
oaths the defeated ruler of Umma is forced to swear in elaborate ceremonies.
All are sworn by "the great battle net," the deity's sacred weapon. Then
Eanatum enumerates his titles and epithets and lists other victories. After a
break in the text the king describes the erection of a stela to commemorate the
restoration of the country's territorial integrity.

Yahweh as Lord of War

Not unlike the Sumerian Ningirsu, Yahweh is the deity of a particular country
and people. Both gods represent a type of deity very common in the ancient

6. *King Eanatum at war.* The upper register of this fragment shows a Sumerian phalanx marching into battle. With their leather helmets, spears, and gigantic, overlapping rectangular shields they present an impregnable wall. Led by King Eanatum, the soldiers are trampling on the corpses of slain enemies. Somewhere above this scene can be placed a fragment that depicts naked corpses being chopped to pieces and carried away by the vultures—hence the name Stela of the Vultures. Below is a similar scene: Eanatum stands in a chariot at the head of a detachment of spearmen; with one arm he supports himself on the chariot, with the other he holds a spear that is pointed toward the enemy.—Fragment of a Sumerian stone relief. Stela of the Vultures, reverse, ca. 2500 B.C.E.

world: the tutelary deity of the state. As the god of a state, both Ningirsu and Yahweh share the same responsibility—to secure royal victory in battle. The state god is the war god. In Iron Age Israel and its neighboring countries, the Bronze Age idea of war continued to be the dominant ideology.[5] War legends replete with this ideology abound in the Bible, and they are particularly characteristic of traditions relating to the exodus from Egypt and the conquest of the promised land. These traditions seem to echo the victory of Asiatic tribes over Egyptians or rather Egypt-dominated Canaanite cities during what historians have termed the Great Catastrophe around 1200 B.C.E., when Egypt lost its long-established control over Palestine. As Egyptian political control waned, new groups formed, typically rallying around charismatic war leaders or warrior clans. Details of the early Israelites' involvement with these events have escaped historical and archaeological scrutiny, but the legends vividly illustrate how peoples such as the Hebrews were quick to adopt the superpowers' ideology of war and victory.

Biblical traditions relating to the Hebrew conquest of Palestine closely resemble the way divine war is depicted in both text and image on the Stela of the Vultures (as well as other Mesopotamian documents). The following features characterize the Divine Warrior's cooperation with the human army: *before the war*, the deity announces victory (according to the Stela of the Vultures, the god appears to Eanatum in a dream to assure him of a successful battle); *during combat*, divine presence and assistance are made visible, usually in the form of the deity's standard carried by priests; *after the battle* has been fought successfully, the leader acknowledges the deity as the actual victor (in the case of the Stela of the Vultures, this is done in the politico-religious iconography on a commemorative monument which receives special visibility, presumably in a temple). All of these features—divine promise of victory, divine assistance during the battle, and erection of a monument—can be found in the story of the Israelites' conquest of the city of Jericho as reported in the book of Joshua.

At the beginning Israel's general Joshua receives the divine announcement of victory. Although the biblical text shows traces of literary reworking, the original account remains visible. "Once when Joshua was by Jericho, he looked up and saw a man standing before him with a drawn sword in his hand. Joshua went to him and said to him, Are you one of us, or one of our adversaries? He replied, Neither; but as commander of the army of Yahweh I have now come" (Josh 5:13–14). Acting as a messenger, the mysterious figure brings God's promise of victory: "See, I have handed Jericho over to you, along with its king and soldiers" (Josh 6:2). The man with the drawn sword echoes the Bronze Age iconography of the Divine Warrior as a male figure with a weapon raised menacingly in his right hand (fig. 7, p. 51). The weapon—a sword or a bow—serves as the Divine Warrior's identifying attribute.

The second element, that of divine presence on the battlefield, is vividly portrayed in the story. The Israelites carry the "ark of Yahweh" several times around the city until the walls collapse—presumably echoing a folkloric motif according to which an act must be performed several times before the desired goal can be achieved. We are not told what the "ark" was. It could have been a portable shrine with a divine image, possibly a small metal sculpture which represents Yahweh as the menacing, weapon-holding warrior just mentioned (fig. 7). Although they remain vague in their detail, scattered biblical passages actually refer to such divine images. The appearance of the "man with a drawn sword" belongs here. According to another revealing passage, warriors of the tribe of Dan first steal the figurine of a deity from a sanctuary, and thus armed they proceed to attack the enemy.[6] Since a later period prohibited the making of divine images, any reference to the problematic contents of the "ark" was suppressed. According to subsequent tradition, the ark served as a receptacle

7. *The Divine Warrior, fully armed.* In Bronze Age Palestine, the warrior-god was frequently depicted as a young, beardless man. Brandishing a sword in his right hand and protecting himself with a shield held in the left hand, the kilt-wearing "menacing god" served as a model for all human warriors. Normally kept in the temple, small metal figurines like the one depicted here may also have been carried to the battlefield in portable shrines to insure victory.—Canaanite bronze statuette, 13 cm high, fourteenth to twelfth century B.C.E.

for the stone tablets of the Ten Commandments—a typical view of later scribes for whom images were the hallmark of idolatry. This substitution constitutes a radical departure from the original custom.

The third element of traditional Near Eastern battle reports, the reference to paying homage to the Divine Warrior, concludes the biblical tale of Jericho: "They burned down the city, and everything in it; only the silver and gold, and the vessels of bronze and iron, they put into the treasury of the house of Yahweh" (Josh 6:24). To bring war trophies into a sacred shrine or temple was not unusual. The sword of Goliath the Philistine was kept in the Israelite temple of Nob, and the Philistines displayed the armor of the Israelite king Saul in the temple of their goddess Astarte.[7] As we know from both texts and excavations, ancient temples, including the one in Jerusalem, frequently had their own foundry, for they wished to store metal in the form of ingots.[8] Accordingly, there is nothing strange about the reference to the special treatment of metal objects gained as spoils of war in Jericho. What *is* surprising, however, is the reference to the "house of Yahweh." In the present context, Yahweh's "house" represents a conspicuous anachronism, for, according to the

Deuteronomist, there was no temple of Yahweh in the early period, before the one King Solomon built in Jerusalem. In its present form, the book of Joshua belongs to the Deuteronomistic Work, i.e. the series of books that starts with Deuteronomy and Joshua and tells the story of Israel from Moses and Joshua to the end of the Israelite and Judean monarchies. Obviously, the Deuteronomist has not always succeeded in imposing his views onto older textual material. The reference to a "house of Yahweh" is clear evidence for an earlier, pre-Deuteronomistic version of the Jericho story. But where was this "house of Yahweh" according to the earlier and no longer extant version of the book of Joshua?

There is only one possible candidate: the city of Gilgal. This is the place where Joshua's army had its camp, and it was from there that the soldiers set off to attack Jericho.[9] Situated only a few miles to the north of Jericho, Gilgal ranks as one of the oldest Israelite sanctuaries. According to the biblical account, it included stone monuments of venerable antiquity.[10] Erected by Joshua as simple, uninscribed stones, they commemorated the army's crossing of the Jordan river. In all likelihood, this explanation represents a secondary interpretation of an earlier account that was more in line with ancient military practice. The earlier version of the Jericho story must have spoken of a sanctuary at Gilgal into which the metal spoils of the conquered city were brought.

Interestingly, the book of Joshua also includes traces of the founding legend of the Gilgal sanctuary. The tale of the mysterious "commander of the army of Yahweh" includes a reference to a previously unknown sacred place where visitors have to remove their shoes.[11] Since this kind of scene generally introduces the account of the founding of a shrine or temple,[12] the angelophany near Jericho most likely represents the residual etiology or founding legend of the Gilgal temple. It is at this point that our argument reaches its logical conclusion: just as the Sumerians erected a memorial stela in the temple of Girsu, so the Israelites displayed the spoils of Jericho in the temple of Gilgal to commemorate their victory. Perhaps we can even reconstruct the original ending of the story. At the end of the account there must have been a counterpart to the angelophany of the beginning. It might have run as follows: "After these events, Joshua returned to Gilgal and built a house for Yahweh at the place at which the commander of Yahweh's army had appeared to him. The silver and gold, and the vessels of bronze and iron, they put into the treasury of the house of Yahweh."

But there is no need to indulge in scholarly speculation about the original form of the legend of Gilgal. For even without our reconstruction it is clear enough that the legend of the battle of Jericho smacks of the traditional Near Eastern ideology of warfare. Yahweh is a war god!

In what follows, we will take a closer look at certain less obvious but equally important themes associated with the Lord of War: the warrior's initiation and the mythology of God's battle with the chaos monster.

7.   The Warrior's Initiation and God's Battle with the Monster

Even before Saul became the first (legendary) king of Israel, he acted as a war leader. How this happened is recounted as follows:

> Now Saul was coming from the field behind the oxen; and Saul said, "What is the matter with the people, that they are weeping?" So they told him the message from the inhabitants of Jabesh [i.e. an Israelite city besieged by the enemy]. And the spirit of Yahweh came upon Saul in power when he heard these words, and his anger was greatly kindled. He took a yoke of oxen, and cut them in pieces and sent them throughout all the territory of Israel by messengers, saying, "Whoever does not come after Saul and Samuel, so shall it be done to his oxen!" Then the dread of Yahweh fell upon the people, and they came out as one. When he mustered them at Bezek, those from Israel were three hundred thousand, and those from Judah seventy thousand. (1 Sam 11:5–8)

The challenge of the enemy provoked Saul's anger, and seized by frenzy he killed a yoke of oxen as a violent call to military action. Here we have the archaic fury of the warrior which both initiates military action and inspires his heroism during combat. Saul's anger parallels that of the Norse berserker who in battle is seized with a frenzy, howls, bites into his shield, foams at the mouth, and is believed invulnerable. Under the spell of holy anger, the warrior transcends his normal state by multiplying his physical forces, losing any sense of pain, and enjoying a proud sense of superiority and invincibility.[13] As might be expected in the circumstances, Saul and his army overthrew the enemy and liberated the city of Jabesh.

At first sight, Saul's slaying of his oxen seems a peculiar act, designed to intimidate his fellow Israelites and force them to join him in battle. While this is obviously what the biblical text implies, comparative evidence suggests another meaning. Traditional tales often refer to the fact that before someone's admission among the warriors he has to kill a wild beast or even a mythical monster such as a dragon. Thus the Roman historian Ammianus Marcellinus reports that, in the Gothic tribe of the Taifali, young men have to kill a wild boar or huge bear before being admitted to the adult warrior community.[14] In a similar vein, Saxo Grammaticus says of Frothi, king of the Danes, that he first killed a dragon and then, having accomplished this heroic deed, set out to fight against his enemies.[15] In the Bible, the sequence of "killing a wild animal" and "fighting against the enemy" is echoed in the story of Samson. As Samson roamed about, "suddenly a young lion roared at him. The spirit of Yahweh rushed on him, and he tore the lion apart barehanded as one might tear apart a kid" (Judg 14:6). Thus, having discovered or proven his strength, Samson began his career as a warrior who, unaccompanied and unaided, was soon to kill thirty men of an enemy town.[16]

Further insight into the warrior's initiation comes from an Akkadian letter dating from around 1800 B.C.E. Found in Mari, a city on the upper Euphrates, it reports a divine message sent by a prophet to the resident king:

> Thus speaks Adad: I have given the whole country to [king] Yahdun-Lim, who, owing to my weapons, had no rival in fighting . . . I have brought you [King Zimri-Lim] back to the throne of your father, and have given you the arms with which I fought against Temtum. I have anointed you with the oil of my victory, and no one can withstand you . . . When you set out on campaign, by no means set out without consulting an oracle. When I, in an oracle of mine, should be favorable, you may set out on your campaign. If it is not so, do not go out of the [city] gate.[17]

The prophet who speaks in the name of the god Adad reminds King Zimri-Lim of his royal investiture. On this occasion, the king was given certain weapons as symbols of his military duties and as a divine pledge of victory. Interestingly, these weapons have special, mythological significance: Adad himself has used them in fighting against his foe, the chaos goddess Temtum (or Tiamat). The two themes of the ritual giving of the divine weapon and the god's combat with the goddess not only invite further comment, but will also supply more information on the warrior's initiation.

The King Receives the Divine Weapon

God-given weapons, especially swords, are not unknown in Western folklore. An example is the sword Excalibur of Celtic mythology. In the medieval epic of King Arthur, the Lady of the Lake gives a sword to Arthur, which he has to return to the goddess before his death, for it is meant for him and no one else; so before he dies, Arthur asks his friends to throw it into the lake. The king's or hero's supernatural weapon seems to reflect the traditional institution of the giving of a weapon to a warrior at his reception into the warrior caste or profession. As they reached the age of adulthood, young Germans were publicly equipped with shield and spear and thereby admitted to the warrior community.[18] Upon completing their initiation, young Indo-Iranian warriors

8. *The Divine Warrior's bow.* Dominated by the Divine Warrior and her attributes: bows and arrows, the Venus star with eight rays, and the lion that serves as her pedestal, the symmetrical scene unites god and king as they face each other. While Ishtar greets the king with her raised right hand and tends him bow and arrows as victorious weapons, the king raises his hands in a gesture of humility that combines adoration with the readiness to receive the divine gifts.—Gold pendant from Urartu, seventh century B.C.E.

received a mace, "the favorite weapon of the warrior god."[19] Similarly, in the Middle Ages, the handing over of weapons stood at the center of the knight's dubbing. These weapons were not ordinary ones; handed down and inherited and sometimes traced to mythical origins, they carried within them the bellicose virtues of the ancestors.[20]

In the ancient Near East, the royal enthronement ritual included the handing over of a special weapon, understood as the warrior deity's weapon, to the new king.[21] Cuneiform literature is full of references to this ritual. Thus the Assyrian king Tiglath-pileser I reports in one of his inscriptions that "the god Ashur and the great gods . . . commanded me to extend the border of their land. They placed in my hands their mighty weapons, deluge in battle."[22] The same king also refers to the bow, one of the most common—and most terrifying—weapons of ancient warfare: "The gods Ninurta and Nergal gave me their fierce weapons and their exalted bow for my lordly arms."[23] Iconography illustrates the transaction (fig. 8 above and fig. 9, p. 58).[24]

With the help of the letter from the royal archives of Mari we can tentatively reconstruct the royal ritual. Adad—the weather-god of the city of Mari—participated in this ceremony in a particular way. Three acts can be discerned:

1) Adad escorts the king to the throne—presumably in the form of a portable statue;
2) the king is given the divine weapons;
3) the king is anointed in the name of the god Adad.

The temple of Adad in Mari must have contained precious arms—perhaps a mace, a spear, and a shield—that were considered the weapons of the deity. With these very weapons the god was said to have triumphed over Tiamat, a mythical dragon of the sea. This is the motif of the miraculous weapon, familiar from mythology and folklore. Imbued with very special powers, the weapon has helped its possessors to prevail over the enemy in the past and therefore will also secure victory in the present. The king is expected to use this weapon or these arms, if only symbolically, to fight against the enemies of the state. Possession of the divine weapons, signs of the monarch's link with supernatural power, makes the king invincible.

Several biblical texts illustrate the idea of the divine weapon. In Ezekiel, we find the following divine message: "I [Yahweh] will strengthen the arms of the king of Babylon, and put my sword in his hand" (Ezek 30:24). According to another tradition, the leader of the anti-Syrian Jewish rebellion dreamt that he was ceremonially installed as the war leader of his people by a priest and a prophet, i.e. by those who in ancient times officiated at the royal enthronement. The high priest prayed for the victory of the people, and then a prophet appeared and gave Judas Maccabeus a golden sword with the words: "Take this holy sword, a gift from God, with which you will strike down your enemies" (2 Macc 15:16). While recorded in the second century B.C.E.—long after the end of the Judean monarchy—these words demonstrate that the ancient rite was still remembered and its powerful symbolism perfectly understood.[25] Further echoes of this rite can be detected in the book of Psalms. The idea of the god-given weapon seems to be present in one of the royal hymns, where the Hebrew text may be understood as referring to the divine gift of a shield to the royal warrior: "You have given me the shield of your help" or "of your protection" (Ps 18:35/Hebr. 36). More explicit is Psalm 2, where Yahweh promises victory to his king. In fact, this psalm shares a number of features with the Mari letter: the reference to the enthronement or investiture of a king; an oracle given to the new king by the deity; the allusion to the anointing ritual in the expression "Yahweh and his anointed one" (Ps 2:2); the reference to a weapon, presumably to one that belongs to the deity.

It is the last-named parallel that is of special relevance here: "Ask of me [Yahweh says], and I will make the nations your heritage, and the ends of the earth your possession. You shall break them with a rod of iron, and dash them in pieces like a potter's vessel" (Ps 2:8–9). Yahweh's enemies are also the king's enemies, and the king will triumph over these foes or, more precisely, he will destroy them with a rod of iron. The background to this divine promise remains vague in the biblical text, but the Mari letter supplies an apt illustration: the king fights with a divine weapon, and the enemy is considered an ally of Tiamat, the dragon of the sea. Thus the royal war is given a cosmic significance—one that goes far beyond what is actually visible to the naked eye. The king's "holy war" against human enemies and the divine war against supernatural foes belong to the same universal war. The Bronze Age ideology of warfare survived the era in which it had originated; in the Iron Age one had only to substitute the "modern" iron rod for the "ancient" bronze mace. Otherwise, nothing changed.

The idea of the divinely given weapon is not confined to the Semitic world; belonging to the stock ideas of ancient thought, it can also be found in Egypt. An example is the sickle-sword (or "scimitar") that the Egyptian god Amen-Re extends to pharaoh Merneptah. The scene is depicted on the famous Israel Stela in the Egyptian Museum in Cairo (fig. 9, p. 58).[26] The words of the deity added by the Egyptian artist prevent any misunderstanding: "Take the sickle-sword for the victory over every foreign country."[27] This scene comes fairly close to Psalm 2, of which it may be taken to provide an ironic illustration— ironic, because here it is Israel's enemy who is given the sword that will triumph. In fact, the last line of the long inscription below the image includes a reference to Israel as a people defeated by the king of Egypt! The divine giving of a weapon to the king remained an important item of Egyptian political iconography down to Hellenistic times. The inscription of the Rosetta Stone, which dates from 196 B.C.E., orders the placing of an honorary relief in all temples of Egypt; this is to depict the local god as he hands "a scimitar of victory" to the king.[28] Found in 1799, this famous multilingual text (two versions of ancient Egyptian accompanied by a Greek translation) served as the basis for Jean-François Champollion's decipherment of the hieroglyphs and thus stands at the beginning of modern Egyptology.

The Myth of the "Chaos Battle"

The myth of the Divine Warrior's successful battle against a being that represents chaos—the unstructured, hostile realm—was widely known throughout the Near East. We have met a reference to it in the Mari letter, which qualifies the king's weapon as the one used by the deity in slaying Temtum, a primeval beast. A myth comparable to that of the (otherwise unknown) story of Adad and Temtum was told in Ugarit, a Syrian city situated on the Mediterranean and living from commerce. This myth, transcribed around 1380 B.C.E. and today known as "Baal and Yam," recounts the story of the conflict between the

9. *The king receives the sickle-sword.* These two almost symmetrical scenes show, reading from the center out: the god Amen-Re with his high crown of two feathers, King Merneptah of Egypt, and a protecting deity standing behind the king. In both scenes, the king receives a sickle-sword, and the accompanying text records the words spoken by the deity: "Take the sickle-sword for the victory over every foreign country." The Egyptian sickle-sword was made of bronze and, unlike the peasant's sickle, had its cutting edge on the convex side. This type of weapon survived in Eastern countries as the scimitar of the Arabs and Persians—the saber with a curved blade.—Egyptian relief, ca. 1207 B.C.E.

weather-god, Baal, and the sea-god, Yam. Baal, whose name means "lord," is the city's main deity and divine benefactor. As a benevolent deity he sends rain and supplies fertility. His realm is the sky, where he rides upon clouds and uses lightning and thunder as his weapons. Baal's opponent, Yam, whose name means "sea," echoes the city's fear of the untamed sea. As the young and warlike Baal asserts himself among the gods and secures for himself a powerful position, he is envied and challenged by Yam. At first, Yam appears to defeat his enemy, but Baal does not submit to his rule. With the help of other gods he is eventually able to kill Yam. Then the text says, quite simply: "Yam is indeed dead! Baal will rule."[29]

The Bronze Age mythology of conflict, of which we have discussed only one example, was remembered long after the end of the era in which it originated and received its classic expression. It has also left its mark on the Bible. One example is Psalm 74, one of the many psalms that celebrate Israel's god as *deus militans*, the warrior deity. Here is a short passage from this poem:

> How long, O God, is the foe to scoff?
> Is the enemy to revile your name forever?
> Why do you hold back your hand;
> why do you keep your hand in your bosom?
> Yet God my King is from of old,
> working salvation in the earth.
> You divided Yam by your might;
> you broke the heads of the dragons [*tanninim*] in the waters.
> You crushed the heads of Leviathan;
> you gave him as food for the creatures of the wilderness.
> You cut openings for springs and torrents;
> you dried up ever-flowing streams.
> Yours is the day, yours also the night;
> you established the luminaries and the sun.
> You have fixed all the bounds of the earth;
> you made summer and winter. (Ps 74:10–17)

The psalmist refers to a myth of creation that involves the creator god's battle with the sea. This myth is somewhat elusive, for while the Bible alludes to it more than once, the story is never told as such and is not included in the creation narratives of the book of Genesis. The basic idea, though, is clear: the Creator has wrested the earth and its ordered structure from the sea. What Genesis describes as a separation of land from water assumes the mythic dimensions of a cosmic battle. The mythic characters associated with the sea—Yam, the Tannins (i.e. a multiplicity of dragons), and Leviathan—do not convey a precise picture of the Creator's enemy. It is far from clear against whom he fights. Are Yam and Leviathan different names for the same character, a mighty sea monster accompanied by its helpers, the Tannins? One detail invites emphasis: the designation of the triumphant Creator as king. "Yet God my King is from of old," sings the psalmist (Ps 74:12), and the statement implies that king and warrior are almost synonymous.

The book of Job is also acquainted with the myth of the antagonism between God and the sea, though the relevant passage avoids any reference to Leviathan. Job uses other names for the enemies of the Divine Warrior:

> He has described a circle on the face of the waters,
> at the boundary between light and darkness.
> The pillars of heaven tremble,
> and are astounded at his rebuke.
> By his power he stilled the Sea [or: Yam];
> by his understanding he struck down Rahab.
> By his wind the heavens were made fair;
> his hand pierced the Fleeing Serpent. (Job 26:10–13)

According to this version of the battle, the Divine Warrior fights against Rahab and the "Fleeing Serpent," who may be identified as companions and helpers of Yam, the dragon of the sea. One detail of the battle merits our particular attention: the "rebuking" or "threatening" (Hebrew *gaʿar*) of the enemy. Ancient warfare is not limited to the use of weapons; words are also used to challenge the enemy, as can be seen in the account of the duel between David and Goliath. The two warriors scoff at each other, saying: "Come to me, and I will give your flesh to the birds of the air and to the wild animals of the field" (1 Sam 17:44). In a similar way the Divine Warrior threatens his enemies. "They are astounded at his rebuke," reports the book of Job. The motif has a long history, and its echo can be discerned in the gospel of Matthew, where Jesus rebukes wind and waves so as to calm the stormy sea and prevent his disciples' boat from capsizing.[30]

How are these stories to be understood? A common interpretation views them as a mythological gloss on the battle between summer and winter, the two climatic seasons of the Near East. The triumphant winter expels the summer and rules over the ensuing rainy season. As for the Ugaritic chaos battle, we have to consider the fact that during fall and winter—between November and April—no ship dared to leave the ports of the Mediterranean cities, for the winds were fierce and the sea unpredictable.[31] In November the storms set in with great violence. These bring clouds heavy with rain, which falls on the foothills of the mountains, especially near Mount Lebanon. The myth thus echoes a conflict within nature. "In the coastal region the extraordinarily rough weather could be understood in terms of a battle between the thunderstorm and the raging sea, between the upper and the lower powers, for sovereignty over the earth. While the one kind of water threatens to swallow up the land, the other kind makes vegetation possible."[32] Baal must of course triumph, for some day the sea calms and the land bears its fruit. It is at the beginning of the rainy season that Baal establishes his "everlasting kingdom" and "eternal dominion."[33] In more prosaic terms, however, Baal's rule does not last longer than the winter rains, for every year Yam reasserts his claim against Baal and brings about the summer, and so there is a permanent conflict between the two powers, with each dominating for a season.

The people of the Near East asked the question of why there should be conflict in nature, and the answer given by the myth refers to fighting among the gods. Accordingly, we can speak of nature mythology or, more precisely, of a *mythological etiology* or explanatory tale. Another theory looks for the conflict not so much in nature as in human society. It is not summer and winter that are fighting, but social classes or even entire nations. According to this view, each deity or supernatural agent represents a human group or individual. In the case of the Ugaritic myth, one may think of the ruling king's need for legitimation: the victory of the warrior god Baal over the sea reflects the royal claim to triumphant authority; by associating himself with victorious Baal, the king asserts his position as the foremost representative of beneficent social and cosmic order.[34] An echo of the ancient idea that the king must triumph over the dragon can be discerned in the imperial art of the Christian emperor Constantine: a publicly displayed picture showed "a resemblance of the dragon beneath his own and his children's feet, stricken through with a dart, and cast headlong into the depth of the sea."[35] In these cases, an *ideological use* of the myth is suggested, for claims to rulership and authority are backed up and ideologically mystified by the mythical tale.

As far as the Bible is concerned, the question "political ideology or natural etiology?" can be settled in favor of ideology. With its clear political focus, the relevant biblical tradition is only marginally, if at all, interested in weather-related phenomena. The conflict between the Divine Warrior and his several enemies—Rahab, Tannin, Leviathan, and whatever their names may be—is not set exclusively in the past, in a mythical time preceding history. As a perpetual conflict, the battle continues into the present. It also relates to human history and gives mythical overtones and cosmic dimensions to Israel's fate in situations of conflict and war. It is in this sense that the psalmist refers to Israel's passage through the sea as an episode in Yahweh's war against the waters.[36] He describes a thunderstorm, or rather its awe-inspiring, sacred character. This is what historians of religion call a hierophany. Thunder, rain, and flashes of lightning are the visible side of the Divine Warrior's appearance in the realm of nature. He fights against the sea, which has to give way to the invisible deity and the people under his protection. Thus the people can cross the sea on dry ground. The Divine Warrior's essential responsibility is to fight on behalf of his people, Israel. Especially during the period of the Babylonian exile, the psalmist turns to the Divine Warrior, reminding him of his fight against and triumph over the dragon of the sea.[37]

The chaos-battle mythology reveals much of the worldview of the ancient warrior societies. According to this, the order of the present world is the outcome of a victory of the gods (or God) over the dark, demonic forces of chaos. The order of the world as established by God or the gods is stable, but it is also somehow fragile and endangered. Hostile forces that still reside within creation and that are normally contained may at any time make their presence felt and thereby endanger the order of the world from within. Nature, society, and state are experienced as fragile and unstable. Earthquakes, floods, drought, famine, and epidemics, attacks from the enemy, defeat in war, exploitation of the lower classes, and so on destabilize the ordered structure of the cosmos and announce the reign of chaos and demonic powers. "The dim awareness of cosmic instability underlies the Hebrew mentality," suggests Ludwig Köhler.[38] This fragility and insecurity of the social and cosmic order necessitates the intervention of the *deus militans*; equally, it is the Divine Warrior's foremost task to reenact the original battle perpetually and, by wresting the earth from the powers of the primeval waters, to restore the original order. The fight for order never ends, for after each defeat the powers of darkness recover and renew their attack. Thus the primeval conflict of the gods continues forever. "The surviving traditions of the chaos battle are evidence of a mentality which flourished for millennia. It must have marked and permeated the thinking, the feeling, and the imagination of the ancient Near East in a way which we have difficulty in appreciating."[39]

The antagonism between divine order and demonic chaos has its equivalent in human society. Evil can be met under many guises in social and political life. Human and divine intervention strive to eliminate evil, to uphold order and make human life possible. Both human and divine warriors may cooperate, for example, in "holy warfare." Religion based on this distinctive worldview can be characterized as religion of warfare. It aims at restoring order to a world that has lost its structure and fallen into chaos. Military campaigns are conducted to restore the ideal primordial state of peace, prosperity, and wellbeing. While mythology tends to emphasize the cosmic, universal dimension of both order and chaos, politics is more realistic and more local, for it aims at healing the territorially defined social and political body, i.e. the state. Hence there is the expectation of a warrior king who will drive the enemy out of the country in order to reveal God's triumphant kingship. The warrior king has a particularly close relationship with the Lord of War. "Blessed be Yahweh . . . who trains my hands for war, and my fingers for battle," reads a passage in one of the royal psalms (Ps 144:1).

Within this ideology, the idea of participation can be considered the key, for human warfare seeks not only to imitate the primeval battle, but also to be synchronous with it and to be part of it. The wish to understand contemporary events in the light of mythological patterns, which are imitated in human warfare, can be explained as the desire to reduce the particular nature of historical events to general notions that remain outside of the realm of the accidental and uncontrollable. To link a particular event to a mythological prototype means to departicularize and thereby dehistoricize it. History is as it were to be avoided, for as a sequence of unique, unrepeatable events it is ultimately chaotic and threatening. Myth, by contrast, offers the security of a meaningful, patterned existence.[40]

8.   From Exodus to Apocalyptic Drama

The archaic ideology of warfare (as discussed in the two previous chapters) did not remain unchanged over all of the biblical period. Three important changes modify the archaic pattern as a new—postarchaic and eventually apocalyptic—mythology emerges. First, biblical authors increasingly emphasize the divine side of warfare, highlighting the Divine Warrior's acts at the expense of human participation: typically, God and his angelic hosts do all the fighting, so that the Israelite army, where it exists at all, loses its function. The enemy will be destroyed, "but not by human hands" (Dan 8:25). Second, as comprehensive apocalyptic scenarios develop, these combine the Divine Warrior's aggressive role with the quieter, judicial activity of the Lord of Wisdom to underline the completeness of divine opposition to both human and transcendent enemies. Third, the battle against the inimical and often transcendent forces of chaos is no longer seen as part of an ongoing conflict; instead, biblical writers envisage the final and permanent overthrow of the enemy. Divine victory can no longer be challenged, for it includes the enemy's complete destruction.

The Exodus Tradition and Jerusalem's Liberation

The development of a new, postarchaic pattern first becomes visible in the account of the Hebrews' legendary escape from Egyptian servitude. The Hebrews lived in Egypt as a guest people who worked on government building projects. The king of Egypt sought to prevent the Hebrew population from multiplying and therefore had their male offspring killed. Eventually one of the Hebrews emerged as their leader and liberator—a man called Moses. He organized a communal flight out of the country, but the fugitives were followed by the Egyptian army. A miracle allowed the Hebrews to escape through a lake in a marshy area. The pursuing chariots were engulfed by the water. Credit for the Hebrews' exodus from Egypt and the annihilation of Pharaoh's pursuing chariots was given to Yahweh, and the biblical account states quite clearly that "Yahweh is a warrior" (Exod 15:3). Into the prose narrative, the scribes inserted a poem that commemorates the Hebrew God's victory over the Egyptian chariot army. This "Song at the Sea," attributed variously to Moses or his sister, Miriam, celebrates Yahweh's drowning of the Egyptian chariot host:

I will sing to Yahweh, for he has triumphed gloriously;
horse and driver[41] he has thrown into the sea . . .
Yahweh is a warrior; Yahweh is his name.
Pharaoh's chariots and his army he cast into the sea;
his picked officers were sunk in the Suph Sea.
The floods covered them; they went into the depth like a stone.
Your right hand, O Yahweh, glorious in power—
your right hand, O Yahweh, shattered the enemy . . .
You blew with your wind, the sea covered them;
they sank like lead in the mighty waters. (Exod 15:1, 3–6, 10)

It is not quite clear what the designation "Suph Sea" refers to. The Septuagint renders it as the "Red Sea" and thus suggests a particular location for the event, placing it at the Gulf of Aqaba (whose name, in antiquity, was the Red Sea). Others translate it as the "Reed Sea" or "Sea of Reeds" and make one think of the marshy lands to the east of the Nile Delta. But philologically, the expression may simply mean "Sea of End" or "Sea of Extinction."[42]

If the song does indeed commemorate a real rather than a legendary event, then the prose account ought to be disregarded and we should consider the poem in isolation. The poem's main thrust is that Yahweh threw the horses and the chariot drivers into the sea so that they sank into the water like stones or lead weights. Thus it seems to exult in the capsizing of ships in a storm, perhaps horse transports making their way toward Palestine through coastal waters.[43] Such an event could have taken place in around 1200 B.C.E., the period in which the Egyptian king Merneptah waged war in Palestine and mentioned Israel in his poem of victory.[44] If we are right in our dating of this event, the slogan "Yahweh is a warrior" would belong to the earliest stratum of biblical tradition.

Due to its exclusive focus on the Divine Warrior, the exodus poem does not refer to Israelite arms, warfare, or military leadership, and thus provides an augury of change, announcing a new ideological development—one that leads to the exclusion of human participation from holy warfare. We happen to know one of the historical events that contributed to this development: the Assyrian army's unexpected departure from Palestine in 701 B.C.E. In that year, King Sennacherib conquered the Judean city of Lachish, but after a short siege of Jerusalem left without having achieved his purpose. The Judeans attributed their enemies' sudden disappearance to Yahweh's angel, who seemed to have decimated their foe, smiting them with the plague. "That very night the angel of Yahweh set out and struck down one hundred and eighty-five thousand in the camp of the Assyrians; when morning dawned, they were all dead bodies. Then King Sennacherib of Assyria left, went home, and lived at Nineveh" (2 Kgs 19:35–36). Here an enemy was defeated, but not by human hands. This idea began to nourish the popular imagination, until it came to dominate the apocalyptic mind.

The Apocalypse of War

Anonymous prophetic poetry and prose dating (presumably) from the sixth or fifth century B.C.E. provides the first evidence for the apocalyptic idea of war. In a victory song replete with shocking images of blood and gore, the poet paints a picture of Yahweh who, after having defeated his unnamed foes, boasts of having trampled them underfoot all by himself, for "from my people, no one was with me . . . I looked, but there was no one to help" (Isa 63:3, 5, Qumran reading). Prose texts that found their way into the books of Ezekiel and Zechariah add imaginative scenes that elaborate the theme.[45] Some day, the armies of several foreign nations will combine to march toward the land of Israel, intent on attacking its unprotected cities and carrying off both its wealth and people. After the enemy's initial success, the Divine Warrior will appear on the scene to determine the final outcome of the battle. He will send terrible earthquakes, devastating plagues, and showers of hailstones and burning sulphur. Moreover, there will be conflicts within the enemy's troops, so that their swords will be turned against their comrades. In this way, Israel's enemy will be utterly destroyed.

The book of Daniel includes several war apocalypses, all dating from the second century B.C.E. and reflecting the crisis provoked by King Antiochus IV, the Jews' Syrian overlord, who interfered with the priestly ritual of the Jerusalem temple. The first of the apocalypses announces the evil king's rise to power:

> At the end of their rule, when the transgressions have reached their full measure, a king of bold countenance shall arise, skilled in intrigue. He shall grow strong in power, shall cause fearful destruction, and shall succeed in what he does. He shall destroy the powerful and the people of the holy ones. By his cunning he shall make deceit prosper under his hand, and in his own mind he shall be great. Without warning he shall destroy many and shall even rise up against the Prince of princes. *But he shall be broken, and not by human hands.* (Dan 8:23–25, italics added)

The "king of bold countenance" whose rule is announced must be the Seleucid king Antiochus. As soon as this ruler rises up against the "Prince of princes," i. e. Yahweh, the God of Israel, "he shall be broken, and not by human hands." Neither Daniel nor his angelic interlocutor explains whose hands will put an end to the foreign king's attempt to destroy the Jewish people. It may be the hands of Yahweh himself or those of an angel. In another Danielic text of the same type, the seer falls into a trance and receives a revelation from an angel.[46] He is told what will happen in the future. There will be wars that lead to the disintegration of a huge empire. Eventually, an evil ruler will appear, a warlike figure worshiping "the god of fortresses" (Dan 11:38). He will pitch his palatial tents near "the beautiful holy mountain" of Jerusalem (Dan 11:45). While the report is somewhat laconic on this point, it is clear enough that, at the very moment of the enemy's attack on Jerusalem, "he shall come to his end, with no one to help him" (Dan 11:45). The one who delivers Jerusalem from his hands is presumably the angel Michael, Israel's mighty protector.[47]

The gospels also depict scenes of apocalyptic war, all of them "synoptically" interrelated and apparently echoing a single source text, imitated and elaborated by the others. The gospel of Mark's apocalyptic sermon, put into the mouth of Jesus, provided the model, and so it may serve as our guide.[48] As in the Old Testament passages, we hear of wars which in this case will lead to the destruction of the Jerusalem temple. Christians will suffer from a terrible persecution. "They will hand you over to councils; and you will be beaten in synagogues; and you will stand before governors and kings because of me, as a testimony to them" (Mark 13:9). Moreover, "brother will betray brother to death, and a father his child, and children will rise against parents and have them put to death" (v. 12). During this terrible period false prophets and messiahs will appear, "producing signs and omens, to lead astray, if possible, the elect" (v. 22). "You will be hated by all because of my name. But the one who endures to the end will be saved" (v. 13). At a particular moment, a transcendent power will intervene, delivering the faithful: "Then they will see the Son of Man coming in clouds with great power and glory. He will send out the angels, and gather his elect from the four winds, from the ends of the earth to the end of heaven" (vv. 26–27).

Specialists have questioned the traditional identification of the "Son of Man coming in clouds" with Christ. In his apocalyptic discourse, Jesus does not seem to have referred to himself as the "Son of Man." Rather, he must have been thinking of the figure that intervenes on behalf of Israel in the book of Daniel's war apocalypse discussed above: an anthropomorphic warrior angel named Michael who delivers the faithful from the apocalyptic woes and horrors.

The "war apocalypses" share a common language and a common repertoire of ideas and literary clichés. We can now establish a list of the shared features of this genre:

1) War is raging between various peoples. Often the domination of the world's leading political power is endangered.
2) The faithful (Jews or Christians) are either directly under attack or affected in some way, so that they must fear for their lives.
3) Eventually, God or a messenger of God intervenes on behalf of the faithful, delivering them from peril.

The key element is the third shared feature, the climax of the apocalyptic myth: divine or angelic intervention. Characteristically, the suffering human community does not engage in any fighting, which is instead done by supernatural powers, i.e. by the Divine Warrior and his angelic representative. The human warrior has abdicated, so to speak. In view of the pagan enemy's enormous superiority, Israel's human warriors had to give up fighting, but they never lost their belief in the Divine Warrior's help.

Concluding this section, we may briefly compare the ideologies we have met in analyzing the Divine Warrior's activity in archaic and postarchaic traditions. These may be described as follows:

— *Divine support.* According to this notion, divine activity combines with human initiative without disrupting the battle's natural framework (see above, chapters 6 and 7). Divine images, often in the form of emblems and war standards, accompany the fighting army, and divine participation is thought to strengthen the soldiers and confuse the enemy. The "support pattern" can be reconstructed from biblical and ancient Near Eastern sources including the Stela of the Vultures. In the Bible, the book of Deuteronomy echoes its central tenet: "Yahweh your God travels along with your camp, to save you and to hand over your enemies to you" (Deut 23:15).

— *Divine support and intervention.* Legendary accounts of ancient battles frequently include scenes in which the Lord of War not only supports the human army but intervenes forcefully on the battlefield, for example by hurling down hailstones from heaven, making the sun stand still to prolong the day, or causing the enemy's city walls to collapse under the priests' trumpet blast. The book of Joshua is replete with legends that highlight the Divine Warrior's intervention and minimize human fighting.

— *Divine intervention.* Divine intervention comes directly out of the heavenly realm, for the Divine Warrior and his celestial army do all the fighting. An example of the "intervention pattern" is the exodus story in which Yahweh destroys the Egyptian army by sending a mighty wind from heaven. As Moses explains: "Yahweh will fight for you, and you have only to be still" (Exod 14:14). Human participation is altogether absent.

In ancient Israelite tradition, the "support pattern" and the "intervention pattern" vie with each other and often overlap and mix in legendary lore, but generally, later accounts show a definite preference for divine intervention.[49] Seen from a broader ancient Near Eastern perspective, the "support pattern" appears to be the older one, based as it is on the notion of the gods' active presence in the world. The idea of divine intervention from "above" appears more recent; its underlying theology thinks of the gods as more transcendent, as residing in and acting from heaven.[50]

The Apocalypse of Judgment

The early high cultures and their central political institution, the state, depended on the cooperation of the latter's leading social types: the scribe and the warrior. These two forces have determined political life for thousands of years. Goethe, well aware of their importance, saw the king as a military man who still needed a chancellor to draw up a contract:

> You are knight and a monarch, you command and do battle;
> Summon your Chancellor, though, when you have contracts to sign.[51]

Thus the state is shaped by power and contract, by warrior and scribe. In the ancient Near East, the warrior mentality's aggressive heroism was generally counterbalanced by the more diplomatic approach of the bureaucrats and the sages. In Assyria, the foremost military state of ancient times, the administration mitigated the aggressiveness of war by a well-devised diplomatic strategy involving bilateral treaties, friendship and assistance pacts, and the installation of local kings who had grown up at the Assyrian royal court.[52] Hebrew culture was quite conscious of the necessity to combine wisdom, the First Function virtue, with valor, the virtue of the Second Function.[53] In Israel, the diplomatic, peaceful approach to social reality was mainly embodied by the legal institutions. Scribes, like warriors, fought against evil, but they did it in a different way. The administrators' participation in the battle against evil is only indirect and restrained, for they are more passive and indulgent and act as judges. Evil is not triumphed over in war but mastered by a decent, "just" administration. Lawsuit replaces war as the latter's more domesticated form. Far from handling weapons, the administrators pronounce a sentence and initiate an administrative act. They are not enthusiastic about the use of weapons, for they regard the word, and not the sword, as their weapon. This is explained in the Teaching for King Merikare: "If you are skilled in speech, you will win. The tongue is a king's sword. Speaking is stronger than all fighting."[54]

Since the scribes were as powerful and influential as the warriors, it will not surprise us to learn that the apocalypse of war with its warrior roots was supplemented by the apocalypse of judgment, a scenario based on scribal values.

The oldest example of a judgment apocalypse can be found in the book of Daniel.[55] In a dream, Daniel is made witness to a session of the heavenly tribunal. He sees how the judges assemble under the presidency of God and how they investigate and pronounce sentence. Evil powers, represented by ugly beasts, are destroyed, and an anthropomorphic mighty angel, called the "Son of Man" to emphasize the contrast he offers with the beasts, is given universal rulership which he will use to grant special privileges to the Jews. The angelic attendant with whom Daniel speaks explains that rule will be given to "the people of the holy ones of the Most High," i.e. to the Jewish people (Dan 7:27).

This transfer of dominion does not involve military action, but is made by divine decree—by an act of administration (see above, chapter 4).

Another, equally fascinating Danielic apocalypse is noteworthy for the idea it contains of the resurrection from the dead.[56] Due to its extreme brevity and elliptical nature, which is no doubt intentional on the part of the author, the text has prompted various interpretations, but the following sequence of eschatological events can be reconstructed on the basis of parallel passages found in the books of Enoch and Jubilees.[57] First, there is a terrible "time of anguish, such as has never occurred since nations first came into existence" (Dan 12:1), no doubt a time in which Jews are persecuted for their adherence to traditional Jewish ways. Many of the faithful die the death of martyrs. It is during this time that Israel's angelic protector, the "great prince" Michael, intervenes. As a result, the persecution ends. The dead, victims of the persecution and the struggle, are judged according to the heavenly books. The truly faithful martyrs—those whose names figure in the book of life—are resurrected, dressed in garments of shining light, and made angels. The unfaithful Jews, by contrast, are relegated to the netherworld, understood as a place of "shame and everlasting contempt" (Dan 12:2). It should be noted that resurrection in this context does not imply return to earthly, bodily life, but rather transfer from the darkness of death to the light of God's celestial abode. One of the comparable Jewish texts is quite explicit on this matter: the righteous will "rejoice with joy forever and ever . . . Their bones will rest in the earth, but their spirits will have much joy."[58]

Turning to the New Testament, we find a similar scene of eschatological judgment, though not set in heaven but on earth. The judge, a figure called the "Son of Man" and the "king," descends from heaven and summons all the peoples of the earth before his tribunal. After having divided humankind into two groups, he announces his judgment. To the first group he says: "Come, you that are blessed by my Father, inherit the kingdom prepared for you from the foundation of the world; for I was thirsty and you gave me something to drink, I was a stranger and you welcomed me" (Matt 25:34–35). The other group receives the following sentence: "You are accursed, depart from me into the eternal fire prepared for the devil and his angels; for I was hungry and you gave me no food, I was thirsty and you gave me nothing to drink, I was a stranger and you did not welcome me" (vv. 41–43).[59]

Yet another example of a judgment apocalypse can be found in the book of Revelation. It reads as follows:

> Then I saw a great white throne and the one who sat on it; the earth and the heaven fled from his presence, and no place was found for them. And I saw the dead, great and small, standing before the throne, and books were opened. Also another book was opened, the book of life. And the dead were judged according to their works, as recorded in the books. The sea gave up

the dead that were in it, Death and Hades gave up the dead that were in them, and all were judged according to what they had done. Then Death and Hades were thrown into the lake of fire; and anyone whose name was not found written in the book of life was thrown into the lake of fire. (Rev 20:11–15)

The passage does not reveal the identity of the one who sits on the throne of the judge, but it must be the same figure as in the book of Daniel—God himself. The scene is styled as a judgment of the dead or of souls. Sea, Death, and Hades are the names given to the same power, or at any rate to closely allied evil powers. As in Daniel's dream, the evil figures sentenced by the divine judge come out of the sea.[60] The reward of the righteous, whose names can be found in the book of life, does not receive much attention; the emphasis is on the punishment of the wicked. They are thrown into a lake of fire—a kind of boiling volcano—to perish. After their first, normal death, they die for a second and final time, so that nothing of them survives. Characteristically, it is not only the evil souls that are annihilated, but also the transcendent, anti-godly powers of evil: Death and Hades. The annihilation of these powers underscores the message that those who do survive—the righteous—will never die again.

Apocalypses of judgment are defined by their shared repertoire of literary motifs and clichés. They can be summarized as follows:

1) The divine tribunal assembles in heaven.
2) The court studies its documents and pronounces its sentence against the accused evil powers and has them punished or destroyed.
3) The reward of the good is generally their postmortem transformation into angelic beings.

Within the history of biblical literature, the apocalypse of judgment is a relatively late creation. Nevertheless, some of its features can be traced back to an early age. Heavenly court assemblies are known from pre-apocalyptic, prophetic traditions. According to one report, the prophet Micaiah was admitted to the heavenly throne chamber, "saw Yahweh sitting on his throne, with all the host of heaven standing beside him," and witnessed how the court deliberated and decreed disaster for the king of Israel.[61] In a similar heavenly scene Isaiah is prepared for his prophetic task and commissioned to proclaim a message of doom in Jerusalem. The apocalyptic version of the heavenly scene differs from its prophetic model in one respect only. Whereas in the prophetic tradition Israel itself is punished, the apocalypse of judgment takes a positive view of the Jewish people (and Christian believers). The apocalypse of judgment brings good news to a suffering people.

In this context, God's justice is consistently underlined. The older apocalyptic sources, which we have discussed, do not refer to a merciful divine judge.

It is only later that mercy complements and mitigates justice. In several sources dating from the second century C.E. we find the notion that the torments of hell may be suspended. According to the Testament of Isaac, punishment in hell lasts until God shows mercy.[62] In the Apocalypse of Peter, a Christian work, the possibility of escape from hell is discussed at length. As soon as one of the blessed intercedes in favor of one of the damned, the latter may be granted mercy, release from hell, and admission to the paradise of the blessed.[63] A consideration of the difference between the apocalypse of war and the apocalypse of judgment can lead us to a deeper understanding of the matter. The apocalypse of war aims at the enemy's annihilation or everlasting punishment. In the apocalypse of judgment, the judge's sentence may be reconsidered, punishment may be mitigated and mercy shown. The warrior tends toward wrath, immoderation, and violence. He considers his adversary a subhuman, abominable beast that must be tormented and destroyed. The wise and conciliatory administrator, by contrast, has to do with human individuals, who, despite all differences, are essentially like himself. Therefore punishment should not be excessive and can be mitigated and limited. According to the book of Job, there is an advocate at God's tribunal—an angel who appeals to God's mercy.[64] The underlying principle can be found in the book of Wisdom, which acknowledges in a hymnic statement that God's sovereign power is balanced by his mildness: "Although you are sovereign in strength, you judge with mildness, and with great forbearance you judge us" (Wis 12:18). "You are merciful to all, for you can do all things, and you overlook people's sins, so that they may repent. For you love all things that exist" (vv. 23–24). In their disposition to mildness, the divine judge and his staff resemble the wise scribes. Interestingly, it is only in the sapiential books, the biblical literature most closely associated with the scribes, that the divine ruler's and judge's mildness are emphasized.

The two apocalyptic genres—apocalypse of war and apocalypse of judgment—convey the same message: the announcement of the deliverance of the elect and the righteous. In the first case, deliverance is staged as deliverance from danger of death in the context of war or persecution; in the second, as the just and favorable verdict of a judge. In the book of Daniel and in the gospels the two independent ways of thinking are juxtaposed without being combined. In Daniel, we find an apocalypse of judgment in chapter 7 and an apocalypse of war in chapters 10–12. In the gospel of Matthew, an apocalypse of war in chapter 24 (paralleling Mark 13) is followed in chapter 25 by an apocalypse of judgment. Again, the two are collocated, but no attempt is made to provide a logical or narrative link. Using a concept from art history that distinguishes between modern perspective and premodern "aspective," we may here speak of a combination or collocation of aspects. Just as premodern art (for example, ancient Egyptian art) and the drawings of our children do not integrate the objects depicted into a comprehensive perspective but juxtapose them, so the older apocalyptic tradition simply collocates the two aspects of the apocalyptic drama—judgment and war—without discussing or even imagining their relationship. "By observing each part on its own, separating it from its environment and closing it off, aspective accords it independence."[65]

In the book of Revelation, things are different. Here the two apocalyptic genres are combined to form a comprehensive, chronologically structured eschatological drama. In chapters 19–20, the following sequence can be discerned:

Apocalypse of war	Rev 19:11–21	The heavenly army conquers the enemy, throwing "the beast" and "the false prophet" into the lake of fire.
Apocalypse of judgment	Rev 20:1–6	The heavenly court's angel overwhelms and binds Satan; the martyrs are received into heaven where they reign for a thousand years.
Apocalypse of war	Rev 20:7–10	Fire from heaven destroys the enemy, Satan is thrown into the lake of fire.
Apocalypse of judgment	Rev 20:11–15	The Divine Judge has Death, Hades, and the damned humans thrown into the lake of fire.

From this analysis the Revelation of John emerges as a well-designed apocalyptic corpus. The two traditional types of apocalyptic discourse—apocalypse of war and apocalypse of judgment—are skillfully combined to articulate a great drama which begins with a war. The fighting is followed by a scene of judgment, which, however, does not serve as the drama's final act. Both war and judgment are repeated. The arrangement is coherent. The first two apocalyptic scenes are about contemporary enemies—"the beast" (= the Roman Empire) and "the false prophet" (= a Christian prophet who did not object to the believers' participation in the worship of the Roman emperor)—whereas the subsequent episodes deal with Satan and his allies as the final, as it were transcendent enemies, who have to be overwhelmed in a campaign of cosmic dimensions reminiscent of the primeval chaos battle. Only after the conflict with and victory over this final enemy can the book of Revelation end in the sublime description of the new Jerusalem and its shining glory.

The Finality of God's Triumph

One feature of the eschatological drama deserves further—and concluding—consideration: the final character of the triumph over the enemy.

The finality of the triumph over the enemy excludes repetition within the apocalyptic drama. There may be various periods of battle, during which the foes may renew their strength, but it all ends in unequivocal, definitive victory. No longer subject to decay, the splendor of the new world will last forever. This notion has come about through a major process of transformation in the history of religions. The traditional worldview of the warriors is based on the assumption that there will be a continuous, never-ending conflict between good and evil forces in a world lacking stability. Although the powers of evil may often be weakened and temporarily controlled, they cannot be annihilated. This, in essence, is the implication of the myth of the chaos battle. Apparently the religion of Zarathustra (Zoroaster) was the first to revise this traditional ideological complex. This prophet, who lived some time between 1400 and 1200 B.C.E. in southern Russia, developed a notion of divine warriordom that permitted the final demise of evil.[66] When devising the eschatological drama, Jewish and Christian apocalypticism followed the Persian model, known through contact between the cultures. The final elimination of evil characterizes all developed forms of Jewish and Christian apocalypticism. In the myth of the chaos battle, Israel's God appeared as superior; but now he is believed to be almighty. By annihilating the beast through his warrior angels, he affirms his omnipotence. As soon as God is defined as *deus omnipotens*, he must also be the *deus victor* whose triumph is final.

The finality of divine victory has left significant traces in Christian teaching. In fact, it has become a basic conviction within the doctrinal tradition and is recognized by most modern believers. After the Lord has come to judge the living and the dead and after he has sentenced the evil powers to everlasting torture or annihilation in hell, there will be no more evil.

The Third Image: Lord of the Animals

*The richness of the biblical record permits the examination of God's special rela-
tionship with animals, and from this study another divine role emerges, for God is
not only Lord of Wisdom and Lord of War, but also Lord of the Animals. He represents important aspects of Dumézil's Third Function: wealth and fertility. For as
long as humans lived as hunters and gatherers or pastoralists, the Divine Gamekeeper (an expression used to denote the same figure, male or female) dominated religious experience, imagination, and ritual life. Even after the advent of agriculture,
this deity—the god "who gives the cattle their food, and to the young ravens when
they call upon him" (Ps 147:9, Septuagint)—continued to fascinate people.*

*In the Bible, traces of the Lord of the Animals abound. The blessing, caring, and
protecting father's character, evident in both Testaments, is matched by another, more
problematic side, for he allows humans to hunt and kill animals, and to consume
meat. The institution of animal sacrifice, understood as a rite acknowledging the
divine ownership of nature, will be discussed here along with the often misunderstood
notion of the godlikeness of the human being (homo imago Dei). Humans are created
in the image of the Lord of the Animals; representing him, they are granted dominion over his creatures. A final section considers the books of Genesis and Job as evidence for a revival of belief in the Lord of the Animals in the generation living
around 500 B.C.E.*

9.   God as Lord of the Animals

For the first ninety-nine percent of their history, humans spent their lives hunting wild animals and collecting vegetable food. The early hunters and gatherers had no domesticated animals and did not cultivate plants. Economically speaking, theirs was a primitive world, balanced by a diverse and sophisticated culture of art, religion, and science. In early times, these three branches of knowledge were intimately interconnected, and the early specialists—we may call them shamans or priests—seem to have been authorities on all of them. They knew how to use healing herbs (science), created simple sculptures such as the famous *Venus of Willendorf* (art), and had notions of the divine (religion).

Anthropologists and historians of religion believe that the worldview of the early hunter-gatherers was dominated by a deity modern scholars term the "Lady of the Animals" or "Lord of the Animals."[1] This is the Divine Gamekeeper, responsible for the increase in game and for giving permission to hunt. The Lord or the Lady of the Animals are essentially benign and friendly to the human race. Belief in a single deity who controls all the animals is widely attested throughout the world. Among certain peoples, however, the various kinds of animals are each accorded their own master or mistress: the Mother of Walruses, the Mistress of Buffaloes, and the like. The archaic world of the hunters has disappeared, but in the margins of modern civilization such societies still exist. Even after the hunting-and-gathering and pastoral cultures have disappeared or declined, the memory of the Divine Gamekeeper lingers on, feeding human imagination and beguiling the mind.

We will begin our discussion with a look at the evidence found by prehistorians and archaeologists in the Near East.

The Lord of the Animals in the Ancient Near East

In the Near East, as elsewhere, the Neolithic revolution introduced the cultivation of plants and the domestication of animals between the eighth and the sixth millennium B.C.E. During this period the human economy shifted from hunting and gathering to planting and herding. By the fourth millennium, hunting and pastoralism, though still supplementing the diet of Near Eastern peoples, no longer supplied the staple. Grains, especially wheat and barley, now

10. *Lord of the Animals in the form of a goat-man.* This figure—with human limbs, raised arms, hands ending in three fingers, horns and a goat's beard—seems to live among the wild animals by which it is surrounded in the images. The earlier seal, on the left, may show the deity as the leader of a dance, whereas that on the right, a later seal, seems to depict the goat-man as the protector of an ibex and other, undefined four-legged animals. Often depicted in works of art, the anonymous "goat deity" is the earliest god on record in Mesopotamia and adjacent areas.—Stamp seals from Mesopotamia, fifth and fourth millennia B.C.E.

came to dominate the diet. From this period onwards, the Divine Gamekeeper can no longer have served as the leading notion of the deity. Nevertheless, there is evidence for deities belonging to this type from the fifth millennium B.C.E.[2] Mesopotamian stamp seals show a figure with human limbs, horns, and a goat's beard, surrounded by wild mountain animals among which it seems to live (fig. 10).[3] Scholars impressed by its beard have termed this deity the "goat demon," but we know virtually nothing about this figure. It seems to be the first deity whose veneration can be documented from Mesopotamia. This "goat demon" lives among the beasts and shares certain features of their physical form; in an early Sumerian sculpture, however, we find an almost naked male figure accompanied by two calves and two birds (fig. 11, p. 79). The birds and the virtual nakedness relate the god to nature, but the fully human body, the carefully parted hair, and the domesticated calves betray his closeness to the human world. It is not only the beasts of the wilderness, but also the herds-man's flock that he cares for.

Further insight comes from the so-called Two-Dogs Palette from Hierakon-polis, Egypt, one of the earliest examples of Egyptian art and certainly the most intriguing early representation of the Lord of the Animals (fig. 12, p. 80). The name "Two-Dogs Palette" derives from the two hunting dogs that frame the

11. *Anthropomorphic Lord of the Animals.* This small vessel is decorated with a male figure—no doubt the Lord of the Animals. He puts his arms around the necks of the two flanking calves in a gesture of protection. On the back of each of the calves sits a huge, big-headed bird, apparently the god's accompanying mythical animal. Here the master of the beasts is no longer exclusively associated with the wilderness, but also with domestic animals.—Sumerian sculpture, ca. 3000 B.C.E.

object's upper part. Working around 3400–3200 B.C.E., a predynastic artist carved animals on a slab of slate—wild dogs, lions, long-necked mythological creatures, but also less fierce horned animals, a goat, and a giraffe. Some of the animals are arranged in unequal pairs, e.g. a lion with a goat or gazelle. Are they fighting? Closer inspection discredits this first impression. The lion and the gazelle are kissing. We discover a certain powerful harmony in the picture, a kind of dance animated by the flute-playing figure at the lower left. This animal-shaped, tailed, but erect and somehow anthropomorphic figure may be the Lord of the Animals. It is to his magic flute's sound that the animals dance the cosmic dance of harmony. The animals depicted are not involved in fighting; instead, they play. As *deus ludens* (the god who plays), the Lord of the Animals is the leader of the dance and the animator of the playing. He plays an instrument, very much like the Greek hero Orpheus, whom artists have often represented as singing and playing a stringed instrument and thereby attracting—and appeasing—wild animals (fig. 13, p. 81). "Ravening lions and tigers Orpheus tamed" (*lenire tigris rabidosque leones*), reads a line in the *Ars poetica* of the Roman poet Horace.[4] A modern commentator has argued that the Egyptian scene "portrays life allegorically as an unequal conflict between the strong and the weak."[5] By employing the term "allegory," the author insinuates that the artist uses the genre of the animal fable to say something about human beings. While such an interpretation cannot be ruled out, we should not forget

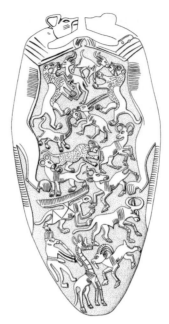

12. *Divine flute-player in animal form.* The animals here depicted—wild dogs, lions, long-necked mythological creatures, but also less fierce horned animals, a goat, and a giraffe—do not seem to be fighting, but playing. The lion and the gazelle are kissing. The playful scene is animated by the figure on the lower left: an animal-shaped, tailed, but erect and somehow anthropomorphic figure playing the flute. This must be the Lord of the Animals.—Egyptian slate palette, ca. 3400–3200 B.C.E.

what is literally true: that the artist has chosen to depict animals—and it is from the animal kingdom that he draws a lesson of universal significance. The world of the Lord of the Animals is ultimately an enchanted world of harmony.

In early written sources, references to animal-related deities abound. One of these deities is the Mesopotamian goddess Ninhursanga, and her portrait, as described by Thorkild Jacobsen, looks very much like that of a more archaic Lady of the Animals.[6] Jacobsen translates her Sumerian name as "Lady of the Foothills" and defines her as the numinous power in the stony soil that rings the Mesopotamian alluvial ground: in the east, the foothills of the Iranian mountains; in the west, the stony Arabian desert. It is in these areas that the herds are pastured in the spring, and it is then that the birth of calves, lambs, and kids normally takes place. It is there that Ninhursanga roams as the Mother of Wildlife, sometimes thought of as a birth-giving donkey, but also often imagined in anthropomorphic form. In ancient imagination, she may have looked like the bare-breasted goddess depicted on the lid of a small ivory pyxis found in a thirteenth-century B.C.E. tomb of Minet el-Beida, the sea port of Ugarit in Syria (fig. 14, p. 82).[7] One text specifies, Ninhursanga's "bosom is bare; on

13. *Orpheus playing the lyre.* The Greek legendary hero and musician Orpheus is here depicted with a Phrygian cap to denote his origin in Phrygia (Asia Minor). His melodies cast a spell over all who hear him play—humans, gods, and animals. Orpheus surrounded by animals became a favorite subject of artists in the Hellenistic and Roman periods. The motif may be a distant echo of the Lord of the Animals.— Marble relief, Roman period.

her left arm she carries a baby so that it can feed at her breast."[8] Tradition makes her the spouse of Shul-pa-e, king of the wild beasts of the desert. As the Mother of Wildlife, she gives form to the unborn animals, and helps their mothers to give birth. After birth, she continues to love her animal children and laments their loss, whether they are killed by hunters or captured and tamed. While her original sphere of influence is wildlife, she can also be considered the tender mother of domesticated herd animals. Moreover, she can be said to preside over the birth of humans, and especially the birth of important individuals such as kings and lords.

The Biblical God Cares for the Beasts

The Israelites of the Old Testament and their early Jewish descendants no longer lived in the archaic world of the hunters and gatherers. They were mostly peasants who supplemented their agriculture by keeping domestic animals—goats, sheep, and cows. Along with agriculture, there was also pastoralism, and tradition reports the impressive number of livestock owned by

14. *Lady of the Animals.* The bare-breasted goddess sits atop a mountain, flanked on either side by a wild goat. The animals are nibbling the leaves that she offers in her upraised hands. The artist depicts the Lady of the Animals as a caring, nurturing figure apparently living in the mountains.—Ugaritic ivory carving, thirteenth century B.C.E.

some of Israel's ancestors and by Job, the hero of the biblical book named after him. The ideal of agriculture mixed with pastoralism can be discerned in a passage in the book of Chronicles: King Uzziah of Judah "built towers in the wilderness and hewed out many cisterns, for he had large herds, both in the Shephelah and in the plain, and he had farmers and vinedressers in the hills and in the fertile lands, for he loved the soil" (2 Chr 26:10). This certainly describes a postarchaic phase of culture that no longer naturally associates itself with archaic religious beliefs. Nevertheless, Israel's early, polytheistic pantheon must have included a Lord of the Animals. It is not known whether early Israel followed the pattern of Ugarit in venerating a Lady of the Animals, for, as a consequence of the monotheistic development, almost all traces of female deities were obliterated.

Being identified with Yahweh, the god of Israel, the Lord of the Animals has in fact left many marks in the Bible. The psalmist puts the following words into Yahweh's mouth: "Every wild animal of the forest is mine, the cattle on a thousand hills. I know all the birds of the air [Hebr.: mountains], and all that moves in the field is mine" (Ps 50:10–11). Uninitiated readers are likely to overlook the passage, and the standard commentaries have little to say about it. It does not seem to be particularly worthy of note that everything that exists belongs to God and that this is also true of the animals. But as soon as we approach this passage from the point of view of the history of religions, we immediately recognize the archaic worldview. The psalm echoes an idea at home in the archaic religion; in fact, it summarizes the experience of the deity shared by most of the early hunters and gatherers. Another passage from Psalms is equally revealing: "Yahweh is my shepherd, I shall not want. He makes me lie down in green pastures; he leads me beside still waters; he restores my soul. He leads me in right paths" (Ps 23:1–3). For the praying individual, who feels safe under the tutelage of the divine shepherd, Yahweh also counts as lord of the domestic animals—and not merely as the owner of the beasts of the forests and the open fields. In view of what we know of the deity's historical development, it seems reasonable to assume that the Israelite Lord of the Animals represents a late form. Under more archaic circumstances, they would presumably have spoken of a Lady of the Animals. More importantly, Yahweh is a celestial deity residing in heaven, not a spirit living in the steppe or the forest. Finally, Israel's Lord of the Animals is also the lord and ultimate owner of domestic animals, which again presupposes an advanced stage of cultural development.

If we consider Israel's Lord of the Animals a late form of the deity, this does not mean that he has lost his original, distinctive traits of character. As a matter of fact, traces of the Lord of the Animals can be found in all traditions and all literary strata of the Bible, including the New Testament. From these traces, his portrait can be reconstructed.

God, according to the Old Testament, is creator, owner, and keeper of the animals. The book of Genesis includes the account of their creation. On the fifth day of creation, the birds and the creatures of the sea are fashioned; on the sixth day, the animals living on the land—"cattle and creeping things and wild animals." God is proud of his achievement; twice his words of appreciation are recorded: "And God saw that it was good." Then follows the blessing of the animals: "God blessed them, saying: Be fruitful and multiply and fill the waters in the seas, and let birds multiply on the earth" (Gen 1:22). To bless means "to bestow the power to reproduce," and this is the power of fertility. Unlike the fish and the birds, the animals living on the earth are not explicitly blessed and provided with the power to multiply, but there can be no doubt that the blessing is meant for all the animals. It may well be that the blessing that God grants humankind on the sixth day actually extends to all the works of the sixth day, i.e. to all creatures living on the earth (as opposed to those living in the air and in the sea).[9]

While the primary meaning of blessing refers to fertility, it also implies the promise of God's protection and care. The idea of divine care for animals is familiar from the Sermon on the Mount: "Look at the birds of the air; they neither sow nor reap nor gather into barns, and yet your heavenly Father feeds them" (Matt 6:26). The Old Testament repeatedly refers to the same idea, and

the book of Job develops it at some length.[10] In the book of Job, God challenges
the protagonist with the following questions:

> Can you hunt the prey for the lion,
> or satisfy the appetite of the young lions,
> when they crouch in their dens,
> or lie in wait in their covert?
> Who provides for the raven its prey,
> when the young ones cry to God,
> and wander about for lack of food?
> Do you know when the mountain goats give birth?
> Do you observe the calving of the deer?
> Can you number the months that they fulfill,
> and do you know the time when they give birth,
> when they crouch to give birth to their offspring . . . ?
> Who has let the wild ass go free?
> Who has loosed the bonds of the swift ass,
> to which I have given the steppe for its home,
> the salt land for its dwelling place? (Job 38:39–41; 39:1–3, 5–6)

Although this is only a portion of Yahweh's long speech on the beasts, its
meaning is clear enough: the Lord of the Animals sends the prey to the lion,
he allows the raven to find its food, he supervises animals' gestation and birth,
he assigns a living space to each species. Particularly impressive is the interpretation of the young ravens' cawing: this is how they pray to the Lord of the
Animals, asking him for food. The book of Job's divine speech can be supplemented by Psalm 104, a text in which the theme of food also figures prominently. While in the book of Job Yahweh asks questions, the psalm supplies the
answer in hymnic form: God is praised for having established a wise and wonderful cosmic order. The psalm is unsurpassed in its descriptive style and poetic
mood:

> You make springs gush forth in the valleys;
> they flow between the hills,
> giving drink to every wild animal;
> the wild asses quench their thirst.
> By the streams the birds of the air have their habitation;
> they sing among the branches.
> From your lofty abode you water the mountains;
> the earth is satisfied with the fruit of your work.
> You cause the grass to grow for the cattle,
> and plants for people to use [or: to cultivate],
> to bring forth food from the earth,

and wine to gladden the human heart,
oil to make the face shine,
and bread to strengthen the human heart.
The trees of Yahweh are watered abundantly,
the cedars of Lebanon that he planted.
In them the birds build their nests;
the stork has its home in the fir trees.
The high mountains are for the wild goats;
the rocks are a refuge for the coneys . . .
The young lions roar for their prey,
seeking their food from God . . .
Yahweh, how manifold are your works!
In wisdom you have made them all;
the earth is full of your creatures.
Yonder is the sea, great and wide,
creeping things innumerable are there,
living things both small and great.
There go the ships,
and Leviathan that you formed
to sport in it [or: whom you have made your plaything, NEB].
These all look to you
to give them their food in due season;
when you give to them, they gather it up;
when you open your hand, they are filled with good things.
(Ps 104:10–18, 21, 24–28)

Here we meet again a motif familiar from the passage we quoted from Job: the crying of the young—in this case, the young lions—is seen as the animals' prayer to the Lord of the Animals. He answers by providing food for all creatures in due season. Worthy of note is the reference to Leviathan. This is not a real animal, but a dragon of the sea whom the ancients saw in the raging waves of the Mediterranean. For the Lord of the Animals, this mythological monster is nothing but a plaything; as a playing deity (*deus ludens*), he enjoys playing with his creatures.

The commentaries on Psalm 104 regularly refer to Egyptian poetry, for that poetry also implies a knowledge of the Divine Gamekeeper. A hymn dating from the fourteenth century B.C.E. depicts Amen-Re in the role of Lord of the Animals. The Egyptian poet never seems to tire of praising the deeds of this deity whom he sees at work in the minutest details of animal life:

[You are the one] who creates the pastures for the animals and food-plants for humankind, who provides for fishes in the river and for birds who mount the sky; who offers breath to all who are unborn, brings life to the offspring

15. *Lord of the Animals.* The two seals show the emblematic symmetrical scene of a male figure holding two animals. In one case, the animals are horned creatures whose mythical nature is evident from their wings; in the other, the animals are lions held by the hindleg. By holding the animals, the male figure, the animals' divine master, asserts his ownership in a playful way. The Lord of the Animals seems to have been given features reminiscent of the Persian king. While this may be an innocent allusion, it might be wondered whether the motif in fact serves as Persian imperial propaganda and is intended to assert that all of creation, including the beasts, is subject to royal authority (this is what Jeremiah said earlier about the Babylonian king: Jer 27:5–6). This kind of political iconography can have meaning only for those who are familiar with the Lord of the Animals.—Fifth-century scaraboid and fourth-century B.C.E. seal impression, both found in Israel.

of the worm, provides for gnats, insects and fleas as well, supplies the field-mice in their burrows and cares for all the bird-shapes in the trees.[11]

Such is the Lord of the Animals!

Peace among the Beasts

Representations of the Lord of the Animals in ancient art, mainly on seals engraved with mythological scenes, often show a male figure holding two wild beasts (fig. 15). The design may refer to the lord as he plays with the animals, or perhaps to the spirit of the wilderness who mediates a peace between aggressive beasts. In other pictorial representations, the presence of the Divine Game-keeper gives the scene an idyllic, peaceful character (fig. 16, p. 87). He is the pacifier. In this context, a passage from the book of Isaiah is of interest. Isaiah's poetry describes the ideal king who will soon rule over the kingdom of Judah. He will be a wise person, known for his justice, and his rule will also affect the realm of nature. The animals will be pacified:

16. *Hittite Lord of the Animals.* In this peaceful, idyllic scene, the bearded Lord of the Animals is surrounded by a lioness with two cubs on the left-hand side, and by two horned animals—a stag and a wild bull—on the right. The wildest of these beasts—the lioness and the bull—are held effortlessly by leg and horn, respectively, while one of the young lions in a playful gesture touches his master's knee with its little paw. As *deus ludens*, the Lord of the Animals presides over a ludic world that we would associate with young animals.—Hittite relief, ca. 900 B.C.E.

> The wolf shall live with the lamb,
> the leopard shall lie down with the kid,
> the calf and the lion and the fatling together,
> and a little child shall lead them.
> The cow and the bear shall graze,
> their young shall eat straw like the ox.
> The nursing child shall play over the hole of the asp,
> and the weaned child shall put its hand
> on the adder's den.
> They will not hurt or destroy
> on all my holy mountain. (Isa 11:6–8)[12]

We excuse the unrealistic elements in a prophet's description. Yet in Isaiah's exaggeration and extravagance we recognize traces of the faith in the Lord of the Animals, for only he can bring about such universal peace.

The Isaianic poem can be better understood when we consider its background in an ancient religious institution known throughout the Near East: the sacred zoo. Several sources give details about enclosures in which certain animals were kept and considered the property of a Divine Gamekeeper. In his book on the campaigns of Alexander the Great, Arrian (second century C.E.) mentions a small, densely wooded island situated just beyond the mouth of the Euphrates river in the Persian Gulf. No one is allowed to kill the wild goats and deer living there, for these animals are sacred to Artemis whose temple dominates the island. An exception is made for those who wish to offer a sacrifice to the goddess.[13] One of the most popular goddesses of the ancients, Artemis was the Divine Gamekeeper of Greek mythology. It seems that in the early period all the animals were sacred to the deity, and the hunters of the archaic age had to engage in certain rituals before and during hunting. At the time of Arrian's writing, the archaic age is past and hardly remembered. Now only a few animals are said to be sacred to the goddess—those living within the enclosure of the temple and forming her modest retinue. The realm of the Divine Gamekeeper has been reduced to the size of a small island.

Another report, also dating from the second century C.E., takes us closer to the land of the Bible. The author, Pseudo-Lucian, writes about the temple of Hierapolis in Syria: "In the [temple's] courtyard large bulls, horses, eagles, bears and lions graze at will. They do not harm people at all. Rather, they are all sacred and tame."[14] Arrian's relatively vast sacred enclosure, which was coextensive with an island, is now merely a sacred zoo, apparently established in the temple garden. Yet the great variety of animals—cows, horses, eagles, etc.—still suggests that the deity of this temple, the goddess Atargatis, is an authentic Lady of the Animals. It is hard to say to what extent Lucian's report can be trusted, but we may safely assume the existence of a small sacred enclosure for animals. This sacred zoo represents and demonstrates the authority the goddess has over the animals. Only the divine Owner of the Animals can bring about peace among the beasts and between humans and animals. That peace is also secured by the ban on hunting and killing the animals in the sacred enclosure (see Arrian's report).

Further insight into the sacred zoo is provided by a first-century C.E. sculpture found in the ancient sanctuary of the Arabian goddess Allât in Palmyra in 1977, and now restored as a monument in front of the museum in Tadmur, Syria (fig. 17, p. 89).[15] It represents a huge, large-maned lion sitting erect. The beast shows its teeth, but it also cradles a small, long-horned antelope between its front legs. Both of these animals belong to the goddess in a particular way: the lion as her animal companion represents her terrifying power and vitality,[16] and the antelope stands for all who are vulnerable and weak and therefore in need of the goddess's special protection. On one of the lion's paws an Aramaic inscription proclaims: "[The goddess] Allât will bless whoever does not shed blood in the sanctuary."[17] Apparently, no blood sacrifices were offered to Allât in her Palmyrene temple. But it was not only animals that were safe there; humans also enjoyed the peace established by the goddess. The temple may be

17. *Peace among the beasts.* A huge, fearsome lion with luxurious mane cradles a small antelope rather than eating it. Visibly, the antelope feels safe in the arms of a tame vegetarian beast which feeds on straw. This tall orthostat, with its unmistakable aura of safety and protection, stood in the sanctuary of the Arabian goddess Allât in Palmyra.—Syrian sculpture, first century C.E.

identified as an asylum, a publicly recognized place of refuge, providing shelter to potential victims of blood-feud, to people wishing to escape from the murderous hands of an avenger intent on killing them. The asylum-seeker may have come from among the notoriously feuding tribes of the desert that surrounds Palmyra.

The sculpture carries an unmistakable message of peace and must have inspired an atmosphere of safety and protection beyond the sacred precinct. Situated in the centre of the Syrian desert, halfway between the valley of the Euphrates and the rich fields, woods, and ports of Syria and Palestine, the oasis of Palmyra has served as a caravan station between east and west for thousands of years. It marked the place where the influences of Rome and the ambitious Parthians intersected. Apparently, the two rival empires of Rome and Parthia granted the city a neutral, semi-independent status so that the goods of these two officially hostile powers might be exchanged there.[18] It was this understanding that led to the amazingly rapid development of the erstwhile modest settlement of seminomadic desert-dwellers into one of the wealthiest, most luxurious, and most elegant towns in Syria. Palmyrene merchants controlled the profitable caravan trade transporting goods from the east to the Roman west. According to the inscription, the sanctuary—and perhaps the entire desert city—was considered a place of peace, where all enmity and conflict had to be suspended. The Lady of the Animals presided over this peace, and the sculpture presented the message to the eyes of the traveler.

The biblical prophet's description of harmony between animals and humans is clearly reminiscent of ideas associated with the Lady—or Lord—of the Animals whose peace reigns in the sacred animal park.

10.   Human Authority over Animals

Gamekeeper, guardian, *deus ludens* and peacemaker—all of these roles characterize the Lord of the Animals, but he is much more besides. Until now we
have focused on his positive, caring and benign side. This account has now to
be supplemented by a look at the other, for us more problematic, side of the
deity. The Divine Gamekeeper is a figure who inspires dread and fear, for he
grants to humans the privilege of killing his creatures. The early hunters and
gatherers depended on killing animals, and the later, plant-growing and animal-
breeding peoples likewise could not survive without consuming meat. Vegetarianism is a latecomer in the history of civilization. The Lord of the Animals
must supply "prey" for humans and animals alike, and this is why the human
race needs divine permission to hunt and kill. We will illustrate this fact from
anthropological literature and the Bible.

Hunting and Sacrifice

Garela-Maisama, our anthropological example of a goddess venerated by
hunters, figures prominently in the pantheon of the Chenchus, a people living
in Andhra Pradesh in India. Racially, the Chenchus belong to the black-skinned
population, with long hair and a certain number of Negroid features. Historically, the Chenchus represent the oldest stratum of indigenous peoples living
in present-day India. Although Aryan and other invaders pushed them back
into the forests and marginal areas, their existence as such has never been
threatened. Economically, most of them work as agricultural laborers and
engage in independent farming, but some still live as hunters and gatherers in
the forests. Around three thousand Chenchus cultivate the land, but when he
wrote his account of them, the anthropologist Christoph von Fürer-
Haimendorf was interested only in those who made a living from food-
collecting, from hunting with bows and arrows, and from fishing. Their main
diet was vegetable in nature, but the Chenchus also ate birds, hares, squirrels,
and monkeys. Around 1940, when the anthropologist visited them, the forest
Chenchus were a small group of 426 people.[19]

All luck in hunting with bow and arrow was attributed to the goddess Garela-
Maisama, for it is she who controls the wild animals of the forest and can grant
or withhold a hunter's success. Thus, in von Fürer-Haimendorf's account,

when a hunter leaves the homestead in the morning, he utters a brief prayer in which he asks the goddess for luck, and he promises her part of the prey. After an animal has been killed, he immediately roasts a piece of meat and with thanks throws it into the forest, inviting the goddess to consume the sacrifice. The offering of a token part of the animal on the very spot where it was brought down is a form of ritual found among many of the most primitive tribes of the world; commonly referred to as "firstlings sacrifice," it represents a symbolic offering of the first item of anything edible one has acquired.[20] On his return home, the hunter again acknowledges the assistance he has received from the goddess. The Chenchus say that in former times they hunted only male animals, for the killing of a female provoked the goddess's anger. If a female animal was killed by mistake, one had to ask for her forgiveness. In everyday life there are various other situations in which the goddess is called upon. Before the Chenchus give themselves to the enjoyment of intoxicating drink, they some-times pray to the divine mother, asking her to protect the revelers from quar-rels and acts of drunken violence. Occasionally the goddess appears to a Chenchu in the form of an old woman and offers help and protection. By way of summary one can say that Garela-Maisama is a tutelary deity of animals as well as of humans.

Garela-Maisama is a complex being, and all references made here to this deity as a goddess have to be qualified, for in certain contexts, Garela-Maisama is male. This dual nature is readily understood: as the spirit of vegetable food, the deity is considered masculine and referred to as "father"; as the spirit of game and hunting, it is seen as female and in prayer is addressed as "mother."[21] Before a certain kind of fruit is completely ripe and fit for consumption, the Chenchus collect a small quantity of semiripe fruits and offer it to the god on a simple altar erected with unhewn stones, asking him to let the fruit ripen fully (again, a firstlings sacrifice). Unlike the hunting ritual, which is performed by the individual hunter in the forest, the rites connected with plants are carried out by the entire residential group (actually, by the men, with the womenfolk watching from the distance). At the time of collecting the wild fruit, the Chenchus once again turn to the deity. They ask the god to protect them against accidents that may occur as they climb the high fruit trees. At this time, they also sacrifice some fruit. The deity is thus an intrinsic part of the economic life of the hunters and gatherers.

In their acknowledgment of a deity who has given permission to kill and who is to be venerated by animal sacrifice, the ancient Israelites were not much dif-ferent from the forest Chenchus of India.

In the Bible the permission to kill is given in the context of the deluge story. After the great flood, God blesses Noah and his sons and grants them dominion over the animals: "The fear and dread of you shall rest on every animal of the earth, and on every bird of the air, on everything that creeps on the ground, and on all the fish of the sea; into your hand they are delivered.

Every moving thing that lives shall be food for you" (Gen 9:2–3). The commentaries regularly explain that the permission to kill constitutes something new, a later concession to human cravings. Before the deluge, they explain, both humans and animals were vegetarians—the creation account of Genesis 1 refers only to a vegetarian diet. The interpretation of the evidence is uncertain, however. Two possibilities have been suggested:

1) The first chapter of Genesis refers only to human dominion over the animals without explicitly speaking of the right to eat meat. However, the notion of domination implies the right to kill and to consume the meat of animals.[22]
2) Genesis 1 must originally have included permission to kill animals and eat meat. The relevant sentence (which corresponded to Genesis 9:2) was deleted by a "vegetarian" editor who believed that all humans and animals were originally vegetarians.[23] This revision may be dated to the fourth century B.C.E., for it was then that the Athenian academy of Plato debated the admissibility of a nonvegetarian diet.

There is no need to decide the issue, for however one determines the meaning of this particular passage, the biblical people had no doubt about their permission to kill animals and to consume meat.

According to the traditional Near Eastern mentality, the privilege to kill animals is mainly reserved for kings. The prophet Jeremiah took up the subject of royal ownership of wildlife in an original way when in the year 594 B.C.E., he proclaimed the following message from his God:

> It is I who by my great power and my outstretched arm have made the earth, with the people and animals that are on the earth, and I give it to whomever I please. Now I have given all these lands [including Judah] into the hands of King Nebuchadnezzar of Babylon, my servant, and I have given him even the wild animals of the field to serve him. (Jer 27:5–6)

According to this oracle, the creator of the universe bestows upon the Babylonian king not only authority over all human beings; he is also to rule over all the animals. The prophet does not give any further details, and therefore we do not know how he would have described or defined the royal rule over nature. One could, however, think here of the right of hunting that the Mesopotamian rulers claimed for themselves.[24] As can be seen in their sumptuous palace art and read in their inscriptions, the kings of Assyria in particular had themselves celebrated as great hunters of lions and other wild beasts; in such a role they decided animal fates.

In biblical Israel hunting was not an activity of economic significance. Nevertheless, the book of Genesis refers to Yahweh twice as the one who grants success to a hunter.[25] The Israelites were only occasional hunters. Professional bird-catchers existed, however,[26] and, while not mentioned directly by Jesus, the activity is alluded to. "Are not two sparrows sold for a penny? Yet not one of them will fall to the ground apart from your Father" (Matt 10:29). The context of this dominical saying suggests that God cares for everything, including the most insignificant matters. At first sight, the juxtaposition of the market value of sparrows and the birds falling to the ground does not seem to make sense. Read from the point of view of the history of religions, however, the saying yields a clear meaning. In New Testament times, fowlers caught sparrows in order to sell them on the market. Jesus' phrase seems to echo a passage from the prophets—"Will a bird fall to the ground without a fowler?"[27] The Lord of the Animals grants success to the bird-catcher, for only when authorized by him can his net catch the bird.

Animals are not only killed in hunting; they are also slaughtered. The relationship between human killing and divine permission to do so has received its most striking expression in the institution of sacrifice. It is only in this context that Israel's sacrificial cult can be understood properly. Whenever an animal is slaughtered, part of it—the entrails—is declared unfit for consumption and has to be offered to Yahweh. This is burned on a stone altar and thus handed over to the deity. By performing the ritual of sacrifice, the Israelite—like the modern forest Chenchu—acknowledges that the permission to kill is not an original human prerogative, but rather a privilege granted by the Divine Gamekeeper. Humans are not allowed to kill on their own authority. Perhaps the widely felt impulse to sacrifice can be understood in terms of a psychological mechanism: whenever someone kills an animal, he has a bad conscience which he calms by performing the ritual. The sacred rite implies that the act of killing is divinely authorized. Originally every Israelite act of slaughtering was accompanied by ritual precautions, and "profane" slaughtering, unaccompanied by sacrifice, was introduced only at a later stage, when the Jerusalem temple claimed the exclusive right to sacrifice. As a late document of Israelite religion, the book of Deuteronomy prohibits hunting rites (i.e. the sacrifice of a wild animal killed in hunting), just as it refuses to tolerate the performance of sacrificial rites subsequent to domestic slaughtering.[28] These prohibitions seem to have originated with King Josiah's reform of ca. 622 B.C.E. But even this drastic royal measure did not obscure the ritual acknowledgment of the divine permission to kill. By offering animal sacrifices on behalf of all the people, the priests of Jerusalem acknowledged Israel's God as the Lord of the Animals.[29]

The Human Owner of Livestock as the Image of God

When we move our attention from hunter-gatherers such as the Chenchus to economically more complex civilizations, we find that the worldview also becomes increasingly rich and sophisticated without losing its archaic harmony.

This can be seen with the huge family of circumboreal peoples—peoples living on the fringes of the northern hemisphere in Siberia, Alaska, and some adjacent areas such as the Labrador peninsula. These traditionally lived from both hunting and herding, with the bear being the game of choice and the reindeer or the caribou the herded animal. Although these northern pastoralists (as they are called) exploited wild and domestic herds, it is on the latter that they mainly relied for their livelihood. In their religious worldview, however, both their own herds and the wild animals figure prominently.

Third layer	Supreme Being	
Second layer	humans	divine animal masters
First layer	domestic animals	wild animals

Worldview of the northern pastoralists (after Tim Ingold)

The social world of the northern pastoralists comprises, in addition to humans, animals, nonhuman animal masters, and the Supreme Being. According to the British anthropologist Tim Ingold, this world can be represented as consisting of three superimposed layers, each of which is occupied by a specific category of living beings or "persons" (see diagram).[30] Organized into two groups— domestic and wild—the animals occupy the lowest level; they count as nonhuman persons. The second layer is that of the humans and the animal-shaped "animal masters," or, in our terminology, the "Divine Gamekeepers." Just as humans preside over the domestic animals, so animal masters control the beasts of the wilderness. The third, top layer can be identified as the celestial realm, the abode of the Supreme Being. Just as the humans and the Divine Gamekeepers have authority over the lowest level, so God rules over the humans and the animal masters. This symmetrical and hierarchical structure forms the ideological theater for all economic and religious activities of the northern pastoralists.

In hunting, humans have to deal with "the other side" of their world, and therefore depend on the animal masters' benevolence and permission to kill and consume. This permission is always granted, for human hunting can actually be seen as a service rendered to the master of the hunted species. In order to understand this notion, we have to know that, as "persons," animals have souls and that these souls leave the bodies once the beasts are dead, in order to be recycled. Three agents are involved in the process initiated by the killing: the hunter, who kills and thus frees the animal soul from its body; the animal master, who takes the soul under his guardianship and offers it up to the Supreme Being; and the Supreme Being, who returns the revitalized soul to the animal master for reincarnation. By killing wild animals, human hunters help the master to free the animal soul and to keep the cycle of life in motion. In return for his service, the hunter receives most of the meat and the other animal products (bones, skin, etc.). In gratitude, the hunter gives small gifts in return in the form of material offerings (such as tobacco), usually thrown into the fire for the benefit of the animal master.

Viewed economically, the killing of animals serves to supply food for humans. Viewed religiously, killing is a sacrifice that sends an animal soul to the Supreme Being, who makes it reappear through a new incarnation. Without the flow of life back to the ultimate source of all being, animals would cease to multiply and people would starve. Hunting and sacrificing not only prevent the cycle of life from coming to a disastrous halt; they also keep it moving. With some modification, the same set of ideas is associated with the killing of domestic animals. In this case, a new idea appears—the ritually staged godlike role of the owner of livestock.

The killing of a domestic animal differs from hunting in that it does not involve an animal master. As the sole guardian of his own herds, the human owner of reindeer enjoys full authority over them. But here, too, killing means the freeing of a soul and its return to the Supreme Being. The two acts, which in hunting are performed by two agents—the hunter and the animal master— are here accomplished by a single agent, the human householder. The householder's first act is of course the slaughtering. The second act involves the slaughterer smearing some of the blood on his face in a particular way fixed by tradition. The face-painting makes him animal-like, identifying him as the animal-shaped divine master of the reindeer. As a master, the slaughterer can pass on the soul of the victim to the Supreme Being, which he does by smearing the home's sacred fireboard with blood and by putting some blood into the fire of the domestic hearth. So every killing of a domestic animal counts as a sacrifice in which the sacrificer acts as an intermediary between the animal and the Supreme Being.

From a comparative perspective, the most interesting feature of the worldview of the northern pastoralists is the structural similarity between the divine master of the animals and the human owner of livestock. Both of them possess animals, and both have the authority to kill. Using biblical terminology, one might say that the human owner of animals is an image of the divine master of the beasts; both of them derive their authority from the Supreme Being, of whom they are also images. Similar ideas appear in the Bible, as will be explained presently.

The account of creation that we read on the first page of the Bible is a thoroughly optimistic text. Animals and humans are created by God. The first chapter of Genesis presents God as creating an excellent world, as a being friendly toward animals and humans, upon whom he bestows his blessing. The human being ranks as God's masterwork, and to him he gives the command:

> Be fruitful and multiply, and fill the earth and subdue it; and have dominion over the fish of the sea and over the birds of the air and over every living thing that moves upon the earth. God said, See, I have given you every plant

yielding seed that is upon the face of all the earth, and every tree with seed in its fruit; you shall have them for food. (Gen 1:28–29)

God owns the entire realm of nature with all its animals and plants, and it is to the humans that he delegates that ownership and dominion. We remember that the Chenchu goddess of the forest had a similar position; she owned everything in the natural sphere, including animals and fruit-bearing plants. Elohim, too, is Lord of the Animals.

In the Bible the privileged position of the human race is explained with reference to a term that has become important in Christian theology and subject to all manner of speculation: the term "image of God." To say, as the Bible does, that God created the human being "in his image" is generally taken to be the essential religious definition of the human. Since the exact meaning of the expression is not obvious, it merits consideration in its original context in the book of Genesis. Here we give two renderings of the relevant passage, found in the account of creation:

Then God said, "Let us make humankind in our image, according to our likeness; and let them have dominion over the fish of the sea, and over the birds of the air, and over the cattle, and over all the wild animals of the earth, and over every creeping thing that creeps upon the earth." So God created humankind in his image, in the image of God he created them.

Gen 1:26–27 (NRSV)

Then God said: "Let us make humankind as our image, as our likeness, so that they have dominion over the fish of the sea, and over the birds of the air, and over the cattle, and over all the wild animals of the earth, and over every creeping thing that creeps upon the earth." So God created humankind in his image, in the image of God he created them.

Gen 1:26–27 (Walter Groß)

The myth states the creator's twofold intention of making humankind in the image of God and of giving it dominion over the animal kingdom. The Hebrew text can be read, as the New Revised Standard Version implies, as simply juxtaposing the two notions, with the implied suggestion that "image" may define the shared outward appearance of God and the human being, whereas "dominion" states human ownership of nature. Others, such as Walter Groß, regard the juxtaposition as more than coincidental, arguing that, as God is Lord over all of creation, the human being reflects the image of God by exercising dominion over the rest of creation.[31] The idea of dominion stands out as the central feature. *The human being is comparable to God, for he also wields authority over the animals.* We take this second view as the proper meaning of the biblical text.

As can be seen from Psalm 8, the same message can be expressed without reference to the notion of the "image of God":

What are human beings that you are mindful of them,
mortals that you care for them?
You have made them a little lower than God,
and crowned them with glory and honor.
You have given them dominion over the works of your hands;
you have put all things under their feet,
all sheep and oxen,
and also the beasts of the field,
the birds of the air, and the fish of the sea,
whatever passes along the paths of the seas. (Ps 8:4–8/Hebr. 8:5–9)

The human being is here depicted as the crown of creation, as the ruler over the animals. Since God has put all creatures under human feet, "all sheep and oxen," the human being shares in God's dominion over the creatures. The most important implication of this dominion is the privilege of killing.

11.   The Rediscovery of the Lord of the Animals, ca. 500 B.C.E.

In biblical literature we not only find scattered and as it were accidental traces of the Lord of the Animals. God's role as the Divine Gamekeeper is taken up and elaborated quite consciously in two works dating from about the same period—the time around 500 B.C.E. In the book of Genesis, the Lord of the Animals dominates the myth of creation, just as he does the philosophy of suffering developed in the book of Job.

The Evidence of Genesis

The book of Genesis begins with a mythological prologue that can be described as a collection of stories about primeval events. Set in a period that precedes historical time, these stories talk about creation, the first sin, banishment from paradise, the first murder, the great flood that almost destroyed all human life, and the origin of multiple languages. One of the main characteristics of these stories is the close association of animals and humans.

The solidarity of humans and animals is nowhere better highlighted than in the story of the flood, which uses the traditional motif of the hero who is close to the animal kingdom. An example of such a person is Enkidu, a figure from the Babylonian Epic of Gilgamesh. Living in the forest as a wild man, he associates with the animals easily. There does not seem to be any essential difference between him and the animals, although he acts as their protector. Foiling the traps dug by human hunters, he sides with his animal friends and helps them to escape.[32] Another example is the Greek demigod Orpheus. An unsurpassed musician, he attracts even the attention of wild animals. "Whenever he played the kithara, the wild animals followed him," reads one report.[33] The ancients often depicted Orpheus sitting among wild animals who, tamed by the magic of his melodies, listen to him (see fig. 13, p. 81).

The biblical myth of the deluge tells of a similar hero who is close to the animal kingdom. When all creatures—humans and animals alike—are due to perish in a great flood, Noah is told to rescue his own family and animals of all kinds in a huge boat. He builds the ark, brings in a great variety of animals, and they all survive the great flood. Noah is the savior of the animals. The beasts obey this exceptional human person, keep peace, and are fed by Noah. The biblical text is quite explicit on the feeding, for God said to Noah: "Also take with you every kind of food that is eaten, and store it up; and it shall serve as food for you and for them," i.e. for the animals (Gen 6:21). At least one non-Jewish deluge story refers to the peace among the animals. Deucalion, hero of the Greek flood myth, welcomed all the beasts into his ship, and, according to Pseudo-Lucian, "none harmed him. Instead, from some divine source, there was great friendship among them, and in a single ark all sailed as long as the flood prevailed."[34] In the Bible, the story of the flood ends as follows:

> Then God said to Noah, "Go out of the ark, you and your wife, and your sons and your sons' wives with you. Bring out with you every living thing that is with you of all flesh—birds and animals and every creeping thing that creeps on earth—so that they may abound on the earth, and be fruitful and multiply on the earth." So Noah went out with his sons and his wife and his sons' wives. And every animal, every creeping thing, and every bird, everything that moves on the earth, went out of the ark by families. (Gen 8:15–19)

Noah, then, controls the entire animal kingdom—with the exception of the fish, which (naturally) remain untouched by the flood.

At the end of the deluge story, animals and humans are given the same divine mandate. Noah is told to bring the animals out of the ark "so that they may abound on the earth, and be fruitful and multiply on the earth" (Gen 8:17). God addresses Noah and his sons, saying, "Be fruitful and multiply, and fill the earth" (Gen 9:1). So animals and humans not only share the earth as their habitat, they also follow the same divine command. They are somehow equal.

We might understand the theme of the solidarity between animals and humans as an important lesson taught by the mythological prologue of Genesis. But there is another possible interpretation, one that considers particular historical rather than merely mythical events. Modern research on mythology suggests that a myth is rarely transmitted with the exclusive aim of communicating a particular story about gods or some event in which deities are involved. Instead, storytellers generally spice the myth up with contemporary allusions that speak directly to their audience, and such is the case with the primeval mythology of Genesis. When the book of Genesis first related the myth of God's blessing of the human race and the animal kingdom, and referred to the deliverance of humans and animals from the waters of the deluge, Jewish readers living around 500 B.C.E. were confronted with a message that touched their existence.

The contemporary references in the biblical account for the most part can be discerned only after careful scrutiny of the Hebrew text. The topical note sounded by the mandate of creation requires some linguistic expertise to be detected: "Be fruitful and multiply, and fill the earth" (Gen 9:1). The Hebrew text can also be rendered as: "Be fruitful and multiply, and fill the *land*." This is a divine command to reclaim and resettle the land of Israel. After having been decimated through war and deportation and having survived a kind of deluge, the population is exhorted to increase and multiply.[35] The power to do so, however, is granted by the archaic deity, the Lord of the Animals, who blesses the families and encourages them to establish a new existence. The full import of Genesis can only be grasped if we interpret it as presenting an alternative to another program, to a road not taken. That road would have involved re-establishing a strong Israelite state, headed by a powerful king, supported by a militaristic ideology and a religion centered on the Lord of War and aiming at the enemy's defeat. Historically, however, no new Jewish state emerged around 500 B.C.E.; the Judeans actually lived under the control of provincial adminis-trators of the Persian Empire. Thus the book of Genesis recommends not a historical but a natural existence, the basis of which is provided by the bless-ing and the command of the archaic deity. After the loss of national independ-ence the compiler of Genesis returns to the archaic image of God and the reassuring world of mythology.[36] This alone can provide the necessary courage to start a new life in the land of Israel.

The Book of Job

The book of Job tells a story whose plot develops as follows: a wealthy man named Job suddenly loses his flocks through an enemy raid; then his children die when, during a party, their house collapses; eventually, he also loses his health. Time and again Job protests that he has never done any wrong, and that his fate is therefore utterly undeserved. God has no right to treat him the way he does. Job discusses his case with his friends, but eventually he also has a vision in which God speaks to him. Completely disregarding Job's arguments, God confronts him with a long questioning of how he cares for the life of lions, deer, wild asses, wild oxen, ostriches, horses, eagles, and other animals.

God's speech culminates in the description of two invincible, awe-inspiring, marsh-dwelling mythical beasts. Called Behemoth (which translates as "great beast") and Leviathan, they are described as a huge hippopotamus and a fire-spitting[37] crocodile.[38] Here is a passage about the crocodile-shaped dragon:

> Can you draw out Leviathan with a fishhook,
> or press down its tongue with a cord?
> Can you put a rope in its nose,
> or pierce its jaw with a hook?
> Will it make many supplications to you?
> Will it speak soft words to you?
> Will it make a covenant with you
> to be taken as your servant forever?
> Will you play with it as with a bird,
> or will you put it on a leash for your girls?

> Will traders bargain over it?
> Will they divide it up among the merchants?
> Can you fill its skin with harpoons,
> or its head with fishing spears? (Job 41:1–7/Hebr. 40:25–31)

Hunters might reply: "Yes, we can do it." But their answer would apply only to a normal crocodile. A confrontation with Leviathan, the mythical monster, is as dangerous as it is futile. No sensible hunter would even dare to try: "Lay hands on it; think of the battle; you will not do it again" (Job 41:8/Hebr. 40:32). "Though the sword reaches it, it does not avail, nor does the spear, the dart, or the javelin. It counts iron as straw, and bronze as rotten wood. The arrow cannot make it flee; slingstones, for it, are turned to chaff. Clubs are counted as chaff; it laughs at the rattle of javelins" (Job 41:26–29/Hebr. 41:18–21).

Compared to the dragon, humans—including Job—appear as small and insignificant. The poet says of Leviathan: "It surveys everything that is lofty; it is king over all that are proud" (Job 41:34/Hebr. 41:26). Leviathan is the proudest of all the creatures and, God argues, rightly so. Far from standing at the upper end of the scale, the human being must recognize its humble, inter-mediate position. It does have a certain amount of control over other beings, but this is severely limited. The human person is a creature among creatures, a middle member in a long series of animals, devoid of special privileges.

Upon Job's vision of the Lord of the Animals all is made well again. Health, possessions, and children are restored to him. But just why his fate is reversed remains a mystery. Commentators feel that it comes about without motivation and explanation. It seems, however, that the reversal can be elucidated and accounted for after all. In his vision, Job is confronted with vital scenes of animal life and thus with the very foundation of life itself. Wildlife manifests the meaning and vitality of the divine blessing that sustains all life, including human life. As Job's anger subsides, he stops arguing with God. Now, ready to receive God's blessing, he feels it begin to work in him and in his life. The book includes a passage that seems to echo Job's eventual insight:

> But ask the animals, and they will teach you;
> the birds of the air, and they will tell you;
> ask the plants of the earth, and they will teach you;
> and the fish of the sea will declare to you.
> Who among these does not know
> that the hand of Yahweh has done this?
> In his hand is the life of every living thing
> and the breath of every human being. (Job 12:7–10)

Having control not only over the animals, but also over humankind, the Divine Gamekeeper can—and does—include Job among those whom he blesses.

As in the case of the Genesis myth of creation, this "anthropological" reading of the story of Job, an interpretation that focuses on individual human existence, is not the only possible one. The book of Job itself hints at the special meaning of this literary work at the time of its writing, a meaning resonant with its contemporary audience as a whole. In chapter 12—the one from which we just quoted—we hear of certain events that marked the existence of the then-living generation in more than a casual way. Acting as the Lord of War, God has thrown Job's society into chaos:

> He [God] leads counselors away stripped,
> and makes fools of judges.
> He looses the sash of kings,
> and binds a waistcloth on their loins.
> He leads priests away stripped,
> and overthrows the mighty.
> He deprives of speech those who are trusted,
> and takes away the discernment of the elders.
> He pours contempt on princes,
> and looses the belt of the strong [?].
> He uncovers the deeps out of darkness,
> and brings deep darkness to light.
> He makes nations great, then destroys them,
> he enlarges nations, then leads them away.
> He strips understanding from the leaders of the earth,
> and makes them wander in a pathless waste.
> They grope in the dark without light;
> he makes them stagger like a drunkard. (Job 12:17–25)

What is described here actually happened in the year 586 B.C.E., when the kingdom of Judah was destroyed by the Babylonians. The counselors, the judges, the members of the royal family, the elders, the owners of large estates, the leaders—they all lost their authority, allowing chaos to reign. Job adds, as if to assure later generations of what his generation had had to live through: "Look, *my eye* has seen all this, my ear has heard and understood it" (Job 13:1, italics added). The Job poet lived in a time in which the memory of the events of 586 B.C.E. was still very much alive. The entire story of Job can be read as a parable of the history of Judah—the history of a wealthy people that loses all its riches. Living in Babylonian exile and in the Diaspora, people start quarreling with their God. It is only the rediscovery of the Lord of the Animals that can gradually restore the divine blessing to the people and the land. After Job—understood as the representative of his suffering people—has had his vision of God and has listened to God's speech about wildlife, he can balance his experience of the political fiasco against another experience: the encounter with God in his role as Divine Gamekeeper. These are Job's words: "I had heard of you by the hearing of the ear, but now *my eye* sees you" (Job 42:5, italics added). Job is a double eyewitness—first of the political disaster and then of the manifestation of the Lord of the Animals. This can only mean that the political experience is as it were deleted by the new religious experience. Around 500 B.C.E.—after the Babylonian exile—people rediscover the archaic image of God and thereby their courage to live is renewed.

Neither the book of Job nor the book of Genesis shows any interest in a God of politics and historical existence. The Lord of War who defeats enemies and grants victory held little promise for them. Disillusioned with and retreating from political life, their authors were concerned about more elementary matters—fertility, flocks, and offspring. What they badly needed was divine blessing. It was in this situation that they rediscovered the archaic worldview and the Lord of the Animals.

The Biblical Name of the Lord of the Animals

We may conclude this chapter by offering an observation that brings the role of the biblical God as the Lord of the Animals once again into sharp focus. The book of Job knows the Lord of the Animals' personal name: Shaddai. In his dialogue with Job, God himself uses this name: "And Yahweh said to Job: Shall a faultfinder contend with Shaddai? Anyone who argues with God must respond" (Job 40:1–2). The name Shaddai is frequently used in Job—thirty-one passages could be listed—much more often than in any other book of the Bible. The New Revised Standard Version and most of the other modern translations follow a long tradition that renders it as "the Almighty." Based as it is on a misunderstanding, this is a problematic translation, and one should stay with Shaddai, as does the translation of the Jewish Publication Society. Apparently, Shaddai is a short form of El Shaddai, a name that can be rendered as "God of the Field" or "God of the Uncultivated Land."[39] The field is, in the words of George Adam Smith, "the rough, uncultivated, but not wholly barren, bulk of the hill-country, where the *beasts of the field*, wild beasts, found room to breed."[40] In ancient times, the vegetation of the hill-country must have ranged from areas of thick, impenetrable forest dominated by the evergreen oak to thickets of tall shrubs called maquis; spotted with low, thorny bushes of less than one meter in height, with bare and stony patches between them, certain areas were—and still are—without a continuous covering of plants.[41] Unclaimed for human exploitation and the abode of wild animals, the hill-country is owned by Shaddai who pronounces the proud words quoted by the psalmist: "Every wild animal of the forest is mine, the cattle on a thousand hills. I know all the birds of the air [Hebr.: mountains], and all that moves in the field is mine" (Ps 50:10–11).

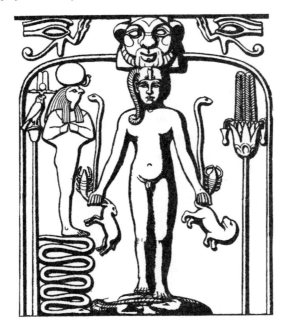

18. *Horus-Shed, the Egyptian Lord of the Animals.* The god is depicted as a boy with a lock of hair, the symbol of childhood, on the right side of his head. Facing forward, adorned with the uraeus on his brow, and standing on the back of a crocodile, the infant god forms the center of a small shrine. In his right hand he grasps a serpent, a scorpion, and a lion, and in his left hand a serpent, a scorpion, and a horned animal—an oryx. These are held by their tails and horns, respectively. On the left, the falcon-headed god Re-harakhte with the emblematic sun-disk above his head stands on a coiled snake. Placed above the boy's head is the mask of the god Bes, another embodiment of the Lord of the Animals.—Detail of a relief from Alexandria. Metternich Stela, ca. 350 B.C.E.

It is not only the Bible that knows the Lord of the Animals by the name of Shaddai. The ancient Egyptians know a god who, having authority over snakes, scorpions, and crocodiles, is considered the Divine Gamekeeper, a deity friendly with humans. Egyptologists spell his name Shed, a transcription reminiscent of Shaddai. This Western Asiatic god retained some of his foreign features, but he was Egyptianized and assimilated to Horus in his form as an infant deity.[42] Especially in the Greek and Roman periods, the divine child Horus-Shed was frequently depicted on small stelae and amulets. On one stela found in Alexandria, the artist shows him as a nude boy with the side lock typical of Egyptian children (fig. 18). The stela was designed to provide protection against and healing of the sting of scorpions or the bite of poisonous snakes and other noxious animals. One of the accompanying inscriptions includes a prayer that addresses the divine child: "Come quickly to me on this day . . . May you drive away all lions on the desert plateau, all crocodiles in the

19. *The Egyptian god Bes as Lord of the Animals.* Represented as a dwarf, Bes was a
very popular deity among the Egyptians, who appreciated his qualities as helper and
protector. Artists occasionally gave him the attributes of some other gods to
emphasize his comprehensive magical power which served to protect against evil.
The illustration shown here endows him with two pairs of arms, a bird's tail, and two
pairs of outstretched wings. Animal heads protrude from the sides of his head and
adorn—or disfigure—his knees, feet, and erect phallus. He is also given the attributes
of the Lord of the Animals. In his left hand, he holds a scorpion, an oryx, and a lion.
The animals on which he stands—a serpent, a scorpion, and others—are contained
in an oval formed by the body of a snake which bites its tail. Dominated by the deity,
all of these animals help Bes to protect those who use his amulet.—Egyptian panel,
Greco-Roman period.

river, all biting snakes in their holes. May you render them for me like pebbles
on the desert hills, like potsherds found along the street . . . Behold, your name
is invoked on this day: I am Horus the Savior [*Shed*]."[43] The concluding reference to the divine name is meant to appeal once more to the god's power and
bring him to act. "Horus the Savior" is Horus-Shed.

Fortunately, we know the myth told to explain the divine child's power over
the beasts, for the stela's long inscription provides the information.[44] Horus,
the infant son of Isis, has been fatally stung by a scorpion. His distracted
mother finds his lifeless body and, amid loud wailing and lamentation, appeals
to the god Thoth to take pity and restore him. Thoth responds to her plea and
successfully invokes the magical power of the gods to bring Horus back to life

20. *Bes as Master of the Lions.* Whereas the artist who produced the amulet shown in figure 19 gave Bes a large number of complex attributes, this depiction retains only the deity's basic form—that of a dwarf. The god embraces two lions in a protective gesture so as to highlight his benevolent attitude toward the beasts.—Egyptian cosmetic vessel in the form of a deity, ca. 500 B.C.E.

and restore him to health, with authority henceforth to own and domesticate the otherwise harmful creatures. These now function as the god's entourage and helpers.[45] Horus-Shed has command over the animals, preventing them from doing harm to humans and, if they have harmed them, providing healing. On the stela, the association of the divine child with animals gives visual expression to his power over them. The mask of Bes signals Horus-Shed's identity with a very popular god who, assuming the role of the Lord of the Animals, averts the dangers coming from wild beasts (see fig. 19, p. 106 and fig. 20). Re-harakhte (the deity standing on the coiled snake in fig. 18, p. 105) seems to have the same danger-averting function. By associating Horus-Shed with the god Re-harakhte and by giving him animals and the mask of Bes as attributes, the artist highlights the young god's power to protect.

Horus-Shed was so popular in Roman Egypt that even Christians became interested in him. They identified the infant god with the Christ child and replaced the myth of Horus with their own stories. The early medieval *Book of the Virgin Mary's Birth* includes several relevant legends. When lying in the manger, the child Jesus is worshiped by ox and ass, and, as the story unfolds, wild beasts also obey him. Surprised by dragons emerging from a cave during their flight from King Herod, Mary and Joseph cry out in terror, but the holy child appeases the beasts, and they worship him. "All wild beasts must be docile before me," he explains.[46] On their journey the holy family is accompanied by a retinue of lions and leopards:

> Wherever Joseph and holy Mary went, they went before them, showing them the way and lowering their heads [in worship]; they showed their servitude by wagging their tails and honored him with great reverence. But when Mary saw the lions and the leopards and all kinds of wild beasts surrounding them, she was at first gripped by violent fear. But the child Jesus looked at her face with a happy countenance, and said: Do not fear, mother; for they do not come to harm you, but they hasten to obey you and me.[47]

In order to assess the full import of the story one has to note where it takes place—Egypt. Only in Egypt could the divine child inherit the role of Horus-Shed, Master of Animals, whose name echoes that of the biblical Shaddai.[48]

The Fourth Image: Lord of the Individual— the "Personal God"

While the Bible generally places great emphasis on the relationship between God and the elected community and thereby highlights the social dimension of religion, divine blessing—in our Dumézilian terminology, the Third Gift—is also granted to the individual who feels personally favored, guided, and privileged. The present section considers this "personal religion" (William James) or "personal piety" (James Henry Breasted) as a subset of ancient Near Eastern religions, which is different from other subsets such as the state cult or beliefs relating to the dead. This religion centers on the particular bond between the human individual and the "personal god" whose special protection, favor, and closeness he enjoys. In each of the great civilizations of Near Eastern antiquity, personal piety took a particular form. For the Semites, the dependence upon the personal deity was seen as existing from birth, whereas for the Egyptians the relationship typically came about as an entry into a client relationship with a divine patron or patroness by way of conversion in adult life. In Israel, two types of personal religion can be distinguished: one derived from the particular form of personal piety current in Egypt, and one closely associated with typically Mesopotamian ideas. Along with these two traditions, the peculiar "oral" orientation echoed in many of the ancient examples of the relationship between a human individual and a motherly, nurturing, and caring deity will be analyzed.

12.   The Discovery of Personal Piety

"I have the sense of a presence, strong, and at the same time soothing, which hovers over me. Sometimes it seems to enwrap me with sustaining arms. God is a personal Being, who knows and cares for his creatures."[1] This is how a North American middle-class woman described her relationship with God in the late nineteenth century. Another declared: "I have often a consciousness of a Divine Presence, and sweet words of comfort come to me."[2] These are only two of many testimonies that the sociologist Edwin Starbuck collected for his book *The Psychology of Religion* (1899). He carefully analyzed his question-naires. The motif of divine companionship reappeared in the responses time and again, and Starbuck reports that twenty-seven percent of his female and twenty-nine percent of his male interviewees, mostly white Protestants, included statements to that effect.[3] He traced this image of God to "one of the deepest instincts of human life, the need for society, for companionship, for kinship."[4]

Today Starbuck's book is largely forgotten, but his insight into people's per-sonal beliefs and individual religious feelings survives in a classic of religious scholarship: *The Varieties of Religious Experience* (1902), by the Harvard philosopher William James. Broadening Starbuck's analysis, James used a term then current in devotional literature to designate the particular form of reli-gion both he and Starbuck were interested in: "personal religion."[5] Personal religion is individual rather than communal; it is the religion of one person. It is not based on belief in certain doctrines taught by tradition, but on feelings and spiritual experiences. Frequently it originates in an experience of conver-sion and the subsequent decision to stay faithful to it. As an activity, personal religion does not depend on ritual acts but consists in the development of a personal relationship with God, culminating in "personal communion with the divine."[6] Starbuck and James were convinced that, by studying personal reli-gion among their contemporaries, they would be able to understand the reli-gious phenomenon itself.

Although some readers complained that the notion of personal religion was too individualistic and did not sufficiently consider its more objective, doctrinal dimension, Starbuck's and James's work did appeal to many who felt very much like Starbuck's interviewees. It also resonated with historians, who were quick to develop a major hypothesis to explain the origins and history of personal piety. According to this hypothesis, personal religion as found today is a secondary phenomenon. Originally, personal religion was developed by and restricted to "heroes," understood as creative spiritual men of genius. Only at a later stage of development did personal piety become known outside of this elite. Eventually, it became available to the masses, who imitated the spiritual heroes' achievement. Among ancient historians, the American Egyptologist James Henry Breasted (1865–1935) pursued this idea. For Breasted, the development of Egyptian religion reached its zenith in the fourteenth and thirteenth centuries B.C.E. It was then that Pharaoh Akhenaten discovered, and celebrated in poetry, his personal relationship with the monotheistic sun-god, Aten. After Akhenaten's death, Egyptian religion reverted to polytheism, but one particular aspect of the solar cult survived: the close attachment of believers to their god. "Although rooted in the teaching of an exclusive few heretofore, these beliefs in an intimate relationship between the worshiper and his god had now, with the lapse of centuries and by slow and gradual process, become widespread among the people. An age of personal piety and inner aspiration to God now dawned among the masses."[7]

Among early twentieth-century theologians and biblical scholars, a similar idea prevailed. This posited that personal religion had been inaugurated by the prophets, great individuals who in their secret meditations communicated with Israel's God. Foremost among these spiritual heroes was Jeremiah who, according to John Skinner, discovered "individual fellowship with God" and developed for the first time a "personal piety"[8] based on "an indissoluble link of communion between his own soul and God."[9] Scholars credited Jeremiah with inaugurating a new notion of the deity: "In the end, Yahweh was no longer a tribal god in the old sense of caring solely for the social group; he was a personal god as well, in the sense of caring for and bringing interior sustenance to individuals, one by one."[10] Accordingly, Jeremiah came to be ranked higher than any other character in the Old Testament: "A braver, gentler, more exquisite, or more courageous soul has not often walked on earth, and his spiritual pioneering in the realm of personal religion made him a forerunner of Jesus and one of the eminent benefactors of the race."[11] Jeremian personal piety later inspired many of the psalms, took hold of numerous Jews, reached Jesus and eventually became part of the Western religious mentality.

Today, a century after the seminal studies by Starbuck and James, scholars still agree on the significance of personal religion. Throughout the twentieth century, the ideal of independence and self-reliance, combined with the Protestant emphasis on the individual believer's faith, persuaded many "to devote most of their spiritual energies to personal faith and private religion."[12] Historians agree that personal religion as described by William James did exist in ancient times. They are reluctant, however, to see it as a derivative form of spirituality, a mere echo of the model established by spiritual heroes. A hundred years ago, many scholars of religion admired the Scottish philosopher Thomas

Carlyle and his book *On Heroes, Hero-Worship and the Heroic in History* (1841), which inspired much of their work. They agreed with him that the "masses" depend on the guidance of great personalities. Today, scholars are likely to argue that cultural developments often happen without such guidance, and that personal piety may have been a popular sentiment from the start, originating in the hearts of the common people. The enthusiasm with which personal piety was celebrated a hundred years ago has subsided; now personal piety may be described as an attitude that has exchanged awe and respect for vulgar familiarity with the divine.[13] The present state of knowledge about and interpretation of the personal religion of the biblical world can be summarized as follows:

1) *Religions consist of subsets.* Many religions—ancient and modern, Western and non-Western—can be described as consisting of several subsets such as ancestor worship, state cult as celebrated in major temples, rituals and beliefs related to the king and to death, and so on. The "complete" religious life of a people tends to be pluralistic in that it forms a collection of subsets, each of which has its own, independent logic, its own rules, specific rituals, and traditions. In this way, personal religion forms an autonomous subset within the general religious culture. Within a religion, the subsets may be controlled and organized into a hierarchy; but frequently, as Durkheim observed, they are merely juxtaposed and only loosely associated.[14] Biblical scholarship has frequently emphasized the distinctions between "official religion" and "personal piety" and sought to describe "family religion" or "popular religion" as a phenomenon distinct from the "great" or "canonical" tradition embodied in the Old Testament legal codes and in the books of the prophets. These distinctions also apply to Mesopotamia and Egypt.[15]

2) *The personal god forms the core of personal religion.* The long-term, close emotional and ritual relationship between a human individual and a god or goddess stands at the center of personal religion in the Near East and Egypt. This relationship is thought to exist either from birth and therefore appears as "natural," or it is entered into later in life so as to constitute a kind of contractual alliance between divine patron and human client, with the client binding himself to serve and be faithful to his divine lord or lady. Prayer language often addresses the personal god as parent or lord, and the human partner calls himself child or servant.

3) *Personal piety may be seen as a phenomenon of crisis, as the response to the challenge of collectively and individually experienced insecurity.* When basic security-providing political structures as well as social and familial bonds loosen or disappear, the unprotected individual seeks refuge with his personal deity.[16] This situation can be seen in the ancient Egyptian Tale of Sinuhe (ca. 1950 B.C.E.): Sinuhe, who lives in a foreign country, suffers from being estranged

from Egypt; at the same time, he feels protected by his personal god. The experience of estrangement is counterbalanced by the strong feeling of individual divine care and protection.[17] We may think of the individual's appeal to a personal god as a mechanism for coping with difficulties in life and overcoming isolation in situations of loneliness, illness, guilt, psychological imbalance, social ostracism, estrangement from family and friends, migration, travel, and any kind of bad luck. Personal piety gave people a sense of being loved, guided, helped, and protected, especially in times of distress.

4) *In Egypt and the Near East, personal religion gained popularity in the second millennium B.C.E.* As an elementary form of the religious life, personal piety is universal; it can be found everywhere and at all times. Yet its particular forms and doctrines are shaped by cultural circumstances. Moreover, its expression, style, emotional quality, and popularity may change according to the mentalities and tastes of individuals, groups, and historical periods.

Biblical Israel's culture developed in an area in which the influence of the two dominant Near Eastern civilizations could be felt: those of Mesopotamia and Egypt. Therefore it is not surprising to find there one type of personal piety inspired by Egyptian and one type reflecting Mesopotamian popular spirituality. For this reason, the following chapters will look at the Hebrew Lord of the Individual in the light first of Egyptian and then Mesopotamian testimonies.

13. God as Lord of the Individual: The Egyptian Contribution

Egyptian religion may be defined in terms of three major subsets: temple ritual, service of the dead, and "personal piety." The modern visitor to Egypt has access to an impressive number of tombs and even structures connected with some of the pyramids and thus can become familiar with the service the ancients rendered to some of their dead. Unlike the ancient inhabitants of the land of the Nile, the modern tourist can also walk through some of the beautifully restored temples and look at the reliefs on the temple walls that often depict scenes of worship, scenes that show the king, but never the common people, for the latter were not allowed to participate in the ritual the state rendered to the gods. As for personal piety, only minor, inconspicuous objects visualize its relevance within the cult and culture of Egypt. A stela in the British Museum shows a blind supplicant as he kneels in front of a seated goddess, whom he addresses, arms outstretched, with a gesture of adoration (fig. 21, p. 116). In the Egyptian museum in Berlin, a stela erected in gratitude by a man whose prayers had been heard by Amen-Re (fig. 22, p. 117) depicts the two listening ears of the god.[18] While these iconographic documents give us a first idea of personal piety in Egypt, it is to ancient texts that we must turn to understand its precise nature.

The Sentiment of Devotion in Ancient Egypt

Egyptians felt a direct link with the deity and thought of individual lives as being governed by a divine power. The relationship between the deity and the individual is characterized on the human side by devotion, trust, obedience, prayer, and sacrifice, or by taking part in processions and feasts, and on the divine side by secure guidance, protection from danger, and even love. Mutual love between a god and an individual is conceivable, and sometimes a person dedicates his life to a particular deity, putting himself under divine protection.

As the basis of this piety one can discern distinctive notions of how the gods act and how human life is experienced, notions that typically originate in periods of social crisis.[19] In quiet times the self-confident man of wisdom and correct behavior emerges as the leading paradigm of Egyptian ethical instruction. This ideal presupposes belief in the intrinsic logic of a stable world governed by generally known and reliable rules that make the course of one's life

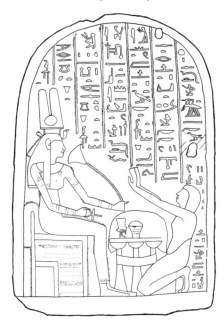

21. *A blind man and his goddess.* The walls of Egyptian temples are regularly
decorated with ritual scenes in which the king is depicted officiating before deities.
This stela showing Amennakhte is exceptional for its depiction of a blind scribe.
Represented eyeless and wearing wig and kilt, he is kneeling before and praying to a
deity, the enthroned goddess Meresger. The petitioner tells the story of his blindness
and asks for divine grace. Kneeling expresses humility, the raising-up of hands
denotes praise and adoration.—Inscribed Egyptian stela, ca. 1140 B.C.E.

predictable. In periods of crisis, this sense of stability vanishes. Now the course
of life appears mysterious and often devoid of rules, and people are unable to
predict the outcome of their actions. What happens is apparently staged by the
gods, but the gods, who enjoy freedom of will, do not necessarily act in response
to someone's good or bad behavior. Instead, they act so as to please their devotees, of whom they expect a humble and pious attitude. In this vein, the traditional Egyptian ideal of a life patterned by the internalization of rules of
behavior is modified and supplemented by the idea of "placing a deity in one's
heart." Being more noble than ethics, piety takes precedence over ethical
behavior, even though ethical behavior in no way loses its importance. The ideal
of the wise and correct person, though not completely displaced, is modified
and supplemented by the new ideal of piety and humility.

Some typical expressions illustrate the essence of personal piety. A painter
employed in the necropolis of Thebes dedicated a votive stela to the god Amen;
one passage of the text reads: "You, Amen, are the Lord of the humble man,
you come at the voice of the poor. I call to you when I am oppressed, and you

22. *Ears that hear prayer.* The dominant image on this stela—the ears—is framed by an inscription: "Amen-Re, Lord of Heaven" reads the top, the bottom "Made by Neb-mehit." The ears are those of the god Amen-Re, who heard Neb-mehit's prayer. We are not told what Neb-mehit prayed for, but it must have been something important, perhaps recovery from a serious illness. In acknowledgement of the divine favor, Neb-mehit erected this stela, praising the deity as the one who listens to and answers human prayers.—Egyptian stela, ca. 1200 B.C.E.

come quickly, to save me in my wretchedness."[20] Here the "poor" are not only commoners such as the painter but also those who have an attitude of humility toward the gods. Another worker at the same necropolis, a draftsman, related in his inscription that he had sworn a false oath by the god Ptah, and that the god had punished him by making him blind; one passage reads: "My eyes may see Amen every day, as is done for a righteous man, who has set Amen in his heart."[21] In one hymn we find the following lines: "How very good is it to sit in the hand of Amen, protector of the silent, savior of the poor, who gives breath to those whom he loves."[22]

This language of piety must first of all be understood as reflecting a common way of thinking, as expressing a culturally conditioned kind of sentiment. There is evidence, however, for a more radical view, held at least by some Egyptians who transformed the pious sentiment into a particular way of life.[23] In this case, the pious individual donates his possessions to a deity by establishing a cultic foundation; at the same time, he refrains from placing himself under the protection of a human patron. One prayer, which was used by schoolmasters as an exercise text, includes a statement of exclusive allegiance to the god Amen: "I do not take a noble as protector, I do not associate with a man of wealth, I do not place my share in another's care. My wealth is in the house of my lord. My lord is my protector."[24] In his tomb inscription, a man by the name of "Simut, called Kiki," tells his story. He came as a beggar into the city, but the goddess Mut, whom he had elected as his guardian, made him wealthy. Now that he is dead, he surrenders all his possessions to the goddess. The inscription extolls Mut: "If Mut takes someone into her protection, then no evil can befall him; he is protected every day until he enters the cemetery. If Mut takes someone into her protection, how fair is the course of his life!"[25] Apparently, Simut did not make use of the patron–client relationship typical of Egyptian social life, an institution that allowed the poor to place themselves under the patronage of a wealthy and powerful magnate. Renouncing all human protection, he relied exclusively on his divine patroness in whose care he felt safe.

The Instruction of Amenemope and the Biblical Book of Proverbs

In Egypt, personal piety made a tremendous impact on how people felt about the gods. Among the scribal class, it was propagated by some of the texts used for scribal training and instruction. The supreme example is the Instruction of Amenemope, a wisdom book compiled some time in the twelfth century B.C.E. When its main manuscript witness, a papyrus owned by the British Museum, was first published in 1923, the Berlin Egyptologist Adolf Erman immediately recognized that one part of the biblical book of Proverbs represents a paraphrase of some sections of the Egyptian instruction text. This of course created a sensation, for it was the first time that modern scholarship had identified an ancient, non-Hebrew text as the model used by a biblical author. Naturally, scholars have since spent much energy on elucidating the relationship between Amenemope and the book of Proverbs. We now can be reasonably sure that Amenemope's Instruction was used in Judean or Israelite scribal education, at least for the training of those who studied Egyptian as a foreign language. At some unknown point in time (presumably not later than the eighth century B.C.E.), one of the leading masters made a Hebrew paraphrase of part of Amenemope; originally an independent work, it was later incorporated into the book of Proverbs (as Prov 22:17–24:22).

Interestingly, the Hebrew master, while generally following his Egyptian model quite closely, did not imitate those passages in which the personal piety of Amenemope is stated most clearly.[26] As a result, the abridged Hebrew work evokes a much more mundane atmosphere than its Egyptian model. Whereas in Amenemope the truly wise person excels in humility, the Hebrew master's "Pragmatic Digest" (as we may call this text) teaches a more confident outlook on life. For him, the world order seems much more reliable, and one wonders whether this could be evidence that he was dissatisfied with the views imbibed by his students in their Egyptian classes. Unlike Amenemope, he perceives God as a calculable aspect of the world order, and not as an independent, free agent. Looking for a period in history that might have given rise to such a perspective, one is tempted to settle on the first half of the eighth century, the golden age of both Hebrew kingdoms. During the long reigns of King Jeroboam II of Israel (782–747 B.C.E.) and King Uzziah (767–739 B.C.E.), the Hebrews were able to cope with their enemies, and economic life must have prospered. Later, the Assyrians made increasingly strong claims of leadership over Palestine, and beginning with the reign of Tiglath-pileser III of Assyria (744–727 B.C.E.), Palestine had to live under the constant threat or reality of foreign rule and exploitation. By then, the times were no longer favorable to optimistic wisdom teaching.

While the "Pragmatic Digest" shows no evidence of personal piety, another collection of wise sayings and precepts, also incorporated into the book of Proverbs, carries a quite remarkable religious message. This is the collection entitled the Proverbs of Solomon (Prov 10:1–22:16); in the canonical biblical book, it comes immediately before the "Pragmatic Digest." In order to avoid confusing it with the collection as a whole, which is also referred to by the same name, we will call it the "Pious Digest." Our terminology is therefore as follows:

Book of Proverbs	Prov 1:1–31:31, the entire canonical collection
"Pious Digest"	Prov 10:1–22:16, a sub-collection entitled "Proverbs of Solomon," anthologizing the Egyptian Instruction of Amenemope
"Pragmatic Digest"	Prov 22:17–24:22, a sub-collection paraphrasing the Egyptian Instruction of Amenemope

In order to appreciate the message of the "Pious Digest," it is helpful to consider the presentation of such an ancient literary work. In the biblical period, books were made from a series of papyrus or parchment strips; glued or sewed end to end, they formed a long sheet. The text, arranged in narrow columns, was written on just one side of the long sheet, the side that was protected when the sheet was rolled up for storage. When a scroll is unrolled and held in the reader's two hands, it is always the central column that is most easy to read, and so scribes took great care to put an important passage in this particular column to give it special visibility. This technique of textual presentation can be seen in the "Pious Digest," where the central section is formed by ten verses with an intense religious message:*

* The literary center of the "Pious Digest" is formed by a group of precisely ten pious sayings, so that the book's numerical structure can be outlined as follows:

(I) The fear of God [traditional reading: Yahweh] is instruction in wisdom, and humility goes before honor. (II) The plans of the mind belong to mortals, but the answer of the tongue is from Yahweh. (III) All one's ways may be pure in one's own eyes, but Yahweh weighs the spirit. (IV) Commit your work to Yahweh, and your plans will be established. (V) Yahweh has made everything for its purpose, even the wicked for the day of trouble. (VI) All those who are arrogant are an abomination to Yahweh; be assured, they will not go unpunished. (VII) By loyalty and faithfulness iniquity is atoned for, and by the fear of God [traditional reading: Yahweh] one avoids evil. (VIII) When the ways of people please Yahweh, he causes even their enemies to be at peace with them. (IX) Better is a little with righteousness than large income with injustice. (X) The human mind plans the way, but Yahweh directs the steps. (Prov 15:33–16:9)

This is essentially a lesson in humility and a recommendation to adopt a sense of reverence toward God, for it is ultimately God who directs everything, hence one should resign oneself to his will. The divine name Yahweh is used nine times; but the expression "fear of Yahweh," used twice (in sayings I and VII), should presumably be restored to its original form of "fear of God," so that the divine name punctuates the lesson seven times, a traditional number that symbolically denotes fullness and completion. The message of this central section corresponds closely to the pious spirit, and even to some of the wording, of the Instruction of Amenemope. If we add some passages from other parts of the "Pious Digest," we can establish an impressive list of four shared subjects:

1) The exhortation to acknowledge the free will of God.
2) The renunciation of retaliation.
3) The recommendation to shun the greedy accumulation of wealth, for moderation pleases the deity.
4) The warning against self-righteousness and the injunction not to think of oneself as being free from sin.

---

part 1:	183 sayings (Prov 10:1–15:32)	
central section:	10 sayings (Prov 15:33–16:9)	
part 2:	182 sayings (Prov 16:10–22:16)	
total:	375 (= 365 + 10) sayings.	

The "Pious Digest" consists of 375 short individual sayings, corresponding to the numerical value of the word "Solomon" (*Sh-l-m-h*) used in the title. If we add the values of the consonants of Shlomoh—*shin* (300), *lamed* (30), *mem* (40), and *he* (5)—we do indeed get the sum of 375. Later sages, who stood in the same tradition, would say that God himself has "arranged all things by measure and number and weight" (Wis 11:20).

Here is a detailed synopsis of the correspondences:

Instruction of Amenemope[27]	"Pious Digest" (Prov 10:1–22:16)
1) God's free will	
"One thing are the words [= thoughts] which man says, and another thing is what God does." (Amen. 19:16–17)	"The human mind plans the way, but Yahweh directs the steps." (Prov 16:9)
"Man's tongue is indeed the rudder of the boat, but the all-lord is its pilot." (Amen. 20:5–6)	"The plans of the mind belong to mortals, but the answer of the tongue is from Yahweh." (Prov 16:1)
	"The human mind may devise many plans, but it is the purpose of Yahweh that will be established." (Prov 19:21)
2) Renunciation of retaliation	
"Put yourself in the hands of God, and then your silence will bring about their [the opponents'] fall." (Amen. 23:10–11)	"Do not say: I will repay evil; wait for Yahweh, and he will help you." (Prov 20:22)
"Withdraw from him [the hot-mouthed], take no notice—the god will know how to answer him." (Amen. 5:16–17)	"Commit your work to Yahweh, and your plans will be established. Yahweh has made everything for its purpose, even the wicked for the day of trouble." (Prov 16:3–4)
3) Economic moderation	
"Better a bushel if the god give it to you, than five thousand with injustice." (Amen. 8:19–20)	"Better is a little with the fear of Yahweh than great treasure and trouble with it. Better is a dinner of vegetables where love is than a fattened ox and hatred with it." (Prov 15:16–17)
"Better is poverty from the hand of God than riches in the storehouse, better is bread, when the heart is satisfied, than riches with sorrow." (Amen. 9:5–8)	"Better a dry morsel with quiet than a house full of feasting with strife." (Prov 17:1)
"It is better to be praised as one who loves men, than riches in a storehouse. Better is bread with a contented heart, than riches with sorrow." (Amen. 16:11–14)	"Better a little with righteousness than large income with injustice." (Prov 16:8)
	"Treasures gained by wickedness do not profit." (Prov 10:2)
4) Everyone a sinner	
"Do not say, I have no sin." (Amen. 19:18)	"Who can say, 'I have made my heart clean; I am pure from sin'?" (Prov 20:9)

The compiler of the "Pious Digest" neither paraphrased nor translated passages from the Instruction of Amenemope; instead, he composed his own Hebrew equivalents, perhaps relying on existing expressions or sayings.

One of the pious sayings merits consideration in detail: the injunction to renounce personal vengeance. The moral code of personal piety tells the angry Israelite to calm down and wait. Not to wait for the anger to cool down and be forgotten, but "to wait for Yahweh" and for divine help. Aggression and retaliation must be left to the deity. This injunction makes sense when placed in the context of social life in the small towns and villages of Palestine. Aggression and vengeance are disruptive, they poison social life, making it emotionally unbearable and destroying peace and harmony. More importantly, they destroy the system of mutual help and solidarity. Leaving vengeance to the deity protects social life. In the New Testament, Paul recommends the very same practice: "If it is possible, so far as it depends on you, live peaceably with all. Beloved, never avenge yourselves, but leave room for the wrath of God . . . No, if your enemies are hungry, feed them" (Rom 12:18–20). With Paul quoting from the book of Proverbs—"If your enemies are hungry" (Prov 25:21)—we are back in the ancient Israelite town, and of course not only in the Israelite local community, but in many communities the world over. For instance, the Lugbara, a people living in Uganda, have a word for leaving vengeance to the ancestral spirits: *ole*. One of the anthropologist John Middleton's informants was quite explicit on the beneficial effect of avoiding family quarrels and leaving punishment to the spirits: "This is good. This is what we call *ole*. *Ole* does not destroy the land."[28] The conviction that vengeance should be left to the spirits or the gods is vital for the development of harmonious social life. Even Sigmund Freud, not exactly a friend of religion, could appreciate this fact in his 1907 paper on "Obsessive Acts and Religious Practices." Freud argued that renouncing primary instincts that affirm the ego's independence contributes to the development of culture. Religions have often preached renunciation. Freud quotes the Bible's "Vengeance is mine, says the Lord," and adds the following observation: "Considering the development of ancient religions one is led to realize that . . . leaving matters to the deity was the way in which humanity freed itself from evil and socially disruptive inclinations."[29] With a belief in the divine punishment of personal enemies, people fight less. Belief in the personal god, therefore, is in the interests of social life. Soothing anger and checking the impulse for revenge, it contributes to stability and harmony and thus promotes the good life, the rules of which are taught by the "Pious Digest."

If our interpretation of the injunction to leave vengeance to God is correct, then it can be read in two ways: as a pious saying that recommends trust in God, and as a pragmatic rule conducive to social stability. Arguably, both in Amenemope and the Hebrew "Pious Digest," the relevant aphorisms unite the two attitudes of piety and pragmatism. These are precisely the viewpoints combined in these writings. Among the commentators, William McKane pays most attention to the ideology implied in the sayings in the "Pious Digest." According to him, it includes sayings that reflect two different ideologies: one concerned with the education of the individual for a successful life in a stable community, and the other characterized by religious sentiment and pious moralism. Sorting the sayings into these categories, he finds that out of a total number of 375 items, 122 (or thirty-three percent) belong in the "pious" category.[30] He suggests that the "Pious Digest" most likely represents the reworking of an earlier book that did not include the specifically pious sayings, which seems a valid assumption. The editor's intention must have been to align the work with his own taste for personal piety, and in the Instruction of Amenemope he found a source that helped him express his ideas. Accordingly, the "Pious Digest" represents a conscious effort to create a work with a strong religious outlook corresponding to Egyptian-style personal piety.

McKane's statistics make it clear that the pious aphorisms are significant and give the book its distinctive devotional flavor; nevertheless, the older ideology, which aims at individual success and social stability and is represented by sixty-seven percent of the sayings, has by no means been displaced. The juxtaposition of the two ideologies suggests a conservative approach to a spiritual revolution: the new spirit of personal piety is welcomed and even made central, yet it is not allowed to displace the older, more rational, mundane spirit. This retention of traditional views is not a matter of coincidence; it reflects a deeply rooted approach to innovation characteristic of traditional thought. The cautious "step-by-step" advance, which seeks to insure continuity, forms part of what Brunner-Traut calls the "aspective" view of reality.[31] Familiar "aspects" of reality transmitted from the past are deemed no less valid than newly discovered ones. New insight is simply added to the existing corpus of knowledge. Given the lack of a coherent, tightly argued worldview, people felt no obligation to rethink its foundations.

Only one possible literary genre can accommodate what seem to be alternative, though to the ancients not incompatible, worldviews: the "collection" of randomly arranged, self-contained aphorisms. In this form, the wisdom of more than one age and more than one temper can be stored side by side. It is not merely the literary form of the collection, however, that allows for this ecumenical generosity. Aphoristic expression itself implies an entire philosophy and worldview. According to this philosophy, experience and thought about experience can be stored best in independent short sayings and poems. The aphoristic worldview also implies that no systematic exposition is intended, for any systematic arrangement or exposition would endanger the independence and originality of an insight stored in a small literary unit. The masters of wisdom have no interest in or conception of completeness or logical presentation of their insights and indeed avoid it. Perhaps one can explain the underlying idea in terms of the distinction between "systematic" and "aphoristic" thought. Systematic thought tends to doctrinalism and the development of comprehensive, complete, and finally closed ideologies. Aphoristic thought, by contrast, remains open-ended and fragmentary. One can always add to the corpus of aphoristic expression, for it can never be complete. Thus aphoristic thinking is more a style of thought than a particular doctrine. As the anthropologist Clifford Geertz explains, "it comes in epigrams, proverbs, obiter dicta, jokes, anecdotes, contes moraux—a clatter of gnomic utterances—not in formal doctrines, axiomized theories, or architectonic dogmas."[32]

In assessing the personal piety expressed in Amenemope and the "Pious Digest," one has to take into account that the instruction genre does not allow for as much individual and emotional expression as does a prayer. Without an effusive outpouring of the human heart, admission of sin, or desperate appeal to divine mercy and compassion, the religious sentiment receives a particularly restrained articulation. Nevertheless, all the essential elements of personal piety are present, and a warm religious tone is not entirely lacking, as can be seen from the following examples:

> Yahweh is far from the wicked,
> but he hears the prayer of the righteous [or: pious]. (Prov 15:29)

> Those who are attentive to a matter will prosper,
> and happy are those who trust in Yahweh. (Prov 16:20)

> The name of Yahweh is a strong tower;
> the righteous [or: pious] run into it and are safe. (Prov 18:10)

The Hebrew word generally rendered as "righteous" (*tsaddiq*) here definitely carries the connotation of "pious," a meaning well known from postbiblical Hebrew. The individual's closeness to God—what William James called the "personal communion with the divine"—can be perceived in these well-crafted sayings.

The "Pious Digest," like the "Pragmatic Digest," was compiled by someone thoroughly conversant with Egyptian phraseology and ways of thinking. This is evident not only from the passages inspired directly by the Instruction of Amenemope, but in others as well.[33] A particularly fine example of a saying marked by Egyptian expression and imagery can be found among the royal aphorisms: "The king's heart is a stream of water in the hands of God; he turns it wherever he will" (Prov 21:1).[34] To begin with, "to be in the hands of a god" is a well-attested Egyptian idiom.[35] Moreover, God's special relationship with the king could hardly have been articulated in a more Egyptian way, for the Nile frequently changes its course in unpredictable ways. Although not in a royal context, the Instruction of Amenemope actually uses the shifting bed of the Nile as an illustration of the unpredictability of human life.[36] The king is here of course the model of a pious person, to be emulated by everyone. It may well be that the anthologist thought of a particular king, for the "Pious Digest" no doubt originated under royal patronage, as presumably did all the collections eventually brought together in the book of Proverbs. But which king did he have in mind?

One might think of Solomon, for this king's name figures in the title of the digest. However, biblical scholars agree that Solomon is neither the author of the book of Proverbs nor can he be considered as the compiler's royal patron. Solomon functions as a merely literary figure to whom all wisdom was attributed. But who was the compiler's real royal patron? When did he live? Gener-

ally speaking, the time between the late eighth and the early sixth centuries—
the era between King Hezekiah (716–687 B.C.E.) and the beginning of the Babylonian exile (586 B.C.E.)—can be considered the most likely period of intensive
cultural contact between Egypt and Judah and therefore the most likely period
for the production of Egyptianizing books.[37] Is it too daring to identify the pious
king, whose heart rests in the hands of God, with Josiah of Judah, promoter of
the great religious reform in the late seventh century B.C.E.? Is it justified to
identify the sin from which no one is free as the worship of deities other than
Yahweh, a practice abolished by King Josiah?[38] If these interpretations are
granted, we might see the "Pious Digest" as a senior teacher's attempt to adjust
a traditional school manual not merely to suit his own religious taste and understanding, but to meet the requirements of an age of religious revival. The sages
then living may have hoped for a return of the legendary era of King Solomon.
Just as the priests sought to restore the temple's original Solomonic purity, so
the teachers hoped to revive Solomonic wisdom and scholarship. The age of
Josiah, the new Solomon, placed not only the whole nation under the protection of Yahweh alone (for the reform aimed at strict monolatry), but also each
person individually. The theme of loyalty to the king, a major theme in the
"Pious Digest," also fits in with the requirements of the Josianic era, for if the
reform was to succeed, it needed general support. It would be hard to believe
that a reform that involved the demolition of local shrines throughout the
country was welcomed by everyone and met with no resistance or opposition.
The age of reform must also have been an age when religious controversy flared
high. Loyalist propaganda served to convince or silence dissidents. New, loyal
scribes had to be recruited and educated in the new teaching. Although we
cannot be certain, the "Pious Digest" may be a book designed for the very specific purposes of a specific period, written, if not at royal request, then at least
with royal approval. Its presence in the book of Proverbs demonstrates that the
work survived the short-lived reform of Josiah and became part of Judah's
literary and religious heritage.

14. God as Lord of the Individual: The Mesopotamian Contribution

In Mesopotamian religion, two phases of development can be discerned. In the first phase, dominated by the Sumerians, the emphasis was placed on praising the gods, who were extolled for their power, majesty, and transcendent splendor; in this context, the praying individual or community is barely visible in the surviving texts. Then, around 2000 B.C.E., the religious climate began to change.[39] Under the increasing cultural and political influence of Western Semites in Mesopotamia, the individual praying person, with his personal agonies and pleas for help and mercy, became a characteristic feature of a new kind of spirituality. Once it had made its appearance, "personal religion" was quick to establish itself as a conspicuous part of the religious culture of the second and first millennia B.C.E. Echoes of the specifically Mesopotamian version of personal religion can be found throughout Western Asia, especially among the Hittites and the Israelites, in whose literatures references to the "personal god" of the human individual abound. It may well be that, when the Israelites came into contact with specifically Mesopotamian forms of personal piety, it resonated with and strengthened sentiments already deeply rooted in their inherited West Semitic mentality.

The Personal God in Mesopotamian Belief

In his classic study of Mesopotamian religion, the American Assyriologist Thorkild Jacobsen largely follows William James in defining "personal religion" as

> a particular, easily recognized, religious attitude in which the religious individual sees himself as standing in close personal relationship to the divine, expecting help and guidance in his personal life and personal affairs, expecting divine anger and punishment if he sins, but also profoundly trusting to divine compassion, forgiveness, and love of him if he sincerely repents. In sum: the individual matters to God, God cares about him personally and deeply.[40]

According to Jacobsen, the notion of the "personal god" forms the center of personal religion. By this modern (rather than Mesopotamian) term, special-

ists describe a divine role the various aspects of which are not easily understood when initially encountered by the contemporary reader. First of all, we
may say that the personal god, like all the other deities of Mesopotamia, is a
being who, like a human person, is an individual self, distinct from other selves,
moved to action by feelings and emotions in the same way that human beings
are. While this sounds rather straightforward, the second characteristic is less
so. The personal god is someone's permanent guardian spirit, responsible for
his or her health, wealth, and success in life. The personal god inspires a king
to restore a temple, and grants someone long life and social or economic success.
When feeling at their best, in full vigor, enjoying economic prosperity and spiritual peace, individuals ascribe this enviable state of body and mind to the presence of supernatural powers. "To experience a lucky stroke, to escape a danger,
to have an easy and complete success, is expressed in Akkadian by saying that
such a person has a 'spirit'," that is, a personal god responsible for luck in
all dealings.[41] The result of one's personal god's presence is "prosperity, high
office, economic success, a large family, respect in public thoroughfares,
government buildings, or assembly places of the worthy, a circle of admiring
friends and colleagues, robust health, radiance of countenance, and authoritative presence."[42]

The relationship between the personal god (or goddess) and his (or her)
protégé is so intimate that certain expressions convey the notion of immanence
within the human body; accordingly, all bad luck begins with the personal god
leaving his human abode. But it is not the mere belief in a personal god that
constitutes personal religion in the sense given to this term by William James;
instead, it is the cultivation and expression of an emotionally charged, intimate,
warm relationship with the tutelary deity, a relationship that typically considers the human partner a child and the divine partner the loving parent. With
the appearance of personal religion, the personal god comes to be considered
the individual's divine father or mother, with whom an intimate, familial relationship can be entertained. From the very moment at which the parental image
appears, we have "personal religion." Many of the early Mesopotamian expressions of personal religion can be found in penitential prayers and letters
addressed to the personal god. Individuals who find themselves in situations of
crisis—estranged from friends, in bad health, in economic distress—call upon
their god, confess their sins, and ask for help. These prayers construe the personal deity as a divine mother or father who nurtures, cares for, and protects
the human child.

Some excerpts from original sources will help us understand how the
Mesopotamians felt about the personal deity. One hymn tells how the goddess
Ninsuna takes the little boy Shulgi (later an important Sumerian king) on her
lap, saying to him: "Shulgi, you sacred seed to which I gave birth, you holy
semen of [the god] Lugalbanda. On my holy lap I raised you, at my holy breast
I determined the destiny for you, you are the best that fell to my portion."[43]

Ninsuna and Lugalbanda are the personal goddess and god of King Shulgi, and they are depicted as his divine parents. In the Sumerian poem "Man and His God," the praying person addresses his god as follows: "My god, to you who are my father that begot me, let me lift my eyes."[44] King Ashurbanipal calls his personal goddess Ishtar "the Lady of Nineveh, the mother who bore me."[45] In his inscriptions, the Babylonian king Nebuchadnezzar II frequently acknowledges Marduk as the god who begot him and destined him for kingship: "Ever since the time that [the god] Marduk, the great lord, exalted me to rulership of the land . . . I have been obedient to my royal begetter with reverence."[46] "Lord Marduk, you are the wise god, the proud prince! You have created me and entrusted me with royal rule over all the people."[47] A formula often found in Mesopotamian prayers addresses a deity as mother and father at the same time: "Like the heart of a mother may your heart return to its place for me! Like a mother and a father, may you return to me."[48]

A complete definition of the personal deity's duties can be found in the Babylonian "Dialogue between a Man and His God." Here the god addresses his protégé with the following word of promise: "I am your god, your creator, your trust. My guardians are strong and alert on your behalf. The field will open to you its refuge. I will see to it that you have long life."[49] What more could one expect from one's divine patron?

Mesopotamian individuals, especially people of rank, thought of themselves as being under the special protection of one or more deities, often a divine couple, who act as their nurturing and loving divine parents. Both men and women enjoyed the presence of personal gods, whose protection they acquired at birth—children had the same personal god as their father. Women were regularly under the protection of their father's and later their husband's tutelary deity.[50] Some of the logic involved can be gleaned from Plutarch: "A wife ought not to make friends of her own, but to enjoy her husband's friends in common with him. Therefore it is becoming for a wife to worship and to know only the gods that her husband believes in."[51] Thus cared for, the Mesopotamians felt, in the words of Dietrich Bonhoeffer, "von guten Mächten wunderbar geborgen," safe in the caring hands of kindly powers.[52] On the one hand, all good luck in life was attributed to their benevolence; on the other, all misfortune was seen as due to the gods' abandonment of their "child."

The Deity's Parental Care

Insight into the dynamics of personal religion can be gained only through close attention to the language used by the ancients. The language of protection and paternal and maternal care is familiar to all who have ever read the book of Psalms. The most striking feature of these texts is that they repeatedly picture the god's protégé as a nursling or little child and the god as a mother, midwife, or someone caring for the baby. "It was you who took me from the womb, you kept me safe on my mother's breast," reads one of the canonical psalms (Ps 22:9/Hebr. 22:10). The notion of God as someone's foster parent, stated in the psalmist's confession of trust, is immediately understandable in this context: "If my father and mother forsake me, Yahweh will take me up" (Ps 27:10). One of the Hymns of Thanksgiving from Qumran elaborates this language:

> [From the womb of] my mother you have filled me,
> from the breasts of her who conceived me
> your compassion has always been upon me,
> from the lap of my wet-nurse [you have looked after me,]
> from my youth you have shown yourself to me in the intelligence of
>   your judgement . . .
> Until old age you support me.
> For my mother did not know me,
> and my father abandoned me to you.
> Because you are father to all the sons of your truth.
> In them you rejoice,
> like one full of gentleness for her child,
> and like a wet-nurse,
> you clasp to your breast all your creatures.[53]

The language of the Psalms inspired the members of an early Jewish sect to celebrate themselves as God's favorite children.

Long before the Hebrew poets, the scribes of Mesopotamia used similar language associating scenes of midwifery, motherhood, and nursing with the notion of the personal deity. A Bronze Age Babylonian text combines anthropomorphic and theriomorphic language to create a vivid image of closeness and protection: the personal god Marduk is compassionate like a midwife and cares for his protégé like a cow for her calf: "like a cow with a calf, he keeps turning around watchfully."[54] For much of ancient culture, the cow epitomizes the idea of motherhood and the maternal instinct; in art, the cow suckling or licking her calf stands for divine blessing and the nurturing love of the deity (fig. 23, p. 130; fig. 24, p. 131; and fig. 25, p. 132).[55] Particularly striking language is used to describe the unique relationship King Ashurbanipal (669–630 B.C.E.) enjoys with his personal goddess, Ishtar of Nineveh. In a poem, the god Nabu addresses Ashurbanipal as follows: "You were a child, Ashurbanipal, when I left you with the Queen of Nineveh [the goddess Ishtar]; you were a baby, Ashurbanipal, when you sat in the lap of the Queen of Nineveh! Her four teats are placed in your mouth; two you suck, and two you milk to your face."[56] The poet combines the image of mother and baby with that of a cow—this is how the four teats are to be explained. In an oracle addressed to Ashurbanipal, a prophetess has the goddess Mullissu (presumably to be identified with Ishtar) say:

23. *Cow and calf—a sacred icon.* In ancient Egyptian and Near Eastern art, the cow suckling its calf has an iconic quality. A common subject, it visualizes the maternal instinct and highlights its special, even sacred character. Owing to its influence, mother goddesses were often given bovine attributes to underline their nurturing attitude (see figs. 24 and 25).—Assyrian ivory carving, eighth century B.C.E.

You whose mother is Mullissu, have no fear! You whose nurse is the Lady of Arbela, have no fear! I will carry you on my hip like a nurse, I will put you between my breasts like a pomegranate. At night I will stay awake and guard you; in the daytime I will give you milk; at dawn I will play *watch, watch your* . . . [?] with you. As for you, have no fear, my calf, whom I have reared.[57]

Again, the images of baby and mother, nursling and nurse, calf and cow are invoked to describe the sacred bond between the ruler and his personal goddess. A similar view can be found in Psalms:

O God, you are my God, I seek you,
my soul [*nephesh*] thirsts for you . . .
My soul [*nephesh*] is satisfied with fat and fatness,
and my mouth praises you with joyful lips
when I think of you on my bed . . .
for you have been my help,
and in the shadow of your wings I sing for joy.

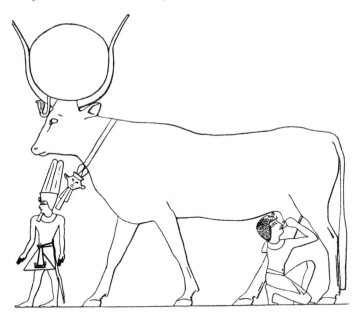

24. *An icon of divine nurture.* The sacred cow of ancient Egyptian art—a cow with a sun-disk between its horns—represents the goddess Hathor. In the illustration, Hathor is led by the god Amen, who wears a crown with two feathers; the child nursing at the cow's udder can be identified as Hatshepsut, who in the fifteenth century B.C.E. ruled as a female pharaoh. According to the accompanying inscription, the cow Hathor says: "I have come to you, my beloved daughter Hatshepsut, to kiss your hand and lick your limbs."—Egyptian relief, fifteenth century B.C.E.

> My soul [*nephesh*] clings to you;
> your right hand upholds me. (Ps 63:1, 5–8/Hebr. 63:2, 6–9).

Far from denoting some vague concept of "soul," as the standard translations have it (including the New Revised Standard Version just quoted), *nephesh* here denotes the mouth.[58] Commentators seem to have a hard time understanding the details of the language of protection and care used here. Taking into account the fact that much of our emotional language echoes early childhood experience can be of help; for it reveals that the praying individual here thinks of himself, perhaps unconsciously, as a nursling who lies in bed, or is held by the hand or whose mouth clings to the mother's breast, sucking milk.

Happiness predominantly experienced with the mouth and derived from eating and drinking reveals an attitude Freudians call "oral orientation" and "oral gratification." Such an orientation is entirely understandable in a culture in which the production of food was precarious and storage limited, so that periods of abundance alternated with periods of scarcity. As we have seen, the

25. *Divine motherhood.* The winged mother-goddess who gives her breasts to two boys, presumably princes, is another version of the motif of the nurturing deity (see fig. 24). The two horns that crown her wig allude to the bovine icon, stating that the mother-goddess shares the cow's maternal instinct (see fig. 23).—Ugaritic ivory panel, fourteenth century B.C.E.

mouth orientation is particularly evident in biblical texts describing the relationship between the individual and the personal god as one between nursling and mother (or others involved with the care of infants). Here we may refer to the observation of Sigmund Freud that, as the infant "sinks asleep at the breast, utterly satisfied, it bears a look of perfect content . . . If the infant could express itself, it would undoubtedly acknowledge that the act of sucking at the mother's breast is far and away the most important thing in life," for by this blissful act it satisfies its two basic needs: eating and love.[59] Accordingly, for Lou Andreas-Salomé, God is "the memory of the most intimate human tenderness whose sweetness a child was given to taste"—by the mother.[60] In biblical Israel, personal piety seems to involve a sort of infantile regression, one that connects the adult person with his or her infancy and with the feeling of security then experienced. As post-Freudians have argued, this regression evokes a sort of dreamtime that serves as a great reservoir of confidence and forms the basis of the courage to live.

As a consequence of personal misfortune or social unrest and disorder, the individual may be thrown back on "oral gratification"—the elementary gratification of appetite characteristic of early infancy. This can be observed in testimonies from all Near Eastern civilizations. Thus an Egyptian sage inserted the following remark into his description of an inverted, topsy-turvy world in which the poor of the land have become rich and the noblemen paupers:

> Lo, a man is happy eating his food.
> Consume your goods in gladness
> while there is none to hinder you.
> It is good for a man to eat his food.
> God ordains it for him whom he favors.[61]

In the Bible it is the grumpy pessimist and skeptic Koheleth who in the midst of ever-present misfortune comes to realize that the good life culminates in moments of joyful consumption, "for there is nothing better for man under the sun than to eat, and drink, and enjoy himself; this is all that will remain with him to reward his toil throughout the span of life which God grants him under the sun" (Eccl 8:15, adapted from the Revised English Bible). When Gilgamesh, the hero of a Mesopotamian mythical tale, mourns the death of his friend, he is given the same advice: "But you, Gilgamesh, let your belly be full, enjoy yourself always by day and by night! Make merry each day, dance and play day and night."[62] Culinary fulfillment also figures in the Egyptian Tale of Sinuhe. If the hero has to live outside of his home country, he should at least be able to enjoy savory food as a compensation. As a matter of fact, Sinuhe's list of the good things that he enjoys gives delicacies a prominent place: "Many sweets were made for him, and milk dishes of all kinds."[63]

The Israelites' and their neighbors' "oral orientation" was no doubt promoted by the long period during which infants were breast-fed by their mothers. The Maccabean brothers' legendary mother said to one of her sons: "I carried you for nine months in my womb, and nursed you for three years" (2 Macc 7:27). Evidence from Egyptian and Near Eastern antiquity also suggests that infants were breast-fed for two to three years.[64] The Tunisian psychiatrist Abdelwahab Boudhiba describes how in his own traditional society the prolonged exclusivity of the mother–child relationship and the virtual absence of the father foster a vigorous network of affection between mother and child. Later in life, however, the male child is almost brutally drawn into the "real," male world, which denies and opposes the dreamlike, fanciful, and playful world of women. As a result, the masculine consciousness is accompanied by a feminine, mother-related unconsciousness. Even in everyday life, explains Boudhiba, the

> prolongation of a man's uterine relation reappears at every instant. The most mature man, the most masculine, will never miss an occasion to recreate, to restore, or to rediscover the uterine milieu—whether through memory,

mimic, dream, or imagination. Alongside the real world is forged an exquisite and personal world of compensation. A veritable realm of mothers is founded, and far more than queen of the hearth or of the night, the Arab woman becomes queen of the unconscious. By the pity which she inspires, and by the affection which she gives without reserve or limit, the mother appears as an effective and unconscious shelter from the castrating impulses of the surroundings.[65]

In other words: an inbuilt regressive tendency toward the maternal provides a balance and a shelter in the harsh life of males. The same or a similar psychological mechanism may account for the unrivaled success of the parental image of the deity within personal religion.

Job's Personal God

The abandonment of someone by his personal god or gods is quite understandable as a reaction to sin, for misdeeds provoke divine anger. As soon as someone loses divine protection, evil demons take over, impairing his health, destroying his possessions, and ruining his reputation. In this case, the repentant confession of sins committed both knowingly and unknowingly was thought to reconcile personal gods and bring back their favor. However, what if sufferers were unable to detect any faults on their part? What if they felt that they should not depend on incalculable divine favor, but have the right to be treated well by the personal gods? This problem was discussed in two classical Near Eastern works of literature: one entitled "I Will Praise the Lord of Wisdom," composed in Mesopotamia in the Late Bronze Age (twelfth century B.C.E.), and the book of Job, written in Israel, presumably around 500 B.C.E. In both works the righteous sufferer, a wealthy, socially high-ranking man, turns in protest to his personal god. Whereas the Mesopotamian sufferer addresses Marduk as his helper, Job looks to Shaddai for assistance. We do not know why the Hebrew poet chose Shaddai as the name of Job's personal god; was he fascinated by the Lord of the Animals, whose Hebrew name he knew?

Mesopotamian language relating to the personal god permeates the book of Job. Shaddai created Job, as the latter himself indicates in his lament:

> Your hands fashioned and made me;
> and now you turn and destroy me.
> Remember that you fashioned me like clay;
> and will you turn me to dust again?
> Did you not pour me out like milk
> and curdle me like cheese?
> You clothed me with skin and flesh,
> and knit me together with bones and sinews.

> You have granted me life and steadfast love,
> and your care has preserved my spirit. (Job 10:8–12)

At times, Shaddai's care for Job has led to splendid moments in his life. In the midst of his complaints, Job remembers with a sorrowful sigh:

> O that I were as in the months of old,
> as in the days when [my personal] God watched over me;
> when his lamp shone over my head,
> and by his light I walked through darkness;
> when I was in my prime,
> when the friendship of [my personal] God was upon my tent;
> when Shaddai was still with me,
> when my children were around me,
> and the rock poured out for me streams of oil. (Job 29:2–6)

Angel-protected, materially solid, and spiritually secure—how else could we describe Job in his bliss?

Of particular interest is the reference to "light." In biblical language in general, according to Sverre Aalen, light is "a figure for success and well-being," while darkness "stands for suffering and failure." Aalen adds that light is sometimes replaced by "lamp," which is also a figure for success and salvation, as in the passage of Job just quoted.[66] However, one may wonder whether this is the whole story. The light that shines over Job's head is not necessarily just the physical sun. Rather, it seems to be a mysterious, generally invisible light that envelops the head of an individual, comparable to the halo or aureole of Christian art. For St. Paul, Christ not only functions in the role of a personal god, but also forms the "head of the man" (1 Cor 11:3), and in the Christian "Odes of Solomon" Christ is the crown of the faithful: "The Lord is on my head like a crown."[67] Such expressions seem to imply that the personal deity could be conceived of as a power whose presence can be felt around someone's head or above someone's residence, as the Job text indicates (God's friendship "upon my tent"). In Akkadian, the personal god is sometimes called "the god at my head,"[68] and a Babylonian correspondent adds the following wish to his letter: "May the guardian of wellbeing and life not depart from your head."[69]

Eliphaz, one of Job's interlocutors in the poem, sketches a beautiful picture of Shaddai as a god who reproves and wounds, but also binds and heals. Moreover, he cares for his protégés in all difficulties; neither famine nor war can do them any harm, and they will have many offspring. Someone guided through life by the personal god will come to his grave "in ripe old age, as a shock of grain comes up to the threshing floor in its season" (Job 5:26). Eliphaz also hints at the special character of Job's personal god, Shaddai, by describing him as the lord of the fields and the wild beasts: "You shall not fear the wild animals of the earth, for you shall be in league with the stones of the field, and the wild animals shall be at peace with you" (Job 5:22–23).

One final lesson can be learned from the book of Job: a lesson on happiness. When at the end of the book God restores the suffering hero's health and wealth, the reader, ancient or modern, is given a brief definition of the Hebrew notion of the good life:

> The Lord blessed the latter days of Job more than his beginning; and he had fourteen thousand sheep, six thousand camels, a thousand yoke of oxen, and a thousand donkeys. He also had seven sons and three daughters . . . In all the land there were no women so beautiful as Job's daughters . . . After this Job lived one hundred and forty years, and saw his children, and his children's children, four generations. And Job died, old and full of days. (Job 42:12–13, 15–17)

In the book of Job human wellbeing is not legitimized as the automatic result of human wisdom and righteousness; traditional notions of the act-consequence relationship in a world of poetic justice do not apply. Health and wealth are in a way independent of human behavior; they are divine gifts. Happiness and the good life depend upon the personal god, for he is the giver of the gift. Blessing Job, he bestows upon him all the benefits that make up his bliss. The blessing extends beyond the life of Job, for it also includes his children and his children's children. It is not only in Mesopotamia that the personal deity of a man is also the tutelary deity of his sons and daughters.[70]

The Personal God as the National Deity

In Mesopotamia, personal piety and the veneration of a personal god were strictly "private" matters for individuals and families. The larger community—local or national—was not involved in this aspect of religious belief and practice. Whenever a larger group of people was concerned, God would be invoked as Lord of Wisdom (i.e. God as the sovereign legislator and judge), as Divine Warrior, or perhaps as Lord of the Harvest (see below, "The Fifth Image: Lord of the Harvest"); but in such a context people would never invoke the personal god. This must have been the original state of affairs in Israel as well. Things began to change, however, presumably during the Babylonian exile of the sixth century. At that time, prophets with an interest in the fate of the nation sought to develop an image of God that was intellectually satisfying as well as emotionally pertinent. As a result, they devised the image of God as the father who considers all the Israelites as his children, caring for them collectively in the same way that a personal god would care for his individual devotee.

The classic representative of this idea is the anonymous sixth-century B.C.E. prophet whom scholars have named Second Isaiah. According to the traditional assumption, he was active among the Jewish exiles in Babylonia, and it must have been there that he witnessed his fellow exiles' fascination with the personal god. Indeed, he must have been deeply impressed with their spiritual experience. Yet he found this individualism unsatisfactory and so propagated a more communal version of personal piety. His message can be summed up in the statement: Yahweh, Israel's national God, acts as the personal god of the collective group. The oracles emphasize the close, filial relationship between Yahweh, the father and protector, and Israel, the community:

> Thus says Yahweh, he who created you, O Jacob,
> he who formed you, O Israel:
> Do not fear, for I have redeemed you,
> I have called you by name, you are mine.
> When you pass through the waters, I will be with you;
> and through the rivers, they shall not overwhelm you;
> when you walk through fire, you shall not be burned,
> and the flame shall not consume you. (Isa 43:1–2)

Another oracle goes even further and describes Yahweh's care from infancy to old age:

> Listen to me, O house of Jacob,
> all the remnant of the house of Israel,
> who have been borne by me from your birth,
> carried from your womb;
> even to your old age I am he,
> even when you turn grey I will carry you.
> I have made, and I will bear;
> I will carry and will save. (Isa 46:3–4)

As a diligent, responsible parent, Yahweh cannot abandon his ward permanently: "Zion said: 'Yahweh has forsaken me, my Lord has forgotten me.' Can a woman forget her nursing child, or show no compassion for the child of her womb? Even these may forget, yet I will not forget you" (Isa 49:14–15). Here we have one of the rare biblical texts in which Israel's God assumes a distinctively female, motherly role.

The extension of the attitude of personal religion to the national realm is not peculiar to Second Isaiah, but rather characterizes much of late biblical spirituality. Some of the psalms, in which individuals address their personal god, include editorial additions that demonstrate that the praying individual has become a collective entity, a kind of "superego" imagined by followers of Second Isaiah.[71] Equally, people imagined Israel's remote ancestor, Jacob, to have acquired Yahweh as a personal god during his wanderings through

Palestine and much of the Near East, a god to whom he attached himself by a vow, saying: "If God will be with me, and will keep me in this way that I go, and will give me bread to eat and clothing to wear, so that I come again to my father's house in peace, then Yahweh shall be my God" (Gen 28:20–21). It was to Jacob that Israel's God appeared in a vision and said to him: "I am El Shaddai. Be fruitful and multiply; a nation and a company of nations shall come from you, and kings shall spring from you" (Gen 35:11). The ancestor's personal god is both the personal god of each descendant of Jacob and also the personal god of the collectivity.

Presumably the book of Job was compiled not to show the fate of an individual who complains to his personal god; instead, it may have been written as a parable illustrating the fate of the Israelites. Read from this perspective, the book seeks to explain Israel's political decline and fall in the sixth century B.C.E. as a loss of national health and wellbeing followed by an eventual restoration. The poet's particular message would be that the Hebrews, like Job, had not committed any sin to deserve such severe treatment from their god. While the biblical books of the Kings explain the state's collapse as a result of noncompliance with the divine commandment to worship Yahweh exclusively, the book of Job denies all responsibility on the part of the people. The lawgiving Lord of Wisdom insists on punishment, but the motherly Lord of the Individual freely grants restitution and provides all the gifts one can possibly wish for in earthly existence.

The Fifth Image: Lord of the Harvest

"Give us this day our daily bread." Although this petition in the Lord's Prayer is addressed to the Christian God, it is actually universal. In all religions one group of deities and demons is utterly indispensable for human life to flourish: the gods of the "Third Function" who provide nourishment and thus life itself. The biblical sources depict God as the giver of three basic gifts that sustain the agrarian economy: water, land, and fertility. From a close reading of the biblical text, two images of the Lord of the Harvest emerge: one that emphasizes the natural gifts of rain and the fertility of the ground; and another that, shaped by historical experience, highlights the gift of the land and announces Palestine's miraculous transformation into a region blessed with rivers and rich yields.

The natural gift of water figures most prominently in the biblical record, and it comes as no surprise that the ancient Near Eastern weather-god, the divine king of the rainy season from October to March, forms an important model for Israel's Lord of the Harvest. In addition to sending water, the Lord of the Harvest also grants fertility. Far from being an intrinsic virtue of the soil, this must be given by God in the form of a divine blessing, for only blessed ground can bring forth high yields of grain and the fruits of gardens and trees.

Without a country of their own, a peasant people cannot exist. In a politically unstable situation, where foreign political powers compel entire populations to leave their home and settle elsewhere, the divine gift of land forms a subject often taken up by biblical authors. Living in Babylonian exile, the people long to return to the God-given land of Palestine. In their imagination, this land assumes miraculous qualities, for God, in addition to giving it to them as a permanent, inalienable possession, will assimilate it to Mesopotamia, transforming it into a region rich with springs and rivers, allowing for miraculous yields.

15.   The Fertile Crescent

Farming has first of all to do with land, soil, climate, and plants, and in order to understand these factors we may begin by considering the geographical and climatic area in which, in the history of humankind, agriculture emerged. There is no historical name for this area in the Middle East, but modern specialists use the poetic term "the Fertile Crescent." This designates a certain portion of the Middle East, shaped like an inverted crescent and characterized by fertility (fig. 26, p. 142). The Fertile Crescent is set off from the less fertile area surrounding it. Introduced by the Orientalist James Henry Breasted in 1916, the elegant expression immediately became current.

Breasted's book *Ancient Times: A History of the Early World* (1916) describes Western Asia as a land marked by three geographical areas, arranged as successive belts on the map. The northernmost part is the mountains. There is then a thin string of fertile land followed by vast desert lands. During the rainy season, i.e. during the Middle Eastern winter, that thin string of fertile land gets enough rain to be green with vegetation and to be used for the cultivation of crops. This green area extends to the east and west in the form of wings, so that, with some imagination, the shape of an inverted crescent can be recognized on the map. "After the meager winter rains, wide tracts of the northern desert bay are clothed with scanty grass, and spring thus turns the region for a short time into grasslands."[1] As is evident, Breasted does not want to exaggerate the fertility of this land—he refers to meager rains, scanty grass, and the short period during which the crescent-shaped area turns into grassland.

Farming in the Fertile Crescent depends on the availability of water, which, in this part of the world, is a scarce commodity (fig. 27, p. 143). What may be termed the "western wing" of the Fertile Crescent—the area closest to the Mediterranean—has annual rainfall figures of between 400 and 600 mm per year, allowing for dependable rain-fed farming. Here the peasant population can hope for sufficient winter rains, for the long summers are invariably hot and dry. The Fertile Crescent's "eastern wing"—the area closest to the Persian Gulf—gets much less precipitation, usually less than 200 mm per year. In this area rain-fed farming is impossible, for cereal cannot be cultivated without an annual rainfall of at least 250 mm; here reliable harvests require irrigation through a system of canals deriving their water from the Tigris and the

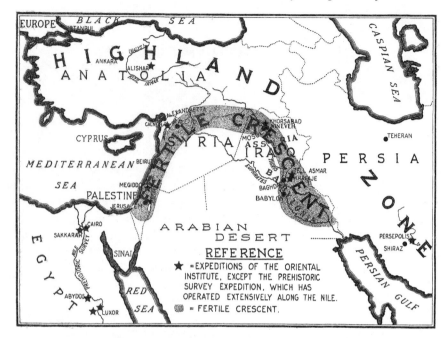

26. *The Fertile Crescent.* This is a narrow, crescent-shaped strip of land, extending through much of the Middle East, that gets sufficient rain during the winter months to be used for agriculture. It is home to an ancient peasant civilization whose religion centered on the harvest.—Map designed by J.H. Breasted.

Euphrates and some lesser rivers. Here are some figures indicating the average annual rainfall in the Middle East:

Jerusalem	496 mm
Beirut	893 mm
Damascus	224 mm
Baghdad	156 mm

While risky rain-fed farming was the rule in ancient Palestine and Syria, irrigation secured Mesopotamian agriculture. In the Middle East, there are only two seasons—summer and winter. According to the book of Genesis, God will not interrupt the cycle of "seedtime and harvest, cold and heat, summer and winter" (Gen 8:22). The summer is reckoned to last from mid-April to mid-October, i.e. from the Hebrew Feast of Passover (Easter) to the Feast of Sukkoth (Tabernacles, Booths). The summers are long and dry; in October the winter sets in abruptly and, in the Fertile Crescent's western wing, brings increasing rainfall.

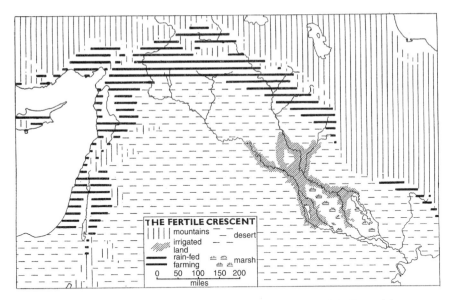

27. *Water resources in the Fertile Crescent.* Only areas of the Middle East with sufficient precipitation or with water available from rivers for irrigation can be used for farming. Baly's map, shown here, gives more information than that of Breasted (fig. 26).—Map designed by D. Baly.

The Fertile Crescent, including Palestine, ranks as the world's first area where the grains of certain wild grasses were not only collected, but also domesticated and systematically grown by the early farmers. It was here that the cultivation of cereals—chiefly barley and a variety of wheats, including emmer—was introduced. Prehistorians date the emergence of cereal agriculture to the eighth millennium B.C.E., and the relevant standard manual's map locates scattered agricultural settlements in Asia Minor and the Fertile Crescent for the period between 7600 and 7000 B.C.E.[2] It was from there that the cultivation of cereals spread to North Africa, Europe, and other parts of the world. After millennia of hunting and gathering, the cultivation of crops changed the economy, and historians rightly speak of the event as belonging to the Neolithic Revolution, which also brought linen-weaving, pottery-making, and the cultivation of fruit trees.

An early description of the flourishing economy of the Fertile Crescent echoes the admiration some of the ancients had for this region. The description is put into the mouth of Sinuhe, an Egyptian who leaves his country to find refuge somewhere in Western Asia, possibly in Palestine:

He [my host] let me choose for myself of his land, of the best that was his, on the border with another land. It was a good land called Yaa. Figs were in

it and grapes. It had more wine than water. Abundant was its honey, plenti-
ful its oil. All kinds of fruit were on its trees. Barley was there and emmer,
and no end of cattle of all kinds.[3]

This idealized literary portrait demonstrates that, by the early second millennium B.C.E. (the date of the story), the mixed economy characteristic of subsequent ages was already in place:

— agriculture: the cultivation of wheat and barley;
— arboriculture: the growing of olive and fig trees;
— viticulture: the planting of grapevines;
— livestock husbandry: the keeping of cattle, goats, and sheep.

In this mixed economy, people apparently appreciated the agrarian sector more
than the keeping of animals. The prophet Isaiah actually contrasts the luxuries
of agrarian existence with the pastoralist's poverty: When in times of war the
flourishing agrarian economy collapses and the once-cultivated land is over-
grown with briers and thorns, people lose all the trappings of higher civilization and are reduced to a primitive pastoral existence marked by a simple diet
of milk, curds, and honey.[4]

Palestine's agrarian situation remained stable throughout the biblical period.
For the book of Deuteronomy, Palestine is "a land of wheat and barley, of vines
and fig trees and pomegranates, a land of olive trees and honey, a land where
you may eat bread without scarcity, where you will lack nothing" (Deut 8:8–9).
In a speech given before the introduction of the monarchy, the prophet Samuel
warns of the future king's right to taxation and labor service; his speech reflects
the same mixed agrarian economy:

> He will appoint . . . some to plow his ground and to reap his harvest . . . He
> will take the best of your fields and vineyards and olive orchards and give
> them to his courtiers. He will take one-tenth of your grain and your vine-
> yards and give it to his officers and his courtiers . . . He will take one-tenth
> of your flocks. (1 Sam 8:12–17)

Although this taxation may have seemed heavy to the peasant population, it
certainly presupposes the production of a surplus: a yield greater than what
was actually needed to support the peasant household.

As agrarian landscapes, the various regions of Palestine vary greatly in
quality, but to modern observers they appear as predominantly rocky and
hilly and therefore difficult to work. George Adam Smith provides an apt
description:

> As to soils, the reader of the Bible feels how near in Palestine the barren lies
> to the fruitful. Apart from the desert proper, which comes up almost to the

gates of Judean cities, how much land is described as only pasture, and this so dry that there is constant strife for the wells upon it! How often we hear of "the field," the rough, uncultivated, but not wholly barren, bulk of the hill country, where the "beasts of the field," wild beasts found room to breed . . . This "field" is a great element in the Old Testament landscape, as we recognize it in the tracts of moorland, hillside and summit, jungle and bare rock, which make up much of the hill-country, and can never have been cultivated even for vines . . . The cultivation of grain was confined to the lower plateaus, broader valleys, and plains . . . To a western eye it must, at certain seasons, seem meager and uninfluential—incapable of stirring the imagination, or enriching the life of a people.[5]

It is not only to the modern, Western eye, that the Palestinian agrarian landscape appears meager; the ancients also described its problems. Neither the olive tree, nor the fig tree, nor the vine counts as Palestine's royal—and therefore dominant—plant; this role is that of the bramble, says the biblical fable (Judg 9:14–15). Jesus, in the parable of the sower, refers to the peasant's "rocky ground," the shallow soil cover, and the ever-present thorns that choke the grain (Matt 13:5–7). "The underlying limestone, thinly covered with soil, barely shows above the surface until the plowshare jars against it," explains one commentator.[6]

Despite the scarcity of rain and the problematic quality of the ground, the Hebrews could often bring in rich harvests of grain, oil, fruit, and wine. Like all ancient inhabitants of the Fertile Crescent, they attributed their harvests to divine favor.

16.   Lord of the Harvest:
Archaic Natural Theologies

A close reading of the biblical text reveals not one but two different archaic descriptions of divine involvement with and support of farming. One description sees God as the weather-god whose gift of rain, freely dispensed during the rainy season, enables the soil to bring forth its produce. While this is the best-attested view, it is by no means the only one. A second view, equally archaic, speaks of God as the one who blesses the ground so as to render it fertile and capable of bearing its fruit. These two peasant theologies will be dealt with in the present chapter.

The First View: The Gift of the Weather-God

Rainfall, as understood by the Israelites, was not merely a phenomenon of nature to which humans were exposed and which they might use for their own purposes. Instead, it was intrinsically purposeful, directed to human ends: "The rain and the snow come down from heaven, and do not return there until they have watered the earth, making it bring forth and sprout, giving seed to the sower and bread to the eater" (Isa 55:10). Behind this scheme of things, people recognized the purposeful activity of the weather-god, whom historians of religion also call the rain-god or storm-god. He is the one "who gives rain on the earth and sends waters on the fields" (Job 5:10), so that humans can till the soil.[7]

The rainy season of the Near East—October to March—was presided over by the weather-god, a young warlike male deity depicted with a hammer or mace, symbols of thunder, and a fork or lance, symbols of lightning (fig. 28, p. 147). To him belong clouds, mist, rain, and dew,[8] but his sphere of influence also includes rivers and streams.[9] His name is variously given as Adad, Hadad, Baal, and, in biblical Israel, as Yahweh, for the role of the weather deity did not remain foreign to Israel's god. Jeremiah, a farmland-owning "weather prophet" living in Jerusalem around 600 B.C.E., exhorts his contemporaries to fear Yahweh, "who gives the rain in its season, the autumn rain and the spring rain, and keeps for us the weeks appointed for the harvest" (Jer 5:24). But Yahweh does not send his precious gifts unconditionally; in a time of drought, the prophet chides the Judeans for having "polluted the land" by their evil behavior—"therefore the showers have been withheld and the spring rain has not

28. *The weather-god.* The helmet-wearing warrior brandishing a mace (for thunder) and holding a fiery spear (for lightning) is the weather-god, the deity presiding over nature from October to March, the period of the rainy season in the eastern Mediterranean. The weather-god of the Near East had many names and titles; in the city of Ugarit, where this depiction was found, people called him Baal, a word that translates as "lord."—Ugaritic relief, ca. 2000–1500 B.C.E.

come" (Jer 3:3). If people heed their divine Lord's commandments, "then he will give the rain for your land in its season, the early rain and the later rain, and you will gather in your grain, your wine, and oils; and he will give grass in your fields for your livestock, and you will eat your fill" (Deut 11:14–15). Jeremiah paints vivid pictures of the weather-god who thunders from on high, stirs up the waters in heaven, and unchains mighty storms: "When he utters his voice, there is a tumult of waters in the heavens, and he makes the mist rise from the ends of the earth. He makes lightnings for the rain, and he brings out the wind from his storehouses" (Jer 10:13).[10]

The most powerful biblical description of the weather deity can be found in the book of Psalms. The text is worth quoting in full and considering in detail:

> Ascribe to Yahweh, O heavenly beings,
> ascribe to Yahweh glory and strength.
> Ascribe to Yahweh the glory of his name;
> worship Yahweh in holy splendor.

The voice of Yahweh is over the waters;
the God of glory thunders,
Yahweh, over mighty waters.
The voice of Yahweh is powerful;
the voice of Yahweh is full of majesty.
The voice of Yahweh breaks the cedars;
Yahweh breaks the cedars of Lebanon.
He makes Lebanon skip like a calf,
and Sirion like a young wild ox.
The voice of Yahweh flashes forth flames of fire.
The voice of Yahweh shakes the wilderness;
Yahweh shakes the wilderness of Kadesh.
The voice of Yahweh causes the oaks to whirl,
and strips the forest bare;
and in his temple all say, "Glory!"
Yahweh sits enthroned over the flood;
Yahweh sits enthroned as king forever.

May Yahweh give strength to his people!
May Yahweh bless his people with peace [*shalom*]! (Ps 29)

In the opening lines, the poet imagines being among the "heavenly beings," i.e. angels or, polytheistically speaking, gods. He poses as their chorus leader and exhorts them to sing the praises of God. Apparently, they have assembled in the heavenly temple, waiting for the *adventus* of the great god Yahweh. Lowering clouds presage both the storm's approach and the arrival of the deity, for God manifests his coming in a mighty thunderstorm, which is subsequently described. Yahweh's voice is the thunder, and from him come forth flashes of lightning. The storm—possibly a hurricane—uproots even the mightiest of the trees, the huge cedars of the Lebanon mountain. At the same time, an earthquake shakes both the desert and the forest land. Yahweh's thundering voice can be heard—note that the expression "voice of Yahweh" is repeated seven times. The number seven stands for intensity and power; a sevenfold thunder is a truly mighty and impressive one, creating an atmosphere of awe. As Yahweh enters his palace, the gods greet him by shouting "Glory." He takes his seat on the throne, and under his feet may be a representation of the unruly waters that surround the earth (see fig. 28, p. 147). In order to understand this allusion one has to know that Near Eastern mythology distinguishes between the rain, over which the weather-god presides, and the waters surrounding the earth, over which the weather-god's enemies rule. Rather than being united, rain and sea, as sweet water and bitter water, are fighting against each other. But once the weather-god has defeated the enemy, rain can fall and bread can become available—as one version of the ancient conflict myth explains.[11]

At the end of the psalm, we again hear the voice of the human poet who at the beginning summoned the heavenly beings to give praise. Now he addresses the deity, asking for a blessing not for himself, but for his people, requesting "strength" and "peace." A strong people is presumably a people that has enough to eat. The last word of the psalm, *shalom*, signifies far more than just "peace"; here, as is often the case, the meaning must be "plenty" and "prosperity." The Bible of the Jewish Publication Society offers a good rendering of the psalm's last line: "May the Lord bestow on his people wellbeing."

The clue to understanding the psalm is provided by the geographical scenario: the Lebanon and the Anti-Lebanon (in the psalm called Sirion). These two parallel chains of mountains are situated to the north of Palestine, i.e. outside of the usual biblical landscape. The psalm reflects, in poetical and mythological form, the change of the seasons from summer to winter as it typically occurs in southern Lebanon. Dark, thick clouds gather in the eastern part of the Mediterranean, and heavy winds drive them eastward. As soon as banks of low clouds become visible, humans and animals impatiently wait for the first rain after the long summer's drought. As they are driven against the mountains, the clouds clash with air masses that differ considerably from them in temperature and moisture, and so dissolve in rain. Frequently, the first precipitation does not reach the ground, but evaporates in mid-air. Several days may pass before the first significant rainfall comes, often in the form of a heavy thunderstorm in the afternoon. Before the end of November, precipitation is not great, but it then increases from December to February. Eventually, we get heavy, torrential rainfall, accompanied by thunder and lightning. In the area of Beirut it is with impressive thunderstorms like the one described in our poem that the rainy season sets in very early, often in September.[12] The most likely scenario for the sublime event that served as the poet's model is a September thunderstorm in Beirut. Thunderstorms, it may be remembered, are much more characteristic of Lebanon than of Palestine.[13]

This is the world, both physical and ideological, not of Israel but of the ancient city-states located on the Mediterranean shore—Sidon and Tyre. It is from one of these that the early Israelites probably borrowed the psalm, which may originally have featured the name of the Syrian weather-god, Baal. The people living in cities like Sidon and Tyre and in the hinterland believed that the change of the seasons was the work of the mighty weather-god. When the rains began people knew that Baal was now king, for the rainy season belonged to him. Rain was considered a divine gift, a manifestation of Baal's beneficent rule. In the case of Baal, and in the case of the weather-god of our psalm, the *reign* of God becomes manifest in the *rain* of God. In the early period of their history, the Israelites seem to have venerated Baal along with their national deity, Yahweh. Later, when their religion developed toward monotheism, the poem was revised and the name of Baal replaced by that of Yahweh.

According to mythology, Baal resides in a palace built on a high mountain. It is from there that he rules as the cosmic king of the rainy season. Mounted on the clouds, he appears as the storm that with thunder, lightning, and rains brings fertility to the earth. Baal's mountain palace reveals the Canaanites' fascination with mountains. With its peak reaching into the skies, the mountain represents the closest connection between earth, the domain of humanity, and heaven, the realm of the gods. The splendor of the highest peaks produces a sense of awe, a sense heightened and made more mysterious when the cloud banks of the thunderstorm veil the summit from view.

The religion of a psalm that reflects the Syrian climate and its dramatic shift from hot summer to rainy winter may be called "nature religion," a faith determined or at any rate colored by natural phenomena. Since natural phenomena are described as the result of vividly imagined divine acts, we may characterize this worldview as "the dramatic conception of nature."[14]

The dramatic conception of nature is echoed not only in the words of the psalm, but also in its actual use. Although the biblical tradition does not give us any information about the ritual setting of Psalm 29, we may think of liturgical celebrations of the weather-god's royal rule at the beginning of the rainy season. While the evidence is fragmentary, we do know of rain-making rites performed in the biblical period. In New Testament times, the Feast of Tabernacles, held in autumn with much pomp and circumstance such as the night-time dancing of men in the temple court, included such a ritual. The central rite, repeated each day for a week, involved the fetching of water from the pool of Siloam and the pouring of water and wine onto the altar.[15] A similar ritual, reported in the Old Testament, helps us to understand the symbolism. To end a long period of drought, the prophet Elijah sacrificed a bull on Mount Carmel and poured water around the altar. After Elijah had sent his attendant for the seventh time to search for signs of approaching rain, "a cloud as small as a man's hand" appeared on the western horizon, followed by torrential rain (1 Kgs 18:43–45). The importance of the rain-making ritual performed at the Feast of Tabernacles was highlighted by the prophet Zechariah, who declared that families who did not go up to Jerusalem for the celebration would not get rain.[16] According to later tradition, it is on the Feast of Tabernacles that God decides upon the rainfall granted throughout the year.[17]

The rain ritual performed in Second Temple times may be a revised version of an older, pre-Israelite ritual serving the same purpose. The older ritual may have included the recitation of mythical and magical texts such as Psalm 29. By reciting this poem, the priests invited the weather-god to enter his palace, to take his seat on his throne, and to rule over the rainy season. The recitation of the poem "pre-imitates" what is to happen soon, and thus initiates the approaching event; the gods realize by "imitation" what humans "pre-imitate." Such magical acts, to the ancient mind, do not merely echo what happens in nature independently of humans; rather, they reflect the belief that the cult promotes and supports the cosmic cycle. Without the proper liturgical acts, the rain may be delayed or may never come at all. Without rain, agriculture would utterly fail and human and animal life would be endangered. In biblical times, terrible droughts often meant minimal harvests and brought starvation and death.

Turning to another poem, the so-called "Psalm of Creation," we come to understand why the ancients did not hesitate to approach the weather-god and ask him to send his gifts: he is a kindly, caring, and all-providing figure.[18] The poem begins with an unmistakable evocation of the weather-god: he resides in heaven, uses the clouds as a chariot, rides on the wings of the wind, is accompanied by his servants "Fire" and "Flame"—i.e. flashes of lightning. Toward the end, the poet resumes the theme of the majestic hierophany: when the weather-god gazes at the earth, it trembles; as he touches the mountains, they smoke. But within this majestic frame, the poet sets a hymn that describes and celebrates the deity as friendly to all creatures, animals, humans, and even plants:

> From your lofty abode you water the mountains;
> the earth is satisfied with the fruit of your work [i.e. with rain].
> You cause the grass to grow for the cattle,
> and plants for the people to use,
> to bring forth food from the earth,
> and wine to gladden the human heart,
> oil to make the face shine,
> and bread to strengthen the human heart. (Ps 104:13–15)

The poet celebrates the weather-god as the owner of the universe who cares for all his creatures, humans and animals alike, not only by sending rain, but also by supplying water through streams and rivers organized into a huge hydraulic system.

Outside of the Bible, verses speak of the weather-god as the "regulator of the waters of heaven and earth, who rains down abundance, who gives pastures and watering places to all lands . . . regulator of all rivers, who enriches all lands, the merciful god to whom it is good to pray."[19] He is the "canal-inspector of heaven and earth, who heaps up abundance and plenty, who provides wealth."[20] The most detailed description of the Near Eastern weather-god's activity reads as follows:

> The god Adad, canal-inspector of heaven and earth, the lofty, lord of all, almighty among the gods, the awesome god whose strength is unrivaled, who bears a holy whip which churns up the seas, who controls all the winds, who provides abundant water, who brings down rain, who makes lightning flash, who creates vegetation, at whose shout the mountains shake and the seas are churned up, the compassionate god whose sympathetic concern is life.[21]

29. *The weather-god and the peasant.* Two parallel scenes contrast the peasant's work with the more leisurely life of his lord, the weather-god. Above, the weather-god, who holds three ears of grain, is greeted by a tambourine-playing goddess, while an attendant takes care of the god's saddled ox. Below, one farmer walks behind the ox-drawn plow, while the other does the sowing.—Assyrian cylinder seal, ninth century B.C.E.

Ancient texts blame the shortage of grain, wine, and oil on the god's failure to send rain to the land.[22] The weather-god's responsibility for the thriving of wheat and vine was most impressively recorded in ancient Near Eastern art. An Assyrian seal associates the weather-god, depicted holding three ears of grain, with a peasant working the ground with an ox-drawn plow (fig. 29). In a Hittite relief, a huge male figure, identified by the accompanying inscription as the weather-god Tarkhunzas, holds ears of wheat in his left hand and rich grape-clusters in his right hand (fig. 30, p. 153).[23] The ear of wheat and the grape-cluster have become common attributes of the weather-god, as can be seen from coins of the city of Tarsus in Asia Minor dating from the fourth century B.C.E.[24] and a first-century C.E. relief showing Baalshamin ("lord of heaven") of Palmyra.[25] They symbolize the god's care for the two harvests—that of grain in the spring and summer, and that of fruit in the fall; they may also symbolize the daily bread necessary for sustaining life and a luxury item, wine. Hittite prayers to this eminently approachable deity abound: "O weather-god, my lord! Send much rain and satiate the dark ground, and, O weather-god, let the bread

30. *Lord of the Harvest.* A huge male figure, more than four meters high, identified by the accompanying inscription as the weather-god Tarkhunzas, is holding ears of wheat in his left hand and rich grape-clusters in his right hand. He stands between a vineyard, represented by a vine which entwines him, and a field of grain, indicated by a few stems of wheat. Although resident above the clouds, the weather-god roams through the fields and vineyards to inspect the produce that he makes grow. Now that everything is ripe, the harvest may begin.—Hittite rock relief, eighth century B.C.E.

grow."[26] On one statue we read: "I have set up [the statue] of the weather-god of the vineyard. Now the grapevine shall prosper, the vine shall grow and thrive. The weather-god shall make this vineyard prosper and the shoots shall rise up."[27] No doubt the god answered these requests by granting rich harvests.

In early Jewish art, the grape-cluster ranks as an important symbol of divine care for Israel. It was not only depicted on coins and in mosaics,[28] but actually formed the only decorative element on the central temple building in Jerusalem (fig. 31, p. 154). According to Josephus, there were golden vines above the gate giving entrance to the sanctuary, and from these vines "depended grape-clusters as tall as a man."[29] The grape-clusters echo a theme associated with the Ara Pacis, the lavishly decorated temple erected in Rome in the years 13–9 B.C.E.[30] It was during the same time that Herod the Great had the Jerusalem temple's sanctuary rebuilt. The grape-clusters thus resonated both with Augustan ideas of a golden age of peace and abundance and Jewish notions of the Lord of the Harvest.

31. *Grape-clusters at the Herodian temple of Jerusalem.* In antiquity, most Jews limited art to the depiction of motifs sanctioned by tradition. One such motif is the grape-cluster, symbol of God's gift of the fruit harvest in the fall. According to the Jewish historian Josephus, huge golden grape-clusters were placed above the entrance of the central temple building; in Busink's reconstruction they are positioned between the door and the windows above it. While the gate gives the priests access to the dwelling-place of God in the holy of holies, it also gives God access to the world. The first and foremost gift God makes to the world is the harvest, represented by the grape-clusters.—Detail of Herod's temple in a modern drawing, ca. 10 B.C.E.

After having reviewed the image of the weather-god outside of the Bible, we must return to the biblical Psalm of Creation (Psalm 104). The psalmist apparently not only reproduced the traditional Western Asiatic image of the weather-god; he also sought to make it comprehensive and attractive. He borrowed and adapted descriptions of divine care from Egyptian poetry to highlight the nurturing, kindly side of the deity he wished to extoll.[31] The Egyptian sun-god, Aten, was said to sustain all life by providing food for all creatures; this must likewise be true of the weather-god, too. We would not do justice to the poet if on account of this dependence we were to dispute his originality and regard the psalm as a mere compilation of quotations taken from other sources. The poem's merit lies precisely in the creativity of bringing together a diversity of materials to shape a new, distinctive vision. One should not hesitate to call the biblical poet a creative theologian or religious philosopher; his achievement resonates even with modern romantic sensibilities. It is to him that we owe the most captivating portrait of the weather-god.

The Second View: The God Who Blesses (or Curses) the Ground

The rural economy rests on the foundations of earth and water. In the previous section, we focused on rain, understood as a divine gift; our task now is to consider the ways in which the Hebrew God was involved with the ground tilled by the peasants. According to the Hebrew mentality, the soil of itself could not bring anything forth without its divine master's blessing. Once this had been granted, the Hebrews celebrated the bounty of the Lord in joyous festivals. Without divine blessing, all labor would have been in vain. But what exactly did they mean by "blessing" (*berakha*), a word replete with archaic meanings and connotations?

Divine blessing conveys the mysterious power to reproduce and to grow. Reproductive power, according to the Bible, is given primarily to female animals and human mothers, and their fertility provides the general model for any kind of blessing, including the blessing of the soil. The account of creation at the beginning of the book of Genesis states that animals and humans are blessed and given the power to increase and multiply. God also blesses the ground so that it yields plenty of produce. (Note that it is the soil, and not the plants, that receives the blessing.) Thus at the thanksgiving festival the peasant is supposed to ask God "to look down from heaven and bless your people Israel and the ground that you have given us" (Deut 26:15). When God blesses "the fruit of the womb, the fruit of the ground, the fruit of the livestock" (Deut 28:4), he gives the power to grow to the fruit within the human mother's womb, the sprouting seed concealed in the womb-like ground, and the unborn animal.[32]

The book of Deuteronomy uses the idiom in the following way:

> Yahweh your God . . . will love you, bless you, and multiply you; he will *bless the fruit of your womb and the fruit of your ground*, your grain and your wine and your oil, the increase of your cattle and the issue of your flock, in the land that he swore to your ancestors to give you. You shall be the most blessed of peoples, with neither sterility nor barrenness among you or your livestock. (Deut 7:12–14, italics added)

> Blessed shall be *the fruit of your womb, the fruit of your ground, and the fruit of your livestock*, both the increase of your cattle and the issue of your flock. Blessed shall be your basket and your kneading bowl. (Deut 28:4–5, italics added)

Here the divine blessing results in the production of all the goods of the Third Function. Interestingly, the Deuteronomic author refers to two inanimate objects as recipients of the divine blessing: the basket and the kneading bowl. Just like the ground, these two material objects are womb-like, for the basket is used for storing fruit, and the kneading bowl for making dough to be baked into bread. Both fruit and bread come from womb-like vessels. Thus the metaphorical association of blessing and womb permeates much of the biblical language.

Claus Westermann, who has written extensively on the biblical meaning of "blessing," emphasizes two aspects as particularly striking: its universality and its unobtrusiveness. God's blessing, despite its concentration on Israel, is his *universal* gift, continually given to all of humankind. Sustaining everyone's physical existence, God's blessing encompasses all people of all times and places. All people "share in the gifts of the blessing, in their physical existence, in food and clothing, in social and economic maintenance of the society in which they live, and in the continuation of life from one generation to the next."[33] This being the case, blessing appears an unobtrusive, quiet matter. As a quiet, continuous, flowing, and hardly noticed act of God, it cannot be captured in spectacular moments or dates. Blessing sustains life's regular and reassuring rhythm in the gradual process of growing and maturing in plants, animals, and human beings. God gives growth and prosperity, quietly letting his children be born and grow up, and granting them success in work. In striking contrast to God's First Function and Second Function activities, his blessing remains inconspicuous. When granting deliverance to his people in dramatic acts (like the miraculous destruction of the pursuing army during the exodus from Egypt), God acts conspicuously, rather than silently, and his saving activity is limited to his chosen people, i.e. it is particular rather than universal. The Divine Warrior who delivers his people from its foes acts quite unlike the Lord of the Harvest or the Lord of the Animals, who bless the entire creation. Israel's tradition also felt that God's First Function acts of revealing the divine law to Moses and concluding a covenant with the people counted as datable, dramatic events, and were on this account also quite unlike divine blessing.

In Israelite thought, then, God is the source of all blessing. As the Lord of the Harvest, he bestows his gift liberally, causing the soil to bring forth its fruit and the sprouting seeds to grow and eventually serve as nourishment for humans. The Hebrews, however, were not always so optimistic about their agrarian situation. At certain moments they could articulate the difficulties of their labor and even refer to the soil as "accursed." In order to account for this harsh verdict we have not only to remember the "stony ground" typical of Palestine (see above, chapter 15); we also have to dig deep into the mentality of the biblical people.

The Israelites apparently disliked cultivating grain, even though it was the most important element in their diet. Its cultivation reminded them of God's curse, pronounced to Adam when he and Eve were banished from the Garden of Eden: "Cursed is the ground because of you; in toil you shall eat of it all the days of your life; thorns and thistles it shall bring forth for you; and you shall eat the plants of the field. By the sweat of your face you shall eat bread" (Gen 3:17–19). Cereal is the food to be eaten "east of Eden." When Cain, a rather innocent peasant, tried to sacrifice grain to the Lord, God did not accept it, for, as the story implies, it issued from accursed ground and was therefore accursed food—food leading to death.[34] Anthropological accounts of peasant life can illustrate and elucidate the Israelite attitude. Robert Redfield, in his essay "The Peasant View of the Good Life," discusses the views peasants have concerning their labors.[35] In some countries, they are immensely proud of their land and their work: here Redfield refers to the Bulgarian, the Irish, and the English. Others, by contrast, engage in agricultural work only with reluctance, and here Redfield quotes the attitude of the south Italian, the Andalusian, and the Syrian peasants, most of whom cultivate the land "with regret." To this latter category also belong the ancient Israelites as well as modern Palestinian peasants. In his monograph on the folk community of Baytin, Abdulla Lutfiyya reports that the local farmers consider agricultural work as essentially degrading and to be avoided if at all possible.[36] There is a curse on agriculture, felt particularly by those whose fields yield little even when tilled with dedication.[37]

Arboriculture and viticulture, by contrast, seem to enjoy divine blessing: this view is implied in frequent biblical references to vines and fig trees as symbols of peace and happiness. "They shall all sit under their own vines and under their own fig trees, and no one shall make them afraid" (Micah 4:4). The Bible has no more apt, more poetic expression than this to condense into a single image the peasants' reconciliation with their otherwise precarious existence. The prophet's dictum betrays a preference for the fruit-bearing plants typical of the Mediterranean countries and requiring relatively little work to get an impressive harvest. Olive trees (to this day highly valued)[38] need no care at all, fig trees very little, and vines at any rate appreciably less than preparing the field and sowing, harvesting, and threshing grain. A Palestinian proverb indicates the level of attention involved in the cultivation of fruit-bearing trees as follows: the olive tree is a Bedouin woman, the fig tree a peasant's wife, and the vine a fine lady.[39] Unlike the vine, the olive and fig trees require little if any special attention. The fig tree bears fruit twice a year (June and late August) and reminds people of paradise.[40] The cultivation of grain, by contrast, reminds people of being excluded from paradise and of having to eat their bread by the sweat of their brow. As is remarked in the Gospel of Philip, there was no grain in the garden of Eden: there were "many trees for food for the beasts, but no wheat as food for humans. They fed like the beasts."[41] In other words: the less work the Palestinian peasant has, the happier he is, and for this reason he has an instinctive preference for fruit-bearing plants. The differentiation between the two main types of work—the cultivation of fruit (vines, olive trees) and of grain—is deeply rooted in ancient peasant mentality.

It may be worth noting the distinction between the real and the emotional economy known from anthropology. The stock example comes from the Nuer of the southern Sudan: although living as much from working the ground as from keeping livestock, they think of themselves primarily as breeders of cattle and regard agriculture as toil forced on them by the poverty of their stock.[42] In a similar way, the Israelites saw themselves as peasant gardeners—planters of fruit trees and cultivators of the vine—but actually lived as much from tilling the soil, forced on them as they lived outside of paradise.

This mentality explains why the ancient peasants celebrated their main festivals after the olive harvest and the end of the vintage in September and October. In the book of Judges mention is made of a vintage festival observed at Shiloh, where the maidens went out to dance in the vineyards.[43] Better known is the Feast of Tabernacles, which the Bible describes as a general thanksgiving celebrated in the fall.[44] Ancient references to the Feast of Tabernacles regularly indicate its joyful spirit and often refer to wine. "The time and character of their greatest, most sacred holiday clearly befit Dionysos," writes Plutarch. According to this pagan author, the Jews celebrate the Feast of Tabernacles at the height of the vintage, setting out tables of all sorts of fruit under tents and huts. He refers to colorful processions during which people carry branches and priests blow little trumpets and play harps. Admitting that this is speculation, Plutarch goes so far as to speak of Bacchic revelries celebrated in secret.[45] So if we can trust Plutarch, for the Hebrew peasants the year culminated in conspicuous and apparently unrestrained consumption.

17. Lord of the Harvest: Theologies Shaped by Historical Experience

The world of the peasants is determined by the more or less stable course of nature. Summer and winter, heat and rain, reaping and sowing form a cycle that repeats itself endlessly and imposes a regular pattern on rural life. Untouched by the forces of power politics, peasant existence remains beyond abrupt and dramatic changes and therefore outside of history. The social class most conscious of, and most readily affected by, the forces of history includes scribes, the higher ranks of priests, and members of the rural and urban elites. In ancient Israel, members of this intellectual class occasionally commented on how historical forces impinged on the agricultural life that they shared with the peasants, and they developed new religious ideologies and expressed new hopes, often in the form of legal utopias and prophetic promises.

All of the ancient Hebrew agrarian fantasies and ideologies reflect the same crisis experienced first in the danger of massive deportation in the late eighth century B.C.E. and then in the reality of the Babylonian captivity, the period between 597 and ca. 500 B.C.E. when a substantial portion of the population of Judah was deported to Babylonia and had to live far away from the Palestinian homeland. The loss of the land not only provoked the development of a new (or perhaps revitalized) doctrine of Palestine as the land given to the people by God; it also led to all kinds of fantastical assertions about the land, culminating in the expectation of unprecedented, paradise-like agrarian productivity for those returning from exile. While some of these notions may date from before the Babylonian captivity, it was among the exiles that they came to flourish, expressing themselves in an increasingly utopian language.

God Owns and Gives the Land

According to the ancient Hebrews, farming rested not only on the availability of water and God's blessing of the soil; it also depended on political and historical circumstances—the legitimate possession and control of their land.

In the second half of the eighth century B.C.E. the possession of the land began to become a political problem. When Tiglath-pileser III (744–727) and his successors renewed the Assyrian supremacy over Syria and Palestine and thus reshaped the political map of the Near East, everyone knew that disobedience to Assyrian rule meant the massive deportation of peoples from

rebellious areas, for the king returned to the unrelenting policy of uprooting
unruly populations from their home country and deporting them for resettlement in some other part of the empire. The prophet Hosea, a contemporary of
Tiglath-pileser III, echoes these fears as he announces doom to his fellow
Israelites:

> Threshing floor and vinevat shall not feed them,
> and the new wine shall fail them.
> They shall not remain in the land of Yahweh;
> but Ephraim shall return to Egypt,
> and in Assyria they shall eat unclean food. (Hos 9:2–3)

As a matter of fact, it was as early as 733–732 B.C.E. that the inhabitants of
several cities and districts of northern Israel were deported to Assyria.[46] Around
720, after the Assyrians had destroyed the city of Samaria, the deportation of
many northern Israelites became a grim reality. By then, living in the land had
also become increasingly insecure for the Judeans of southern Palestine. In 701,
the Assyrians came and captured the Judean city of Lachish and deported those
of its inhabitants who were not killed during or after the siege. When, in the
same year, the Assyrian army also laid siege to Jerusalem, one of the Assyrian
king's envoys sought to persuade "the people sitting on the wall" to give up
their resistance. If they handed themselves over to the Assyrians, they would
be treated fairly and eventually taken away "to a land like your own land, a land
of grain and wine, a land of bread and vineyards, a land of olive oil and honey,
that you may live and not die" (2 Kgs 18: 32). The land of Ashur would be like
the land of Yahweh. Eventually, the Assyrians left without having conquered
Jerusalem.

The impact of the Assyrian policy of deportation was tremendous, for it
modified not only the political map of the Near East, but also the mental map
of all its inhabitants—the way people thought about the relationship between
ethnic group, state, national territory, and patron deity. The Assyrians understood their state as a territorial state in which membership was determined by
residence within the territory controlled by the king and, ultimately, owned by
the state god, Ashur.[47] As Ashur's representative, the Assyrian king viewed
himself as the owner of all the land and thus could freely decide where to put
the deportees.[48] In a similar vein, the Hebrews came to see their national god
as the one who had elected them and planted them in Palestine. For them,
Yahweh was the ultimate landowner, and it was to him that they owed their
land tenure. This was a new development, for earlier the Hebrews had seen
their state not as a territorial state; rather, theirs was a national state with membership defined by affiliation to the ethnic group and its patron deity, Yahweh.
A tomb inscription dating from around 700 B.C.E., the time of the Assyrian
crisis, gives a first lyrical expression to the new idea:

> Yahweh is the God of the whole country,
> the highlands of Judah belong to the God of Jerusalem.[49]

Even the prophet Hosea, who was strongly committed to a theology of the personal relationship between the ethnic group—Israel—and Yahweh, could now speak in Assyrian fashion of "the land of Yahweh" (Hos 9:3).[50]

After the destruction of the state of Judah and the deportation of Judeans in 597 and 586 B.C.E. by the Babylonians, the idea of the divinely given country hardened and inspired national pride, even among the Jews living in exile.

It was presumably in the exilic period that two conflicting ideologies of God's promise of land originated: Did God in ancient times promise the land to the patriarchs Abraham, Isaac, and Jacob (as recorded in the book of Genesis)? Or did he grant it to the generation that, led by Moses, left Egypt to settle in Canaan (thus in Exodus and Deuteronomy)? (See below, chapter 19.) When speaking of the divine promise of land ownership, one school of thought considered the land as rightfully inherited from their patriarchal ancestors and looked forward to returning to their ancestors' country after the exile. The other school, in contrast, made ownership dependent upon loyalty to God's commandments as given to Moses, explained the loss of the land as being due to the people's disobedience, and linked resettlement to Yahwist orthodoxy. Both groups shared one conviction, however: whether thought of as the God of the patriarchs or considered the God of the exodus, Yahweh owned the land.

The implications of divine ownership of the land were repeatedly articulated by prophets who predicted the return of the deportees and by scribes who compiled new rules and laws that should be respected in a new, postexilic agrarian community. In Ezekiel's prophecy, pronounced in the years before 568 B.C.E., the notion of the land figures prominently. According to Ezekiel, a prophet of priestly stock, the Judeans had defiled the land by their sins, just as a woman defiled herself with her menstrual blood.[51] However, Yahweh will cleanse his people and, apparently, the land as well. Addressing "the mountains of Israel," the prophet gives them Yahweh's own command: "But you, O mountains of Israel, shall shoot out your branches, and yield fruit to my people Israel; for they shall soon come home" (Ezek 36: 8). God will take pity on his people, gather them in from the nations, and secure the yield of their fields. The prophets never tired of announcing the peasant paradise:

> Then you shall live in the land that I gave your ancestors; and you shall be my people, and I will be your God. I will save you from all uncleanness, and I will summon the grain and make it abundant and lay no famine upon you. I will make the fruit of the tree and the produce of the field abundant, so that you may never again suffer the disgrace of famine among the nations. (Ezek 36:28–30)

The time is surely coming, says the Lord,
when the one who plows shall overtake the one who reaps,
and the treader of grapes the one who sows the seed;
the mountains shall drip sweet wine,
and all the hills shall flow with it.
I will restore the fortunes of my people Israel,
and they shall rebuild the ruined cities and inhabit them;
they shall plant vineyards and drink their wine,
and they shall make gardens and eat their fruit . . .
and they shall never again be plucked up
out of the land that I have given them,
says Yahweh your God. (Am 9:13–14)

On that day the branch of Yahweh shall be beautiful and glorious, and the fruit of the land shall be the pride and glory of the survivors of Israel. (Isa 4:2)

The God-given land will become like the garden of Eden—a garden assigned to humans for "tilling and keeping" and freely enjoying its fruits (Gen 2:15).

The priestly legislation transmitted in the book of Leviticus is based on the divine proclamation of land ownership: "The land is mine; with me, you are but aliens and tenants" (Lev 25:23). As aliens and tenants, the peasants are utterly dependent on their divine lord's favor, which is granted only as long as they obey his commandments: "You shall observe my statutes and faithfully keep my ordinances, so that you may live on the land securely. The land will yield its fruit, and you will eat your fill and live on it securely" (vv. 18–19). These commandments include a particularly strange one—one that prohibits all agricultural work in every seventh year; this "shall be a year of complete rest for the land" (v. 5). But what shall the people eat during the seventh year? This question seems to receive two answers: according to one view, people will find enough food on the unworked fields (v. 6); according to the other, in the year preceding the Sabbatical Year, due to special divine blessing the fields will yield much more than usual—in fact, three times as much, so that no one starves (v. 21). Here the fertility of the land assumes unheard-of, mythical qualities.

According to agricultural historians, Palestinian farmers seem to have used a rotating system that had about half of their land lie fallow each year, using the other half for cultivation.[52] The biblical idea that every seventh year *all* the land should lie fallow presupposes belief in a periodically occurring considerable enhancement of the land's natural productivity. This belief may have had many roots, and modern scholarship can only guess at what they were. Possibly, people expected that every seventh year would see rain of a force and duration that would produce an extraordinary harvest—a belief still entertained by some modern Syrian desert dwellers.[53] This belief may have inspired the prohibition of all agricultural work during every seventh year.

One final passage about the Divine Landowner and his care for his people deserves attention: the peasant's thanksgiving at the temple. The relevant law prescribes the words of the declarations the peasant has to pronounce when offering his firstfruits to the priest. When giving his basket of fruit to the priest, he is to say: "Today I declare to Yahweh your God that I have come into the land that Yahweh swore to our ancestors to give us" (Deut 26:3). He then has to pronounce a set text known as Israel's "historical creed." Its final words sum up the message: God brought "us (Israelites) into this place and gave us this land, a land flowing with milk and honey. So now I bring the first of the fruit of the ground that you, O Yahweh, have given me" (vv. 9–10). After a declaration of his freedom from sin, the peasant asks for God's blessing: "Look down from your holy habitation, from heaven, and bless your people Israel and the ground that you have given us, as you swore to our ancestors—a land flowing with milk and honey" (v. 15). All these words acknowledge or imply Yahweh as the Divine Landowner.

Palestine Transformed into a Land of Rivers

Only in one biblical passage is Palestine's agriculture derived from rivers rich in water rather than from precipitation during the rainy season. Palestine, explains the book of Deuteronomy, is "a land with flowing streams, with springs and underground waters welling up in valleys and hills, a land of wheat and barley, of vines and fig trees and pomegranates, a land of olive trees and honey, a land where you may eat bread without scarcity, where you will lack nothing" (Deut 8:7–9). Despite the historical accuracy of the list of agricultural and horticultural products, the lyrical description echoes wishful thinking more than actual fact, for springs are rather uncharacteristic of Palestine. Nevertheless, the idea must have been dear to some of the Israelites. One of these, Second Isaiah, a prophet active among the sixth-century Babylonian exiles, announced the sudden transformation of Palestine into a land rich with water:

> When the poor and needy seek water,
> and there is none,
> and their tongue is parched with thirst,
> I, Yahweh, will answer them,
> I, the God of Israel will not forsake them.
> I will open rivers on the bare heights,
> and fountains in the midst of the valleys;
> I will make the wilderness a pool of water,
> and the dry land springs of water.

> I will put in the wilderness the cedar,
> the acacia, the myrtle, and the olive. (Isa 41:17–19)

The same notion is even more clearly expressed in one of the psalms, in a passage reminiscent of the oracle delivered by Second Isaiah:

> He turns a desert into pools of water,
> a parched land into springs of water.
> And there he lets the hungry live,
> and they establish a town to live in;
> they sow fields, and plant vineyards,
> and get a fruitful yield. (Ps 107:35–37)

How can we account for the utopian expectation of a dramatically changed Palestinian landscape, of its transformation from an arid wasteland with limited possibilities for farming into a land rich in gurgling springs and sparkling streams, a land that can be irrigated so as to produce abundant harvests?

The Bible's aquatic utopias did not originate in Palestine; in order to understand them, we must look instead to Mesopotamia, known for "the waters of Babylon" (Ps 137:1). From fifth-century B.C.E. cuneiform sources we know that some of the Babylonian Judeans made a living as canal managers or irrigation experts, while others engaged in the reparation of canal dams or in irrigation farming.[54] During this time, the Greek traveler Herodotus visited Mesopotamia, where he was impressed with the country's fertility. He comments on the virtual lack of rainfall, describes the labor-intensive irrigation system, and praises, with characteristic exaggeration, the rich harvests. "Of all the countries we know, this is the best at bringing forth the fruits of Demeter [grain] . . . It brings forth grain so plentifully that its yield is two hundred-fold and, when it surpasses even itself, three hundred-fold. The blades of corn and barley are easily four fingers wide."[55] Herodotus adds that some people, who have never seen Babylonia, refuse to believe what he has told them about the country's astonishing fertility. The Judeans transplanted to Mesopotamia were certainly no less impressed than Herodotus with the high level of agricultural know-how typical of Mesopotamian farming; even modern scholars admit that, by reaching a level of efficiency comparable to that of nineteenth-century C.E. Europe, it was superior to the less developed agriculture of ancient Greece and Rome.[56]

It is to the Judeans living in the land of the two rivers that we owe the utopian image of Palestine as a land transformed into one rich with water. These people must have speculated about the character of the deity whom they expected to produce Palestine's great geomorphological transformation. They assimilated the Palestinian god Yahweh to the Lord of Sweet Water, a deity well known in Mesopotamia. In what is now Iraq, especially in Babylonia proper, there is little

32. *Lord of Sweet Water.* The high relief depicts Ea, god of the fresh water, twice: in the center of the basin's face (left) and as a corner sculpture (right). The bearded god wears a horned cap and a long garment. In his hands he holds a bottle into which water flows from round, rimmed vases placed above, in the sky; from the same vessel water then flows down to the earth in two symmetrical streams. He distributes the fresh water, gift of the gods, that ultimately originates from the heavenly ocean. The god is attended by a bearded priest clad in fish-shaped vestments. The priest carries a small ceremonial vessel—a situla—and his raised hand holds what may be an aspergillum for sprinkling holy water. The symmetrical scene is repeated on the four outer faces around the rectangular monolithic water basin.—Detail of Assyrian stone relief, ca. 700 B.C.E.

rainfall, and none at all between May and October, so people depend upon water from rivers and wells for the irrigation of their fields. This fresh water is presided over by the Sumerian god Enki. Called Ea by the Babylonians, he is a peaceful god, kind to humans and generous with his gifts. He is often depicted holding a vase: a round-bodied, short-necked, flared-rim jar with streams issuing from its mouth (fig. 32). Sometimes fish are shown swimming along the streams. The vessel's name, *hegallu*, means "abundance," and so the "flowing vase" ranks as an important symbol of fertility and plentifulness. Associated with Ea was the Abzu, the subterranean ocean, a huge reservoir of fresh water, thought of as the residence of Ea and the ultimate source of life. In mythical imagination, it was from the Abzu, called "the great watery abyss" by the Hebrews (*tehôm rabbah*—Gen 7:11), that springs, wells, streams, rivers, and lakes drew their fresh water and were continuously replenished. Being assimilated to Ea, who was considered a creator god,[57] Yahweh might be expected to transform Palestine into a land that could be irrigated so as to promise *two* high-yield harvests instead of the one generally permitted under Mediterranean conditions.[58]

Yahweh the Ea-like water-god is most prominent in his association with Jerusalem's Gihon spring. If the ancients were justified in calling Egypt the "gift of the Nile," then we may argue by analogy that Jerusalem was the gift of Gihon, for this was the city's only permanent source of fresh water. Under the special patronage of Yahweh, both the spring and the watercourse enjoyed a kind of sacred status. Although archaeologists and historians still dispute the exact location of the ancient temple area, it may well be that the Gihon spring was included in the holy precinct.[59] One of the psalms mentions this spring's quasi-mythological status: "There is a river whose streams make glad the city of God, the holy habitation of the Most High. God is in the midst of the city" (Ps 46:4–5/Hebr. 46:5–6). God and water are here closely associated, and God is thought of as an Ea-like figure, a deity blessing the city with a spring. Other references continue this mystification by abandoning all realism and endowing the source with truly mythical qualities. Thus the name of Gihon is given to one of the four rivers that watered the garden of Eden—the original paradise of the first human couple[60]—and the same river figures prominently in prophetic announcements of the great transformation of the landscape of the Jerusalem area. Rich waters were expected to gush forth from the temple and transform the arid land into a land watered by mighty streams. "Living waters shall flow out from Jerusalem, half of them to the eastern sea and half of them to the western sea; it shall continue in summer as in winter," announces the prophet Zechariah (Zech 14:8), who seems to be describing not so much the actual Gihon spring as the flowing vase of Ea, out of which two streams of water always issue. According to Ezekiel, this mythical stream will be full of fish, just like the water issuing from *hegallu*, the vase flowing with abundance.[61] The idea has also found its way into the New Testament, where we read of the "river of the water of life, bright as crystal, flowing from the throne of God and of the Lamb through the middle of the street of the city" of Jerusalem (Rev 22:1–2).

One cause of these speculations may be the fact that the Gihon spring supplies its water not in a steady stream, but in an intermittent fashion, so that it ebbs and flows. As George Adam Smith reports, "the water breaks from the hole in the basin three to five times a day during the rainy season, but during summer twice a day, and after any failure of the spring rains (as in 1901, as well as in other years) less than once. Even when the spring rains do not fail, the flow in autumns frequently falls to this minimum."[62] Thus in the fall the population has to rely on the rainwater collected in domestic cisterns. Inspired by their Babylonian experience, prophets hoped that the spring would overflow some day and, under particularly favorable circumstances, feed a real stream. It was this hope that inspired them to announce a great and in fact utopian increase in the water supply.

These utopian notions no doubt belong to the pious lore and learning of Judean intellectuals living in the Babylonian Diaspora. Just how pervasive these ideas were can be seen from the opening lines of the Psalter, which describe the pious man as one whom God has planted "like a tree by streams of water"— the streams or canals of southern Mesopotamia or a transformed Palestine (Ps 1:3). Despite their popularity with the sages, these mythological notions presumably made little impact on the way Palestinian peasants conceived of the deity on whose gracious gift of water they depended for their farming. Thinking of water, they would not so much imagine the divine forces that from the depths of the earth feed the streams and canals, but would instead look up to the sky, the realm of the weather-god whose "way is in whirlwind and storm, and the clouds are the dust of his feet," who "makes the storm clouds, who gives showers of rain to you, the vegetation in the fields to everyone" (Nah 1:3; Zech 10:1). For them, Palestine remained "a land of grain and wine, where the heavens drop down dew" (Deut 33:28).

Conclusion

In conclusion we can say: whether he is depicted as the giver of rain, the God who blesses the ground, or the Divine Landowner, Yahweh emerges in each case as the Lord of the Harvest or, as one might also say, an agrarian fertility deity that, by granting its gifts, sustains all human life. Thus all human fulfillment ultimately depends on God. On the face of it, this notion seems straightforward enough and appears to have been commented upon before. When, in 1904, Adolf Guttmacher wrote the entry on "happiness" for the *Jewish Encyclopedia*, God's involvement with the good life appeared to him to be the main fact relevant to the discussion. In Guttmacher's words:

> Everywhere in the Old Testament the joyous and harmonious notes of life are accented. Life is synonymous with good and blessing. This predominant note of happiness was undoubtedly the outcome of faith and of a complete dependence upon and trust in God the Creator of all. Happiness is to be found in the personal relation between man and his Maker: the closer this relation, the greater the happiness . . . The joyous strain of existence bursts forth everywhere.[63]

For the Israelites, the good life had two sides—material and spiritual—and therefore involved both the rich harvest and the God who gave it to them. They enjoyed the Third Function gifts, attributing them to the caring love and blessing of the Lord of the Harvest.

For a modern appreciation of this "attribution," it may be helpful to consider an argument developed in the psychology of knowledge and perception. The Greek philosopher Plato observed that knowledge should not be defined

33. *Rubin's vase.* As was discovered by the Danish psychologist Edgar Rubin (1886–1951), our visual apparatus distinguishes between "figure" and "ground." Rubin's famous drawing can be seen as a vase on a black ground or as a pair of silhouetted faces on a white ground. Whenever we perceive the faces, however, then the vase disappears, for our perceptual system does not allow us to see both at the same time.

as the fact of knowing but as the act of reflecting on it: "Knowledge does not consist in the impressions of sense; it consists in reasoning about them."[64] This is also true of happiness: it does not consist in the presence and availability of goods and services (material goods, social goods, etc.), but in the act of reflecting and reasoning about them.

Applying this insight to the biblical experience, we may define joy in very general terms: a joyful experience is had when worldly goods such as food, children, and social and economic success are experienced *as being granted by God.* While the goods themselves constitute the good life, it is their God-givenness that reflects happiness and therefore defines it. The fact that these goods are appreciated as coming from the hand of God and are considered as signs of divine presence and friendship is of capital importance, for the Hebrews could not speak of the good life without speaking of God. It is apparently the act of associating the good life with God that transfigures life into something sacred and of ultimate value. The very act of associating God and the good life constitutes happiness. If we are to find the culturally specific Hebrew notion of what we call happiness, then we can say that the Israelites did not aspire to *mere* worldly enjoyments. Whatever goods the Hebrews enjoyed, they enjoyed them also as signs of divine blessing and benevolence. As Leo Gorssen explains, "it is never the mundane happiness *in itself* that satisfies, but the encounter with Yahweh, who manifests his love and solidarity in the good life. The loving presence of Yahweh frees human happiness from its radical limitations and gives it a transcendent dimension, thereby completely transfiguring the structure of happiness."[65]

The psychology of religious perception as developed by Hjalmar Sundén can help us to explain what is involved in Gorssen's idea that the good life is restructured by this addition of a transcendent dimension. Sundén argues that, for understanding reality, human beings normally develop two complementary perceptional sets, the one everyday and profane and the other special and religious.[66] As individuals grow up in a certain culture, they develop not only a pragmatic approach to life, but also a specifically religious frame of reference that is peopled by God, gods, saints, and angels (and whatever else tradition leads them to believe in), i.e. supernatural beings who, like real people, interact with them. Sundén compares the presence of the two sets and the possible shift from the one to the other with what we see when exposed to Rubin's vase (fig. 33, p. 168). We may either see a white vase against a black background, or a pair of black silhouettes against a white background. When perception moves from the one structure (the vase) to the other (two silhouettes), we speak of a restructuring. By analogy, the change in wider perception—the structure shift or Gestalt shift—takes place involuntarily, with the religious outlook asserting itself from time to time, for instance on festive occasions or under stress. It is not difficult for Sundén to demonstrate that, even today, people have a religious frame of reference, a fact often commented on by specialists in religion. A fine description of the coexistence of multiple interpretations of the world can be found in William James's *Varieties of Religious Experience*. To the modern mind, he argues, neither science nor religion "is exhaustive or exclusive of the other's simultaneous use . . . On this view religion and science, each verified in its own way from hour to hour and from life to life, would be co-eternal."[67]

Applying Sundén's insight to the Hebrew experience of the good life, we may say that it is frequently accompanied by a structure shift from profane to religious. The Israelites experienced not just the foreground of the good life, the oil, the wine, and the figs, but also the background of God's beneficial presence. They could not avoid the structure shift that imposed itself on their vision of things, for it was part of their mental and emotional furniture. And, once the shift occurred, the Israelites were well content with themselves and with their divine lord.

Epilogue
The Hebrew God: Fragments of a History

The Hebrew God, like any other ancient deity, has a history. The ideal study of this God would consist of two parts: the first on his nature and character, and the second on his history, resulting in a monograph that would be entitled "The Hebrew God: His Character and His Story." The second part of such a work would tell the history of the Hebrew God as it developed in biblical times and perhaps beyond. But due to the absence of reliable sources, only the first part, the one dealing with the deity's essential character traits, can actually be written. Only rarely is it possible to add historical detail to the structural description. The history of the Hebrew God remains elusive, so we can offer no more than an epilogue that seeks to supplement the portrait with a few historical fragments. Two story-lines are to be followed: the story of God with his people, the Israelites, as it is told in the canonical tradition, and the story as it can be reconstructed by historical scholarship. Finally, we comment on the Hebrew God's impact on the belief of an early Jewish movement that later developed into a new religion—Christianity.

18. Manifestations of the Divine and Historical Beginnings

The first contact between a deity and a group of devotees fascinates the historian of religions as much as it captures the believer's imagination. Yet despite their common interest, the language that they use to describe "the first time" differs widely and sometimes resorts to incompatible vocabulary. Pious tradition, often of venerable antiquity, prefers the poetic idiom to report of "origins"; rooted in the encounter between the divine lord and the human ancestor or founder, and transmitted from generation to generation, origins are deemed sacred. "Beginnings," as reconstructed by the historian and explained in scholarly prose, are different in kind; revelation is replaced by the social practice of sacred acts, rituals, and notions of the divine, used by an early society to master its life and give it meaning. When the following section discusses the story of Jacob's dream and the early historical background of the Hebrew God, then the former subject can be identified as the believers' tradition of origins, whereas the latter corresponds to historical enquiry; nevertheless, even the tale of the dream needs historical elucidation and commentary if it is to make sense to us.

"Revelation" and "Origins"

The Israelites traced their ancestry to a legendary hero whom tradition calls either Jacob or Israel. This man met the Hebrew God in a dream, and the event is recorded in the book of Genesis, book of the "origins." Journeying alone through an inhospitable land, Jacob camped out of doors: "And he dreamed that there was a ladder set up on the earth, the top of it reaching to heaven; and the angels of God were ascending and descending on it" (Gen 28:12). While this could be a complete dream, the biblical storyteller informs us that Jacob also saw a god named Yahweh standing above this ladder (or stairway, as some recent philologists have suggested), and that Yahweh spoke to him kindly, promising him land and offspring. The Lord of Jacob's dream, moreover, also promised to be with him and to protect him wherever his journey would lead. Among the stories about Israel's ancestors, this ranks as one of the most important, for every Israelite saw himself in Jacob, the patriarch somehow embodying all his descendants. His dreaming is the dreaming of all of his sons and daughters, grandsons and granddaughters, and their children and children's children as well. The Lord of his dream is also their Lord and the Lord of their dreams.

Like other passages in the book of Genesis, the story of Jacob's dream shows traces of editing. Apparently, an originally short, old story has been expanded several times, with each editor adding his own understanding to the account, giving it an additional feature. We believe that three successive stages of religious awareness, corresponding to three kinds of revelatory experience, can be discerned. Using the terminology of religious studies, we will call these forms of revelation hierophany, epiphany, and theophany. Our reconstruction of the text's stages of growth can be visualized in a chart that highlights the editorial expansions by using bold type.[1]

The gradual growth of the story of Jacob's dream

First stage: hierophany (Gen 28:11–12,16–19)	Second stage: epiphany (Gen 28:10–12,16–22)	Third stage: theophany (Gen 28:10–22)
He came to a certain place and stayed there for the night, because the sun had set. Taking one of the stones of the place, he put it under his head and lay down in that place. And he dreamed that there was a ladder [or ramp, stairway] set up on the earth, the top of it reaching to heaven; and the angels of God were ascending and descending on it. Then Jacob woke from his sleep and said, "Surely Yahweh is in this place—and I did not know it!" And he was afraid, and said, "How awesome is this place! This	**Jacob left Beer-sheba and went toward Haran.** He came to a certain place and stayed there for the night, because the sun had set. Taking one of the stones of the place, he put it under his head and lay down in that place. And he dreamed that there was a ladder [or ramp, stairway] set up on the earth, the top of it reaching to heaven; and the angels of God were ascending and descending on it. Then Jacob woke from his sleep and said, "Surely Yahweh is in this place—and I did not know it!" And he was afraid, and said, "How awesome is this place! This is none other than the house of God, and this is the gate of heaven." So Jacob rose early in the morning, and he took the stone that he had put under his head and set it up for a	Jacob left Beer-sheba and went toward Haran. He came to a certain place and stayed there for the night, because the sun had set. Taking one of the stones of the place, he put it under his head and lay down in that place. And he dreamed that there was a ladder [or ramp, stairway] set up on the earth, the top of it reaching to heaven; and the angels of God were ascending and descending on it. **And Yahweh stood beside him [or above it] and said, "I am Yahweh, the God of Abraham your father and the God of Isaac; the land on which you lie I will give to you and to your offspring; and your offspring shall be like the dust on the earth, and you shall spread abroad to the west and to the east and to the north and to the south; and all the families of the earth shall be blessed in you and in your offspring. Know that I am with you and will keep you wherever you go, and will bring you back**

is none other than the house of God, and this is the gate of heaven."

So Jacob rose early in the morning, and he took the stone that he had put under his head and set it up for a pillar and poured oil on the top of it. He called that place Bethel; but the name of the city was Luz at first.

pillar and poured oil on the top of it. He called that place Bethel; but the name of the city was Luz at first. **Then Jacob made a vow, saying, "If God will be with me, and will keep me in this way that I go, and will give me bread to eat and clothing to wear, so that I come again to my father's house in peace, then Yahweh shall be my God, and this stone, which I have set up as a pillar, shall be God's house; and of all that you give me I will surely give one tenth to you."**

to this land; for I will not leave you until I have done what I have promised you." Then Jacob woke from his sleep and said, "Surely Yahweh is in this place—and I did not know it!" And he was afraid, and said, "How awesome is this place! This is none other than the house of God, and this is the gate of heaven."

So Jacob rose early in the morning, and he took the stone that he had put under his head and set it up for a pillar and poured oil on the top of it. He called that place Bethel; but the name of the city was Luz at first. Then Jacob made a vow, saying, "If God will be with me, and will keep me in this way that I go, and will give me bread to eat and clothing to wear, so that I come again to my father's house in peace, then Yahweh shall be my God, and this stone, which I have set up as a pillar, shall be God's house; and of all that you give me I will surely give one tenth to you."

In the story's most ancient form, the hierophany account, Jacob dreams only of angels who are ascending and descending a flight of stairs. In response to his dream, Jacob erects a sacred stone to mark the place of the event. Historians of religion call this a hierophany: a manifestation of the sacred in nature, in this case in a dream, which opens the door to a different and higher world, the world of God and the angels. The dreamer perceives God only indirectly through his vision of the angels, messengers who establish a link between heaven and earth by descending and ascending the ladder. This link has to be made from the beyond, for no mortal can hope to reach out to the divine world without God having authorized him to do so by first manifesting himself in a sacred place. Here we have a case of an early, unsophisticated, yet clear and unmistakable religion, one that we may call a nature religion, for it relies on natural experience for its establishment of a shrine which, as a simple stone, is not yet a temple. Although Jacob comes into view as a divinely privileged person, the emphasis seems to be on the sacred place marked by him.

A more developed form of the narrative, the epiphany account, takes the dream to be simply an initial, though promising, manifestation of the divine to

Jacob, whose relationship with the deity becomes the focus of the story. Due to this shift in emphasis, the earlier story is supplemented by Jacob's own promise: if the hierophanic deity proves to be an efficient tutelary, he will build him a temple. How can we explain this addition which shifts the meaning of the earlier story? Apparently, the descendants of Jacob were no longer content to have a sacred place; having lost their main temple, that of Jerusalem, when the Babylonians set fire to it in 586 B.C.E., they shifted their interest to a god who would no longer primarily be linked to a sacred spot, but who instead would manifest his presence mainly in the biographical and historical experience of a people displaced through flight from the enemy or deportation and resettlement in a foreign country. In such a national history and personal biography they would recognize the directing hand of the god who blesses them with protection and survival, or the raised arm of the god who punishes them with illness, war, and disaster. This is the kind of divine manifestation called an epiphany: the revelation of God through the events of history.

A second and final addition produced the theophany account. According to this new passage, it is Yahweh who appears in the dream, addressing Jacob and promising him numerous offspring. This revised version of the story again shifts its meaning. Apparently, the story of Jacob's dream came into the hands of scholars who not only collected ancient traditions but also edited and interpreted them according to their own taste and theology. They introduced Yahweh himself into the dream, imagining that he had stood above the ladder and given their ancestor a promise. They may have heard such promises in the prophetic discourse around 500 B.C.E., a time in which many Jews returned from the Babylonian exile to their ancestral homeland and needed encouragement to establish their families and take root in Palestine. Through textual expansion, the vagueness of the dream of the angels and the ladder is here replaced by clear notions of the deity, now made to identify himself unambiguously, saying: "I am Yahweh, the God of Abraham your father and the God of Isaac" (Gen 28:13). The manifestation of a speaking deity may be called a theophany, to distinguish it from the other two forms of manifestation, the archaic hierophany and the epiphany. We may see in the theophanic paradigm the scholarly theology, a religion interested in texts and in the words they imagined God to have spoken in the past. Much care was taken to make Jacob/Israel, Israel's eponymous ancestor, a relevant figure. Jacob's dream and his wanderings were only episodes in a story that described how he returned from the fringes of Mesopotamia to Palestine, where he settled and had numerous offspring. This story resonated with those Jews who, when repatriating themselves after the Babylonian exile, hoped for a new life.

All the Hebrews, irrespective of whether they emphasized their God's manifestation in hierophanies in nature, in epiphanies in history, or in theophanies in their theological writing, believed in Yahweh as a living power who would not stop revealing himself and his divine will.

Yahweh and "Beginnings"

Our analysis of the tale of Jacob's dream in terms of the history of religions makes us learn much about the way in which the Hebrews experienced their deity; but it did not lead us to the historical beginnings of the alliance between God and Israel. With other, comparable stories such as the one about God's revelation to Moses at the "burning bush," we do not fare any better, for they, too, give us no access to historical facts. Historians do not believe in a divine act of revelation that establishes a religion; foundational revelations are considered the subject of popular etiologies, as mere imaginative answers to the question of what the origins were, as tales from the inexhaustible repertoire of pious storytellers. While these tales give invaluable insight into the religious mentality of the Hebrews, they are historically of little worth.

If the accounts of revelatory experiences cannot lead us back to historical beginnings, how can these be traced? In order to understand the earliest history of the Hebrew God, specialists rely on the name "Yahweh," the most conspicuous, and in the Bible most frequently used, name of the Hebrew God. The search for the earliest discernible circle of devotees and the oldest region where Yahweh was venerated has led to a surprising result: Originally, Yahweh was not the god of the Hebrews, but one of the Edomite deities.[2]

One, apparently early—according to some, the earliest—biblical poem has Yahweh come to the aid of the Israelites from outside of Palestine, from Seir in Edom:

> Yahweh, when you went out from Seir,
> when you marched from the region of Edom,
> the earth trembled, and the heavens poured,
> the clouds indeed poured water. (Judg 5:4)

The poem gives Yahweh a home and a function. His abode is in Seir, a mountainous part of Edom. Modern scholarship identifies the heartland of Edom with the rocky plateau immediately southeast of the Dead Sea. Situated between the Negev in the west and the Arabian desert in the east, it now belongs to the Kingdom of Jordan. In addition to a home, the poet assigns a clear function to Yahweh: he is a weather-god, responsible for sending rain. Pointing out further, archaic-sounding biblical passages that associate Yahweh with Seir— "Yahweh came from Sinai, and dawned from Seir upon us" (Deut 33:2)— scholars have concluded that Yahweh must have been an Edomite deity. In support of this assumption one can also invoke an inscription found in Kuntillet Ajrud in the Negev; dating from ca. 800 B.C.E., it refers to "Yahweh of Teman."[3] In the Bible, Teman is occasionally used as another name for Edom.[4] The Temanite or Edomite deity's abode seems to have been a sacred mountain. When later tradition refers to Mount Sinai as the place of divine revelation, it may have preserved a trace of memory of the Edomite mountain of Yahweh.

How to account for the presumed fact that a mountain- and weather-god, on whom the Edomite peasants and pastoralists depended, came to be venerated by the Israelites? The tales surrounding the figure of Jacob also speak of a brother of Israel's ancestor, a man named Esau; he was considered the ancestor of the Edomites. Just as Jacob and Esau were thought of as twins, so the Israelites and the Edomites were considered people related by common blood. "You shall not abhor an Edomite, for he is your brother," commands biblical legislation (Deut 23:7/Hebr. 8). Further information about the kinship of the two peoples and their religion is not available, and so we must be content with the notion that the Hebrews adopted a deity of their Edomite brothers as their own god. Here we can see once more how radically the "beginnings," as traced by historical scholarship, differ from the "origins" as told in popular lore. In the tale of origins, Jacob and his God meet as distinct personalities, and the act of revelation leaves no doubt about its finality and relevance. By contrast, the historian has to be content with modestly and tentatively suggesting an Edomite background for Yahweh. Historical truth lacks the ornaments of poetic fiction, for, unlike the "origins" as they are remembered—or invented—by tradition, "beginnings" are generally unchronicled and remain too vague to permit more than provisional interpretations.

19. The "Sacred Story" and Monotheism

The previous chapter's task was to find the point at which the history of the Hebrew God begins. We found a double beginning: a biblical one which we characterized as belonging to popular tradition, and a historical one which could be determined only tentatively. The present chapter continues the two accounts. The first narrative, the one which sets in with tales such as the dream of Jacob, maintains its popular and traditional character; its "sacred story" tells how the Hebrew God, through election and legislation, formed a people to his liking and assigned it a land to live in. The second, historical-critical narrative—the one starting with suggestions about Yahweh's Edomite background—may find its continuation in a discussion of the early stages of Israel's monotheistic notion of the divine.

The God of Israel's Foundational Story

The Hexateuch (the five books of Moses plus the book of Joshua) narrates the sacred story of the Israelites from the creation of the universe through the Hebrews' conquest of Palestine. There are leading human characters in this account: patriarchs such as Abraham and Jacob and leaders such as Moses and Joshua, but the real hero is the Hebrew God. Modern scholarship has invented the term "history of salvation" (or "history of redemption," translating the German *Heilsgeschichte*) to designate the substance of the story, the purposeful interaction of God and human protagonists to form God's people. The canonical history of salvation precedes history proper—the story of Israel, its monarchy and enemies, as told in the books of Judges, Samuel, and Kings.

Underlying the Hexateuch are three great traditions: the divine promise of descendants and land, given to Israel's ancestors; the divinely ordained exodus of the enslaved Hebrews out of Egypt, followed by their conquest of the land; and the giving of the divine law at Mount Sinai. True, other subjects are also dealt with in this compilation—for example, there is the primeval mythology of the first eleven chapters of Genesis, or the theme of the desert wanderings of the Israelites—yet it is the three elementary traditions that give it its basic shape. These traditions, moreover, can be assigned to the three functions:

The promise of descendants and ownership of land made to the patriarchs corresponds to the Third Function, which always has to do with fertility and wealth. The emblematic figure in this tradition is Abraham, bearer of the divine promise, whose grandson Jacob is also called Israel. God blesses, i.e. he bestows the power of reproduction and fertility. Outside of the patriarchal narrative, the Third Function also figures prominently. Thus Palestine is described as a rich land flowing with milk and honey,[5] and the book of Deuteronomy promises that "God will make you abundantly prosperous in all your undertakings, in the fruit of your body, in the fruit of your livestock, and in the fruit of your soil" (Deut 30:9).

The traditions of the exodus from Egypt and the conquest of the land correspond to the Second Function. Two great warriors are presented to the reader: the God of Israel and Joshua. God is the Divine Warrior of the exodus and Joshua the commander of the conquest. The victory over the Egyptian army is attributed directly to God, for the people who flee from the country of their oppression have no army of their own: hence the divine intervention in the form of a miracle of nature that allows the Israelites to cross the sea on dry ground, while the Egyptian chariots sink into it. Earlier we discussed the story of Joshua's holy war against the city of Jericho (see above, chapter 6). Another typical Second Function text is the list of the conquered towns in the book of Joshua.[6]

The Sinai tradition has to do with the promulgation of law and therefore with a theme that belongs to the First Function. Again the function is ascribed both to the deity and a human being, for the story associates the human mediator Moses with the wise divine legislator. The most famous First Function text is, of course, the Decalogue, a summary of Israel's sacred and civil law in ten commandments.

The Hexateuch ascribes the promise of descendants to the same deity as the exodus from Egypt, the conquest of the land, and the Sinai legislation. On the human side, we have a more differentiated story: Abraham is a protagonist of the Third Function, Joshua a hero of the Second Function, and Moses a First Function figure. Each of these has a particular functional office, but none is a king, for a king would have all three functions (see above, chapter 1). Therefore a convenient way to summarize the image of the deity that unites the three functions is to say that he appears as a king. Most readers of the Bible visualize the Hebrew God as a grave old man sitting on a throne, and the biblical text does little to dissuade us from such a notion. This image, "a gigantic anthropomorphism," "reflects the picture of the earthly king projected onto the cosmic stage." The Hebrew God's disparate features—of supreme lord at Sinai, Divine Warrior fighting for the Hebrews' liberation in the exodus story, and protector of the patriarchs—"make sense only if constantly referred to the image of human kingship,"[7] for it is the human king's duty to provide leadership, to engage in warfare, and to nurture the people. Thus it is mainly the figure of God that conveys a sense of tripartite completeness, a completeness achieved through the presence of the three themes of war, wisdom, and wealth.

On the human side, a similar sense of completeness is conveyed only once— in the book of Deuteronomy's remarkably dense statement of the relationship between the three domains. At harvest time, the peasant is told to visit the temple and bring a basket filled with "some of the first of all the fruit of the ground" (Deut 26:2) to the priest. From the priest's point of view, it is by ritual means that the land's fertility and productivity are ensured. But the thanks-giving ritual also includes the invocation of the Warrior God who liberated the peasant out of Egyptian servitude and gave him, by right of conquest, the fruit-bearing land. The First Function, represented by the priest and the temple, and the Second Function, represented by the invocation of the Warrior Deity, are in complete control of and superior to the peasant who tills the soil and stands for the Third Function. The ritual's message is clear enough: it is not primarily to his own work that the peasant owes the crops, but rather to the priestly ritual and the Divine Warrior's conquest of the land. Here we have the usual situation according to which the First and Second Functions are deemed superior to and nobler than the Third Function. This is the view of proud aris-tocrats who define themselves as forming Israel's social and cultural elite.

Within the Hexateuch, the story of the patriarchs in Genesis forms a dis-tinct body. Although Genesis is now integrated into the tripartite system of the Hexateuchal framework, it may not be amiss to pay attention to this book's indi-vidual—and quite surprising—message.

Genesis can be seen as a book of divine blessing, for, with their eighty-eight occurrences, the words "to bless" and "blessing" form its leitmotiv, the book's prevailing and ever-returning theme. Through blessing, God bestows fertility. This theme is present already in the account of creation, where animals and human beings are blessed, i.e. provided with the power to reproduce. "Be fruitful and multiply, and fill the earth" is the divine mandate given to human beings (Gen 1:28). The main theme of the patriarchal stories is the divine promise of numerous offspring given to Abraham, and the realization of that promise. "I will make of you a great nation, and I will bless you, and make your name great" (Gen 12:2). "I will make your offspring like the dust of the earth; only if the specks of dust on the ground could be counted could your offspring be counted" (Gen 13:16). The promise cannot be fulfilled easily, for there are serious difficulties. Sarah, spouse of Abraham, is infertile and has already entered menopause; or, according to another story, she is passed off as Abraham's sister rather than his spouse, and is taken into the harem of a foreign ruler. All of this does not help Abraham to have numerous offspring. Eventu-ally, he does have a son, but then God commands him to sacrifice this only child. This also seems to obstruct the original promise given to Abraham. But Abraham's son survives, for at the last moment God abandons his wish to have this child as a human victim. With Isaac, the next generation is in place and can expect the fulfillment of God's promise. Isaac's son Jacob emerges as the one who is finally to have numerous descendants—but not immediately, for certain problems have to be dealt with. First of all, it is not easy to find a suitable wife for Isaac; she must be sought among relatives who live far away. Eventually, a prospective bride is found, but her father is unwilling to deliver her within a reasonable time. As soon as one difficulty is removed, another appears.

The plot that traces the line of Abraham's offspring is supplemented by another plot, one that focuses on the theme of the Israelites' access to food. Here the story is also one of a people permanently challenged by the scarcity of elementary resources, for again and again the patriarchs are visited by drought and famine. Several times they are granted refuge in a neighboring country where they find food and water for both themselves and their flocks. This episode repeats itself three times, and each time the story is told of a different patriarch; first of Abraham and Isaac,[8] and then of Jacob. The most developed account of the migration episode is in the Jacob story, which takes the form of a full-blown novella. Like his ancestor Abraham, Jacob finds refuge in the land of Egypt. In this case, help comes from a quite unexpected source. In Egypt, Jacob's son Joseph, whom his father thought dead, turns out to be the most influential figure in the king's administration. We learn that Joseph has stored so much grain during the seven "years of plenty" that he could feed not only the Egyptian population, but also his Israelite father and his brothers and their flocks during the ensuing seven "years of dearth." The well-known story of the pharaoh's dreams—first of seven fat cows and seven lean ones, and then of seven fat ears of grain and seven meager ones—is a particularly impressive instance of a Third Function motif. No less impressive is the statement that concludes the account of Jacob's settlement in Egypt: "Joseph provided his father, his brothers, and all his father's household with food, according to the number of their dependants" (Gen 47:12).

In addition to the "promise of offspring" and the "famine" motifs, a third plot occasionally comes to the fore. This is the increase of the flocks—a subject important among pastoralists. An entire chapter of the book of Genesis is devoted to the miraculous increase of Jacob's sheep and goats. The last sentence of this chapter reads: "Thus the man grew exceedingly rich, and had large flocks, and male and female slaves, and camels and donkeys" (Gen 30:43). The book of Genesis never leaves any doubt about what the Hebrews took to be the visible effect of divine blessing: numerous offspring, large amounts of food, and ever-increasing flocks of sheep and goats.

How can we account for the great interest that the book of Genesis has in the Third Function? This question is susceptible of an answer that is as precise as it is surprising, if we agree with those scholars who prefer a late date for the book of Genesis. In recent years some scholars have come to consider Genesis the latest part of the Pentateuch and have assigned it to the fifth century B.C.E. If this dating is correct, then Genesis is contemporaneous with and thus comparable to the book of Job. As will be remembered, we have read the book of Job as a book of the Third Function. The two biblical writings share a number of features:

1) Both books are set in a Hebrew world that is not closed upon itself but is open to its non-Israelite surroundings. Job's friends are neither Israelites nor Judeans but foreigners. In fact, some modern commentators have felt that Job himself, who lives in the "land of Uz" (Job 1:1), may be an Edomite rather than a Hebrew. A similarly cosmopolitan atmosphere characterizes the patriarchal stories of the book of Genesis. Here Israel's ancestors entertain friendly relations with other people, such as the Egyptians and the Philistines. This cosmopolitan climate is absent from the rest of the Pentateuch. In this respect the books of Exodus and Deuteronomy in particular are vastly different from the book of Genesis: programatically separatist, they are hostile toward other nations.

2) In both Job and Genesis the primary form of the economy is the breeding of livestock and the idea of wealth is to own large flocks. Many commentators have signaled this fact and argued that Job is depicted as a contemporary of the patriarchal period. Unlike the pastoralists of other cultures, who consider raids for cattle as laudable pursuits, both Job and the patriarchs of Genesis are peaceful people. They never indulge in such adventures; instead, they may be nonretaliating victims of raids, as is the case with Job.[9]

3) The notion of God is very similar in the two books. Both Job and the patriarchs interact with a deity that blesses human beings and animals and makes them increase and multiply. In our terminology, this deity is one of the Third Function.

Apparently, Genesis and Job belong to the same cultural milieu. Written about 500 B.C.E.—i.e. after the Babylonian exile—they echo that period's vital interest in restoring the material basis of Israel's existence and its spiritual identity. People became conscious of the fact that the state, with its emphasis on the Divine Warrior and the wisdom god, had been responsible for the national disaster of 586 B.C.E. Now, after the destruction of the military-bureaucratic complex, there was (to borrow an expression from psychology) a movement of cultural regression in which people remembered the archaic Lord of the Animals. He and no other deity could provide the obvious spiritual basis for economic restoration, for he is the one who blesses and nurtures animals and humans alike. Here we can discern one of the reasons why these books—the only ones in the Old Testament—have been adopted into the canon of world literature. In them the specifically Jewish and parochial message is relegated to the background, and the human message is thrown into relief. With their focus on the recurring themes of human existence that appeal to readers of all times and cultures, the two books could become part of humanity's literary heritage. Translated into the more technical terminology of our trifunctional analysis, this idea might be stated as follows: the Third Function holds universal appeal and is much less shaped by culturally specific forms than the Second and First Functions. War and wisdom seem to be less universal than life and wealth.

If our reading of Genesis is granted, how does this book, with its distinctive notion of the Hebrew God, relate to the rest of the Hexateuch? The answer must be that the book of Genesis does not of itself, naturally as it were, fit in with the sacred story of salvation. Within the Hexateuch two conflicting ideological patterns can be discerned: one that insists on tripartite completeness and another that shows a clear preference for the Third Function. Found only in the book of Genesis, the latter pattern neglects the First and Second Functions in order to focus completely on and extoll the Third Function. Marked by the absence of priesthood and warriordom, the world of Genesis is peaceful, idyllic, and committed to a pastoral ideal. Patriarchal authority, as it occurs naturally in families and clans, is the only archaic form of authority compatible with this ideal. Royal, administrative, priestly, and military authority are all conspicuously absent.*

Here we can get a rare glimpse of those who did not belong to the aristocratic elite or who no longer believed in the values traditionally upheld by this elite. Reading the book of Genesis, we can listen to people who after the downfall of the monarchy in 586 B.C.E. ceased to believe in "tripartite completeness" and developed their own ideology of the one, fundamental function of fertility. Having children, raising sheep and goats, and producing food were for them all that mattered in life. The peasant and pastoralist view of the good life—the alternative to "tripartite completeness"—receives here one of its most convincing expressions on record in ancient history.

---

* There seem to be exceptions to this rule, but all of them can be explained. (a) Occasionally, kings appear in the book of Genesis, but they are neither warriors nor intellectual leaders; instead, they are seen as super-peasants, royal rulers of countries that produce such an abundance of food that in times of famine they can invite the Hebrews in and share their wealth with them; this is why we find Abraham and Joseph in Egypt, and Isaac among the Philistines of Gerar. (b) Abraham as a warrior figure, as he is depicted in one rather cryptic chapter (Gen 14), is very exceptional, and it may well be that the chapter was not part of the original book. But even if it was, one can detect an element that balances out the picture, for Abraham is not the aggressor, but the defender and rescuer of others. He returns captives to their royal master and spoils to their original owners; Abraham thus emerges as a diplomatic leader who respects others rather than as a conqueror intent on enriching himself (Habel, *The Land Is Mine*, 127). (c) In all of Genesis, a really warlike mood is expressed only in the aphorisms that characterize some of Israel's twelve tribes as prone to raids or acts of violence: "Benjamin is a ravenous wolf, in the morning devouring the prey, in the evening dividing the spoil" (Gen 49:27); in this case, the entire chapter seems to be intrusive and foreign to the original design and spirit of Genesis. Alternatively, one may think of it as a surviving trace of the original warlike atmosphere which was elsewhere deleted by pacifically minded editors (M. Weber, *Ancient Judaism*, 49–54; Rose, "Entmilitarisierung"). At any rate, the book's emphasis on Third-Function realities is consistent and not undermined by an aristocratic warrior perspective.

Historically, the ideological pattern represented by the book of Genesis was meant to offer an alternative to the tripartite one, a plebeian pattern as opposed to an aristocratic one. The present collocation of the two views of society in one literary corpus—the Hexateuch—conceals the fact that there is an enormous tension between them, a tension that defies reconciliation.[10] Nevertheless, at the level of what scholars have termed the "final edition" of the Hexateuch, Genesis is incorporated into the larger, trifunctional structure and thereby neutralized. Finally, the aristocratic pattern of society prevailed and, with it, the ideology of tripartite harmony and completeness.

Monolatry and Monotheism

As much as the critical analysis of the canonical "sacred story" can open our eyes to the multiplicity of ancient Israel's religious mentalities, this reading contributes little to the understanding of monotheism, the foremost feature of biblical religion. For this reason we have to begin afresh. Our discussion must set in with the fact, today recognized by most scholars, that monolatry and monotheism—the exclusive worship of and belief in one single deity—were latecomers in the history of Hebrew culture.[11] Israel's religion originated in a world of polytheism, and its first discernible phase was characterized by the worship of multiple deities—gods and goddesses. This early phase of Israelite religion has left traces in the biblical record, which otherwise tends to suppress whatever seems contrary to monotheistic orthodoxy. In ancient times, no one doubted that Yahweh was Israel's national deity, just as other polytheistic nations also had their divine tutelary: the Assyrians had Ashur and the Babylonians Marduk, for example. But like other ancient nations, the Hebrews not only served and acknowledged their national god, they also worshiped a number of other deities. Thus the prophet Jeremiah, who lived around 600 B.C.E., reports that people did not hesitate "to make offerings to the Queen of Heaven and to pour out libations to her" (Jer 44:25). The people who did so, and who were chided for it by the prophet, pointed to the gifts of the goddess: plenty of food, general prosperity, absence of misfortune. Jeremiah was one of those prophets who promoted the exclusive worship of the national deity, Yahweh.

While the biblical tradition itself traces the mandate to practice exclusive worship of Yahweh back to very early times, to the patriarch Abraham or the prophet Moses, modern historians of religion attribute these views to a movement that, within Hebrew polytheism, for a long time represented only a minority of the population. The first attestations of this idea may be dated to more than four hundred years after the presumed historical lifetime of Moses, whose work and personality are shrouded in legend. The first datable source is the book of Hosea, a prophet active in the northern kingdom around 750 B.C.E. This book transmits the following divine word: "I have been Yahweh your God ever since the land of Egypt, you know no God but me, and besides me there is no savior" (Hos 13:4). Here the exclusive worship of Yahweh is connected with the exodus tradition. A close reading of this oracle leads to what we consider basic insight into the origins and meaning of monolatric worship:

— It was most likely in the northern kingdom of Israel, rather than in southern Judah, that the monolatric idea originated.
— The deity to be worshiped exclusively is the war-god who has led the Israelites out of Egypt. Moreover, the very term "savior" implies a military notion, for it refers specifically to divine help in battle.[12] It is in this "military" sense that we have to understand the Hosean passage.

The prophet, however, does not seem to have had much influence during his time. It was not until a hundred years later, toward the end of the seventh century B.C.E., that the Yahweh-alone movement became more influential and eventually succeeded in coming to dominate the biblical tradition.

How can one account for the emergence of the unusual idea of restricting worship to just one deity? Where did Hosea get this idea from? A tentative answer may be suggested by an ancient military custom documented in the book of Judges, a book that apparently originated in the northern kingdom. Here we learn that during warfare Israel got rid of its other gods in order to offer worship exclusively to Yahweh: "So they put away the foreign gods from among them and worshiped Yahweh; and he could no longer bear to see Israel suffer" (Judg 10:16). When the army of the tribes of northern Palestine or the army of the northern kingdom took the field, then all ritual activities related to the gods were suspended; only Yahweh, Israel's Divine Warrior, received ritual attention. Worshiped exclusively, he promised to assure victory. But after victory, after the situation of war was at an end, people could again worship their local deities, their family gods, and whatever supernatural beings they were used to addressing with prayer and sacrifice. The obligation of exclusive worship was limited to the weeks or months of war.

This institution of temporary monolatry was not peculiar to Israel, but can be found in at least one other Semitic religion—that of Mesopotamia. A particularly good example is included in the Atrahasis Epic known from Babylonian cuneiform tablets dating from around 1700 B.C.E.[13] This epic is a mythical account of early humanity. The gods create humankind to serve them, but eventually humans become so numerous, boisterous, and noisy that some of the gods can no longer sleep. For this reason the gods decide to kill humanity by no longer sending rain. One of the gods disagrees, however. This is Enki, the cunning god of wisdom, who turns to the man Atrahasis, telling him how to outwit the gods: people must stop venerating their deities altogether. They should concentrate their worship on only one deity—the rain-god, Adad. So people actually stop worshiping other gods, build a new temple for the weather-god and offer him sacrifices. Pleased with this honor, Adad sends dew during the night so that grain can grow in the fields. The text explicitly states that, after the crisis is over, people return to their previous ritual practices.

The war leaders of early Israel may have adopted a similar strategy. By proclaiming exclusive worship of the Divine Warrior, they hoped to enlist this god's cooperation. It was easy to reinterpret—or misunderstand—the ancient call to exclusive worship and so turn a temporary measure into a permanent practice. Temporary monolatry in times of war can be considered the proto-type or embryonic form of the Yahweh-alone idea and thus the precursor of monotheism. At any rate, the exclusive veneration of Yahweh in a situation of crisis makes sense during the eighth and seventh centuries B.C.E., for it was then that Assyrian pressure on Palestine grew and increasingly marked its political life. As the crisis became permanent, all Israelites and Judeans were asked to attach themselves exclusively and permanently to the one deity that promised help. Thus incipient monotheism can be understood best as a ritual response to the challenge of a severe political crisis.

Even though he was worshiped with increasing exclusivity, the Hebrew God remained a figure from the ancient Near Eastern pantheon. Israel's intel-lectuals—priests, prophets, and scribes—compared their God with the deities of the major civilizations they knew, and this led to repeated borrowing from other religions in the interest of extending or achieving a better description of Yahweh's supremacy. The reconstruction of this historical process constitutes a major challenge; unsurprisingly, it has attracted numerous brilliant minds. Among the relevant titles there is a book by Sigmund Freud: *Moses and Monotheism* (1939). According to the founder of psychoanalysis, the Egyptian sun-god, Aten, would have been the model for Yahweh, but this suggestion does not stand up to present-day critical scrutiny. In addition to Aten, scholars have been impressed with other powerful deities: the Egyptian god Amen-Re; the Ugaritic high god El; Ashur, state god of the Assyrians; Marduk, the main Babylonian deity; and, finally, Ahura Mazda, Zoroaster's monotheistic god. To all of these deities people attributed supreme power and, about all of them, monotheistic or almost monotheistic theologies were developed. Each of these deities may, at one period or another, have served as a model for the Hebrew God.[14]

How exactly the image of foreign deities has shaped that of the Hebrew god is hard to say. A discussion of two biblical passages will give us an idea: the psalm of creation and an oracle of Jeremiah. The psalm of creation (Ps 104) is strongly reminiscent of hymns which Amenophis IV alias Akhenaten (1364–1347 B.C.E.) composed for his exclusively venerated sun-god Aten. The Hebrew poet's contact with the hymnic tradition of Egypt cannot be dated, however, for the influence of Akhenaten's poems on Egyptian ritual poetry can be traced to Hellenistic times.[15] Clearly, the belief in the Hebrew God could be expressed in a language that was borrowed from another monotheistic tradition. In 594 B.C.E., Jeremiah delivered the following divine message to his king, Zedekiah, exhorting him to accept foreign rule:

> Thus says Yahweh of hosts, the God of Israel: . . . It is I who by my great power and my outstretched arm have made the earth, with the people and the animals that are on the earth, and I give it to whomever I please. Now I have given all these lands into the hand of King Nebuchadnezzar of Babylon, my servant, and I have given him even the wild animals of the field to serve him. (Jer 27:4–6)

Jeremiah's notion of God is less indebted to Israelite tradition than to the theology of King Nebuchadnezzar II, then the ruler of all of Western Asia. In an inscription, Nebuchadnezzar addresses his divine lord: "Lord Marduk, you are the wise god, the proud prince! You have created me and entrusted me with royal rule over all the people."[16] Marduk was both the creator of the universe and Nebuchadnezzar's personal god. Thus the careful scrutiny of biblical texts occasionally reveals Israel's indebtedness to its larger cultural milieu.

The various factors that presumably played a role in the formation of biblical monotheism—not only temporary monolatry and the figures of Aten and Marduk, but also the belief in Amen-Re, Ashur, and Ahura Mazda—come from several cultures and must have made their contributions at different times. It should be clear, however, that foreign influences cannot be considered decisive factors, for there must have been masterminds who exploited the opportunities for creative encounter, adaptation, and assimilation, devised the new religious idea, and promoted it through their disciples. Neither a school initiated by a known master nor an organized party, this is best described as a movement, understood as an informal, uninstitutionalized group motivated by a religious idea to which great importance is ascribed. On the analogy of modern equivalents such as the American Civil Rights movement, Third World liberation movements, or the ecological movement, one would expect its activists and sympathizers to come from various sectors of the population and to specialize, at least occasionally, in contentious interaction with opponents. In fact, there is reason to assume the existence of a Yahweh-alone movement which, no later than ca. 750 B.C.E., inspired by prophets and religious enthusiasts, came to attract the intellectuals and to gain increasing influence. Soon, as northern Israel disappeared as a state, the movement moved south and gained influence in the southern kingdom of Judah. With the cult reform of King Josiah of Judah (ca. 622 B.C.E.) it accomplished a further move of equal importance, that from the social periphery to the center of the state. Although the exclusive cult of Yahweh did not remain without opposition, it eventually came to dominate the religious culture.

20. Christ as Second God

When in the present chapter we turn to early Christianity, we can continue our by now well-established method of following two story-lines: one that corresponds to the sacred story of the gospels, and another that seeks to reconstruct historical reality. Our point of departure will be the tradition about the temptation of Jesus in the desert, a tale that again invites an interpretation from the perspective of the history of religions.

The Temptation of Jesus

When the early Christians spoke about the hero whom they venerated as their Lord, they could draw on a vast repertoire of stories, reports, and anecdotes. One such story tells of Christ's lonely retreat into the wilderness of Judea, where he fasted for forty days and forty nights; apparently retreats and fasting belonged to the regimen preparatory to visionary experiences.[17] It must have been in a vision that he had in the desert that the devil appeared to him. He tells the famished prophet to reveal his divine powers by changing stones to bread; Jesus refuses. As the vision continues, we see the devil and Jesus on the pinnacle of the Jerusalem temple; the devil suggests that Jesus should throw himself down, relying on the help of God's angels to prevent him from killing himself; again, Jesus refuses. The third challenge has another location still: the devil takes Jesus up onto a high mountain from which all the kingdoms of the world can be seen. The devil offers him rulership over these kingdoms, on condition that Jesus prostrate himself, humbling himself in a gesture of worship and acknowledging him as his master. And again, Jesus refuses.

The three temptations can easily be correlated with the three functions of Dumézilian theory: bread, extracted from stony ground by the Palestinian peasant, is a Third Function reality; the demonstration of one's extraordinary courage and the expectation of rescue from danger belong to warriordom and therefore to the Second Function; and the offer of universal rulership completes the challenges with the First Function. Interestingly, each temptation happens at a different place, so that an ascending line can be discerned: the bread temptation on the surface of the earth, the test of courage on the pinnacle of the temple (i.e. the highest building), and the offer of universal rulership on the peak of a mountain, close to heaven. Thus the entire cosmos is traversed and the hierarchy of the functions highlighted. The cosmic structure can be represented in the form of steps:

> (I) summit of mountain—universal rulership
> (II) pinnacle of temple—courage of warrior
> (III) desert plain—production of bread

The triad of earth (desert), intermediate space, and sky merges into the triad of fertility, force, and sovereignty.

What is the meaning of the temptation story? Jesus is clearly understood as a person endowed with special powers and with access to the nonhuman world of spirits and demons. In the version given by Matthew, the story ends on an angelic, rather than satanic note: "Then the devil left him, and suddenly angels came and waited on him [Jesus]" (Matt 4:11). The story is apologetic in character, for it defends Jesus against two charges: that of working in the service of the devil, and that of performing miracles for self-aggrandizement and other selfish purposes. Withstanding the devil's three tests, Jesus appears as someone whose powers derive not from satanic but from angelic connections. Thus he emerges as a relative of Zoroaster and Buddha, two other religious founders whose character was tested with similar threefold temptations.[18]

Jesus also emerges as a transfunctional character, as someone who, incorporating all three functions, can be active as wise ruler, terrifying warrior, and protective fatherly—and even motherly—figure. In the gospels themselves, however, the tripartite completeness is not yet developed. Mixing as they do legend with historical knowledge, these early biographies depict him as a sage and magician who heals people's bodily ailments; in terms of Dumézil's pattern, he can be assigned to the First Function. Moreover, there is a special affinity with the Third Function, for on one occasion Jesus supplies his audience with food—so generously that seven baskets of leftovers can be collected.[19] Only as a being who after the death of his body lives and reigns eternally in heaven is Christ depicted as encompassing all the three divine roles. Now he is considered primarily as judge (First Function), Divine Warrior (Second Function), and good shepherd of the individual believer (Third Function).

The First Function is in clear evidence for Christ, who ranks as God's representative and vice-regent. God, as explained in the letter to the Ephesians,

> put his power to work in Christ when he raised him from the dead and seated him at his right hand in the heavenly places, far above every name that is named, not only in this age but also in the age to come. And he has put all things under his feet and has made him the head over all things for the church, which is his body. (Eph 1:20–23)

Seated at the Father's right hand, Christ shares God's sovereign authority. The very assertion that Christ is God—an assertion explained and defended

34. *Christ at the Last Judgment.* The Christian Creed states that Christ will return "to judge the living and the dead." This scene, often found in art, places the enthroned Christ, shown in majesty in a circle of light (the mandorla), at the center of a drama of universal dimensions. Surrounded by angels and saints, he invites the blessed with his right hand into the kingdom of heaven, while with his left hand he sends the damned into hell. As is fitting, right and left are defined from Christ's, not the viewer's, perspective.—Giotto, *Last Judgment* fresco, 1309.

through the centuries with remarkable tenacity—implies his vice-regency over creation.[20] Christ the Pantocrator and judge forms the center of the doctrine of the universal judgment. The Creed explains that Christ sits enthroned at the Father's right hand wherefrom, at the end of time, he will come to judge the living and the dead. In the Bible, the gospel of Matthew gives the clearest description of Christ the Judge: "When the Son of Man comes in his glory, and all the angels with him, he will sit on the throne of his glory. All the nations will be gathered before him, and he will separate people one from another, as a shepherd separates the sheep from the goats" (Matt 25:31–33). Whereas the good people will be welcomed into the Father's kingdom, the bad ones will be sent away to eternal punishment. Giotto's great fresco in Padua is only one example of the standard iconography of Christ who, majestically enthroned and surrounded by angels and saints, presides over the final events of the history of salvation (fig. 34).

Christ the warrior represents the Second Function. The visionary of Patmos sees him wearing bloodstained garments and leading the heavenly cavalry on horseback. His command is "a sharp sword with which to strike down the

35. *Christ the Warrior.* Depicted as a helmeted Roman general in full armor, Christ treads the lion and the dragon under foot and thrusts his spear into the beast's throat. The Latin superscription provides the scriptural warrant: "Upon the asp and the basilisk you shall tread, and you shall trample upon the lion and dragon" (Ps 91:13). While this theme is more commonly associated with St. George, the medieval imagination did not hesitate to see Christ as a dragon-killing warrior.—French medieval illumination, ca. 830 C.E.

nations, and he will rule them with a rod of iron" to execute God's vengeance (Rev 19:15). Ever since the days of Emperor Constantine (306–37), the first Christian ruler of the Roman Empire, Christ the Warrior has figured in religious language.[21] Many scriptural passages, including poems from the book of Psalms, were quoted to support or illustrate the idea. Early commentaries on Psalm 91 (numbered as Psalm 90 in the Vulgate) understand Christ as the one who subdues and triumphs over "the lion and the dragon." "*Super aspidem et basiliscum ambulabis, et conculcabis leonem et draconem*"—Upon the asp and the basilisk you shall tread, and you shall trample upon the lion and dragon.[22] The Stuttgart Psalter, a French manuscript dating from ca. 830, illustrates the scene: Christ, in full armour and with waving military coat, running full tilt, treads upon the crouching lion and the twisting serpent, thrusting his spear into the latter's wide-open throat (fig. 35).

When the doubting disciple, Thomas, worships Christ by addressing him as "my Lord and my God" (John 20:28), we have an explicit reference to the well-known figure of the personal god (Third Function).[23] Lucid metaphors highlight Christ's nurturing role vis-à-vis his followers: he is "the hen that gathers her brood under her wings" (Matt 23:37), and as the paternal "good shepherd"

36. *Christ the Good Shepherd.* Represented as a young, beardless man clad in shepherd's attire—a short, belted tunic—Christ carries a lamb on his shoulders. The lower part of this idyllic picture is filled with a flock of six sheep with their heads turned to the shepherd, the upper part with seven stars and allegories of the sun and the moon. Christ is framed by biblical scenes. On the left, we recognize the whale who casts up Jonah and the dove perched on Noah's ark; on the right, another bird and Jonah sleeping under a bush. The Lord of the Animals not only cares for the Christian sheep; as can be seen from the whale and Noah's dove, he was also active in Old Testament times.—Oil lamp from Italy, ca. 200 C.E.

he knows the name of each individual lamb (John 10:3, 11). The theme of Christ the Good Shepherd, reminiscent of the Lord of the Animals, was always present in Christian iconography and spirituality. Around 200 the bucolic Christ can be found throughout the Mediterranean world—in Italy, North Africa, and Asia Minor. An Italian terracotta lamp decorated with biblical scenes and a dominant shepherd figure may well be the first identifiable object of art showing specifically Christian iconography (fig. 36).[24] While the shepherd figures prominently in pagan art as well, the Christian understanding of the scene is evident from several contemporary textual sources. Tertullian of Carthage refers to a chalice adorned with the motif and explains how it was understood: the shepherd is Christ, the lamb carried by him the individual believer, and the flock represents the church.[25] In a dream she had while awaiting her martyrdom in Tertullian's Carthage, Perpetua (ca. 200) saw a white-haired man wearing shepherd's attire. As she approached him, he was milking sheep; welcoming her to paradise, he offered her a little cake of

CATECHISM
of the
CATHOLIC
CHURCH

SECOND EDITION

*revised in accordance with the official Latin text
promulgated by Pope John Paul II*

contains glossary and analytical index

LIBRERIA EDITRICE VATICANA

37. *The Good Shepherd as "logo."* In the 1990s, the pope issued an authoritative
standard catechism and thereby departed from the church's traditional policy of
leaving the compilation and publication of such textbooks in the hands of individual
bishops. On the title page of the Latin text and all vernacular translations one finds
the image of Christ the Good Shepherd, adapted from a tombstone in the catacombs
of Domitilla in Rome. This pastoral scene showing a lamb and a panpipe player is
reminiscent of the iconography of the pagan hero Orpheus (see fig. 13). On the title
page of the catechism it is used to symbolize the sweet rest and happiness that the
faithful experience when they place themselves under the mild authority and
protection of Christ.—*Catechism of the Catholic Church* (2000).

cheese—an apt gift from a shepherd.[26] In the earliest extant Christian epitaph,
found in Anatolia, the deceased Aberkios calls himself "a disciple of the Holy
Shepherd who pastures his flocks of sheep in the mountains and in the plains,"
thus identifying himself as a Christian.[27] In those days the psalmist's phrase
"The Lord is my shepherd" must have been familiar to all believers. Recently,
the Catholic Church has rediscovered the ancient icon of the Good Shepherd
and placed it on the title page of its catechism (fig. 37).

Transfunctional and exercising all three functions, Christ appears as the truly
universal divine man. Christ the Good Shepherd, the Warrior, and the Judge parallels the Hebrew God, Lord of the three gifts of wellbeing, victory, and wisdom.

Mystical Ascent as a Key for Understanding the Historical Jesus

The story of the temptation of Jesus, which we have discussed above, provides much insight into the thought of the early Christians for whom their lord was a divine being. But neither the tale itself as told in the New Testament nor our Dumézilian interpretation can shed much light on the fundamental question of how this tradition could originate in the first place. How can we account for the fact that, in addition to the one God of Jewish belief, a second divine being could establish itself in a new popular movement? To answer this question, we must come back to a subject dealt with in an earlier chapter—the subject of the heavenly ascent (see above, chapter 3).

Within that variety of Judaism to which Jesus belonged and in which Christianity originated, heavenly journeys and the transformation of some of those who traveled were not forgotten. Instead, the tradition of the ascent to the divine throne actually flourished in the first century C.E. There is evidence of both kinds of heavenly journey that we have distinguished: the "major" ascent that involved the ascending mystic's transformation into a divine being, and the "minor" one that honored a prophet or seer by making him experience God's dazzling splendor. The celestial ascents reported by Paul[28] and John of Patmos belong to the "minor" variety, for they report only of things heard and seen but include no reference to the visionary's dramatic transformation. The book of Revelation is remarkable for its description of what John—and other visionaries—saw: "There in heaven stood a throne, with one seated on the throne. And the one seated there looks like jasper and carnelian, and around the throne is a rainbow that looks like an emerald" (Rev 4:2–3). A poem found in Qumran can be understood as referring to the "major" heavenly journey of the Essene brotherhood's founder. It is with pride that this anonymous priest speaks of himself:

> None can compare to my glory;
> none has been exalted save myself,
> and none can oppose me.
> I sit on high, exalted in heaven,
> and none surround me.
> I am reckoned with the angels,
> my dwelling is in the holy council.[29]

"Major" heavenly journeys of the same kind—i.e. ascents during which the visionary is invested with special divine powers—may be postulated for several religious leaders of the same period; an example is Simon the Magician whom his followers called "the power of God that is called the Great" (Acts 8:10). Recent scholarship has found good reasons for placing Jesus among those who had the same kind of transforming mystical experience.[30] Like the founder of the Qumran fraternity, Jesus seems to have practiced the mystical ascent to the divine throne and to have experienced transformation into a divine being. If this notion is granted, then Jesus' claims about himself find a natural explanation, as does the early Christian community's belief in Jesus Christ as a divine being to be placed and worshiped next to God.

Several New Testament traditions can be understood without difficulty in terms of the hypothesis of Jesus the mystic who ascends to heaven. A first stage of the mystical journey can be discerned in the report on Jesus' baptism. When he was baptized by John the Baptist, Jesus saw heaven open and heard God call him his beloved son.[31] This event can be understood as the initial vision that invites and enables the elected one to undertake the heavenly journey. Not unlikely, John the Baptist had prepared his disciple for this event. As an ascetic he must have been familiar with mystical experience and was able to instruct others.

While the tradition of the baptism of Jesus may reflect the early mystical experiences made in the circle of John the Baptist, the gospel of John supplies evidence of Jesus as an accomplished heavenly ascender who has reached the highest stage of meeting God and being transformed. As Jan Bühner has demonstrated, the gospel of John presupposes a tradition according to which Jesus' heavenly ascension did not take place at the end (after his death), but at the beginning of his activity; although obscured in the present text, it can nevertheless still be discerned.[32] During his mystical ascent, Jesus must have received his heavenly initiation. The statement that "no one has ever seen God. It is God the only Son, who is close to the Father's heart, who has made him known" can be explained in terms of a "major" heavenly journey (John 1:18). The same is true of the following passage: "No one [greater] has ascended into heaven than the one who descended from heaven, the Son of Man" (John 3:13).[33] Bühner's interpretation receives support from the gospel of Philip: "Those who say that the Lord first died and then rose up are in error; for he rose up first and then died."[34]

The mystical practice of Jesus does not consist only of the master's own, exclusive experience of the ascent to the heavenly throne. Rather, there seems to have been a communal experience under the master's guidance and instruction. An echo of this can be found in the account of Jesus' transfiguration or transformation into a being permeated by divine light. This happened on an isolated hillside in the presence of specially selected disciples, joined by saints who appeared from heaven—Moses and Elijah.[35] While some commentators dismiss this story as a legend without historical background, others consider the transfiguration's essential historicity as being compatible with phenomena known from the history of religions.[36] What the disciples saw was no doubt due to a hallucination, experienced in a state of hypnotic trance. As a matter of fact, the biblical story itself refers to the "sleeping" of the disciples with whom Jesus shared the experience.[37] We may get a better understanding of this tradition if we suppose that Jesus, with the inner circle of his disciples, actually practiced theurgical rituals of some kind. He may have taught them how to ascend to heaven and have actually taken them up to the third heaven, i.e. paradise, abode of the righteous among the dead. "Jesus in his lifetime believed he had ascended into the heavens, told his most intimate disciples of his experiences, and . . . induced similar hallucinations in some of them."[38]

The plausible assumption that Jesus was a practicing mystic who could initiate others into the secrets of the heavenly ascent accounts well for the fact that he could be considered a divine being. But at this point a question seems unavoidable: Is the divine status of Jesus compatible with monotheism—the Jewish belief in a single deity?

As a matter of fact, in the early history of Judaism and even later, strict monotheism did not succeed in establishing itself completely. Besides the pure monotheism another tradition existed, one indebted to Israel's premonotheistic religion. Particularly striking, and of great importance for the history of religions, is its belief in *two* deities, so that we may refer to it as ditheism. According to this tradition, the Most High appoints a second god, delegating to him certain tasks or even the complete authority over all creation (see above, fig. 3, p. 30).[39] Without a flourishing Jewish mythology of two deities, one called the Most High and the other called Yahweh, Wisdom, or the Prince of Angels, Christianity with its belief in "one God, the Father, and one Lord, Jesus Christ" (1 Cor 8:6) would not have been able to develop and to attract first Jews and then Gentiles. The Christian perception of the Hebrew God adds another chapter to the canonical story of this God by giving it not one, but two heroes: the God Most High and his son, Jesus Christ. Although overshadowed by monotheism, the belief in two deities rather than one God is deeply rooted in Hebrew tradition.

Appendix I
The Names of the Hebrew God

Habet ferme haec lingua 10 nomina dei et plura nomina, quibus complectuntur opera dei, auff deutsch non reddi.[1]

This language has almost ten names of God and several names which refer to the works of God—which cannot be rendered in German.

Martin Luther

When the prophet Jonah, on a ship in the Mediterranean, was asked by his fellow travelers who he was, he answered: "I am a Hebrew. I worship the Lord, the God of heaven, who made the sea and the dry land" (Jonah 1:9). From this passage it is clear that the Hebrews called their god "the Lord," and from other passages it is equally obvious that they sometimes referred to him, quite simply, as "God." This is what we find in the most common English translations of the Old Testament. On closer inspection, two discoveries suggest a more complex picture. First, both "the Lord" and "God" conceal more than one underlying Hebrew term—in the case of "the Lord," it is Yahweh and Adonai, in the case of "God" we find Elohim, El, or Eloah. Second, there are actually more divine names than the two (Lord, God) or the five (Yahweh, Adonai, Elohim, El, Eloah) we have just mentioned—Shaddai, for instance, a name generally rendered as "the Almighty." All of these names are meant to refer to the same deity—the monotheistic God. The present appendix is designed to provide a basic understanding of the divine names as they appear in the biblical text (in Hebrew and Aramaic) as well as in commonly used English translations.

As can be imagined, scholarship has expended a great deal of energy on elucidating the divine names. While not all of the problems have been solved, there is unanimity on a number of issues, some of which will be explained in what follows.

The multiplicity of divine names often serves the poetic purpose of variation, for Hebrew poetry likes repetition with variation. It is through the accumulation of similar names and expressions that Hebrew rhetoric seeks to impress. The way in which the divine names function in poetic texts can best be illustrated from the book of Psalms:

> It is for you, O Yahweh, that I wait,
> it is you, O Adonai, my God [*elohim*], who will answer.
> (Ps 38:15/Hebr. 38:16)

These two lines use three words for the Hebrew God: "Yahweh," the Hebrew God's proper name, is placed first. The second line uses "Adonai" as an alternative, for variation ranks as an important poetic device. "Elohim," the third designation, is not actually a divine name, but the generic word for "god." In other contexts, however, it can be employed as a name for the Hebrew God.

A similar accumulation of divine names can be found in the following introduction to a prophetic oracle:

> The oracle of Balaam son of Beor . . .
> the oracle of the one who hears the words of God [El],
> and knows the knowledge of the Most High [Elyon],
> who sees the vision of Shaddai. (Num 24:15–16)

Here the biblical poet again exploits the multiplicity of divine names for the sake of poetic variation. He appears to use two divine names: El Elyon and Shaddai. The first of these he "breaks up," distributing it over two parallel lines. Shaddai, though traditionally—and incorrectly—rendered as "the Almighty," is another name of the Hebrew God (see the glossary below). It would be wrong, however, to see the poetic device of parallelism merely as a means of varying expression; instead, it aims at producing a cumulative effect: repetition seeks to underline and to impress. The following passage may serve as an example:

> For your Maker is your husband,
> Yahweh *tseva'ot* is his name;
> the Holy One of Israel is your Redeemer,
> the God of the whole earth he is called. (Isa 54:5)

God is called Maker and Redeemer, and the two traditional names "Yahweh *tseva'ot*" and "the Holy One of Israel" are supplemented by a newly coined one: "God of the whole earth." Similar accumulations also occur outside of poetry; an example listing three divine names can be quoted from Isaiah: "Therefore says the Sovereign [Adon], Yahweh *tseva'ot*, the Mighty One of Israel" (Isa 1:24). Here the writer uses two divine names, each of which is a paired expression—"Yahweh *tseva'ot*" and "the Mighty One of Israel"; moreover, the first pair is enlarged by the added title of "the Sovereign" (Adon). As a final example, the following passage may be quoted: "Swear by Yahweh, the God of heaven and earth" (Gen 24:3). The accumulation of divine names fits solemn occasions and creates a numinous atmosphere of majesty and awe.

A close reading of the biblical text suggests that certain names serve to characterize God in a specific way. Each of the various divine names may carry a specific connotation. Although this connotation is not always clear, it can be recognized or tentatively established in some cases. Thus the book of Job's hero venerates *Shaddai* as his personal god; this god's name means "god of the uncultivated fields" and characterizes the Lord of the Animals (see above, chapter 11). The divine name *Yahweh* often implies a specific reference to Israel, to Moses and the exodus, whereas *Elohim* carries a more general meaning—he is the Creator and the universal god, ruler of all creation. Thus the account of creation in the first chapter of Genesis uses the divine name Elohim, for it deals with the establishment of the entire universe. By contrast, the story of Moses, the exodus from Egypt, and the revelation of the law at Mount Sinai with its focus on Israel are dominated by the name Yahweh. A mediating position is taken by the myth of Adam and Eve and paradise lost (Gen 2–3), for it uses the combined form of the divine name—"*Yahweh Elohim.*" With the name Elohim, the narrator highlights the creation of all humankind; with the added name of Yahweh, a more specifically Israelite message comes into view, one that seems to equate the expulsion from paradise with the deportation of the Judeans out of Palestine in the sixth century B.C.E. The temperaments of the two deities also differ: whereas Yahweh appears to be a stern, austere figure, prone to anger and meting out punishment, Elohim seems to be an intrinsically kindly god (just like El Shaddai). It should be clear, however, that this kind of distinction between Yahweh and Elohim does not operate in all biblical texts.

One biblical tradition accounts for the multiplicity of divine names by suggesting a history of the use of these names. The passage can be found in the book of Exodus: "God [Elohim] also spoke to Moses and said to him: 'I am Yahweh. I appeared to Abraham, Isaac and Jacob as El Shaddai, but by my name Yahweh I did not make myself known to them'" (Exod 6:2–3). Here a distinction is made between the earlier period of Israel's ancestors of the book of Genesis and the later time of Moses in the book of Exodus. Whereas the earlier period uses the divine name El Shaddai, traditionally (though without linguistic or historical warrant) translated as "God Almighty," the later period prefers Yahweh. Obviously, the biblical narrator wanted to put order into the use of the divine names, and so decided that there was an earlier and a later name. Modern historians of religion generally reject the idea of two periods using two different divine names and suggest more complex reasons for the presence of El Shaddai and Yahweh. Nevertheless, the passage is interesting in that it sees the presence of more than one divine name as something to be accounted for. Moreover, the passage seems to be aware of the difference between the religions and spiritualities underlying the books of Genesis and Exodus. In Genesis, El Shaddai is a kindly figure who promises land and offspring; in Exodus, Yahweh liberates Israel from Egyptian servitude and reveals his law. Incidentally, the introduction of the divine name Yahweh through Moses, as explained in the passage from Exodus, is contradicted by a statement in Genesis, which explains that the name of Yahweh was introduced much earlier—during one of the earliest generations of human existence (Gen 4:26).

The story of the biblical names is complicated by the fact that within the biblical era the name Yahweh came to be considered a particularly sacred name and therefore should be used either with caution or not at all. Originally, the name Yahweh was an ordinary divine name like all the other names of ancient Near Eastern deities; when and by whom a sacred taboo was placed on it to restrict its pronunciation remains unknown. In modern Judaism, the name Yahweh is not spoken. When in the second century B.C.E. the Pentateuch was translated from Hebrew into Greek, the divine name Yahweh was not left as a proper name in the text; instead, it was replaced by *kyrios*, the Greek word for "the Lord." The Greek translator did not have to invent this alternative name, since Adonai, another common biblical designation for God, also means "the Lord" and constituted a convenient substitute. Presumably, when scriptural passages were read in public in the ancient synagogue, the reader replaced Yahweh by Adonai or some other word, and it must be from such a practice that the Greek translator took the idea. Ever since the earliest times Bible translators have followed the tradition of substituting Yahweh by another term. In the twentieth century, James Moffatt used "the Eternal" as a substitute for Yahweh in his translation, echoing a traditional rendering used by German and French Jews. Most translations prefer "the Lord." To distinguish between Adonai and Yahweh, some editions use small capital letters according to the following rule: Adonai = the Lord, Yahweh = the LORD.

Some biblical texts show evidence of ancient scribal or editorial tampering: certain divine names have been replaced by others. The scribes working in the biblical period were the first to be confronted with the problem of the divine names. Some felt a preference for Yahweh and edited their texts accordingly; others thought that the use of Elohim was more appropriate—and not only in order to avoid the sacred name Yahweh, but also to convey a more universal message. It seems that at an early stage of textual transmission the name Yahweh was deleted from Psalms 42–83 and replaced by Elohim. The opposite was frequently done in the book of Proverbs, from which "Elohim" was almost completely eliminated.[2] The scribes who tended to introduce the name of Yahweh apparently wanted to give the text more of an Israelite flavor.

Some of the divine names seem originally to have referred to gods other than the Hebrew God. They permit a glimpse of Israel's originally polytheistic religion. In certain biblical texts, the use of more than one divine name can be seen as revealing an earlier, premonotheistic level of development. This is the case with one passage in the book of Deuteronomy (Deut 32:8–9, discussed above, chapter 4). Here "the Most High" (Elyon) figures along with "Yahweh," and the two appear to belong to different levels within a polytheistic pantheon: Elyon occupies the superior rank, while Yahweh holds the inferior position. Monotheism has identified the two divine figures, making Yahweh just another name of the Most High; in this way, a minor figure of the pantheon acquired the highest rank by being identified with the actual high god. Only a small number of the divine names listed in the glossary below seem to have designated, in polytheistic times, the actual high god; good candidates for this tentative interpretation are El, Elohim, El Elyon, Ancient of Days, and God of Heaven. Names such as El Shaddai, Yahweh, God of the Fathers (Ancestors), Eloah, and the Holy One of Israel are clearly the names of former lower-rank deities. Some of the divine names also reflect new developments within monotheism. This is the case with Yahweh Elohim and Adonai Yahweh, names that were presumably never given to any deity other than the monotheistic God of Israel (or, if we refer to the time after 586 B.C.E., early Judaism).

Some Names of the Hebrew God

For the following glossary, the most frequently occurring and, among the less frequently occurring, the most interesting names, epithets, and attributes of the Hebrew God have been selected. All the expressions listed can be found either in the Hebrew Bible or in major English translations such as the King James Version (KJV, also called the Authorized Version, 1611) and the New Revised Standard Version (NRSV, 1989). The passages indicated are meant as examples; complete listings of relevant passages are not given.

Adonai. *Adon* in Hebrew means "lord." The form *Adonai* can be translated either as "my lord" or simply as "lord" (and linguists offer various explanations for the untranslated element "ai"). Used 132 times in the Bible, the designation is traditionally rendered as "Lord." "The sanctuary, O Lord [Adonai], that your hands have established" (Exod 15:17, NRSV). This passage can also be rendered differently: "The sanctuary, my Lord [Adonai], which your hands have established."[3] (The NRSV sometimes has the spelling "LORD," in small capital letters, for Adonai; thus Exod 15:17; Ps 38:5. But this is misleading, for it suggests that the underlying Hebrew term is Yahweh, which is not the case.)

Adonai Yahweh. The expression can be translated as "Lord Yahweh." Most of the 310 occurrences appear in the prophetic literature. "Thus says Adonai Yahweh" often introduces prophetic speech (Amos 3:11; Ezek 2:4). KJV and NRSV render the expression as "Lord GOD" (avoiding the awkward "Lord LORD").

Almighty, The. The Greek Old Testament and the New Testament (Rev 1:8) occasionally use *pantokratôr*—"the Almighty"—as a divine name or epithet. Modern English translations also use it to render the Hebrew *Shaddai*; in doing so they follow the Greek Bible. "Shall a faultfinder contend with the Almighty [Shaddai]?" (Job 40:2, NRSV). Contemporary exegesis tends to reject this translation and prefers to leave Shaddai untranslated.

Ancient of Days, The. This is how the KJV renders a divine name that is only attested once in the book of Daniel (Dan 7:9). The deity thus designated is presumably El Elyon.

Ancient One, An. Thus the NRSV for "the Ancient of Days."

Ehyeh. This name of obscure meaning is attested only twice (Exod 3:14; Hos 1:9). The book of Exodus includes the following dialogue between Moses and the God of Israel: "But Moses said to God [Elohim], 'If I come to the Israelites and say to them, The God [Elohim] of your ancestors has sent me to you, and they ask me, What is his name? what shall I say to them?' God [Elohim] said to Moses, 'I AM [Ehyeh] WHO I AM.' He said further: 'Thus you shall say to the Israelites: I AM [Ehyeh] has sent me to you'" (Exod 3:13–14, NRSV). Here the narrator refers to the deity as Elohim; it is understood that this is not an actual name but only a general description. God gives his name as Ehyeh. This Hebrew word can be rendered "I am," but is apparently also used as a divine name. The meaning of God's answer is obscure, so that commentators are still coming up with new explanations. The uncertainty of the expression is evident from the alternative renderings suggested by the New Revised Standard Version: "I am what I am" and "I will be what I will be." At any rate, it is clear that the passage uses three divine names: Elohim (God), the God [*elohim*] of the Ancestors, and Ehyeh.

El. Though not as often attested as Elohim, this is another standard Hebrew term for "god" and (Israel's monotheistic) "God." Example: "I am God [El] and there is no other" (Isa 45:22). In some Genesis texts, El may be, or reflect, the name of the Canaanite high god "El" (Gen 14:18–22; 33:20; 46:3; 49:25), but this is not certain.

El Elohê Yisra'el. "El the God of Israel" (Gen 33:20). This expression is found only once in the Bible as the name given to a sanctuary. KJV and NRSV leave it untranslated: "El-Elohe-Israel." See also "Elohê Yisra'el" and "El."

El Elyon. "The most high God" (KJV) or "God Most High" (NRSV) figures only in one passage of the book of Genesis and is identified with Yahweh (Gen 14:18–22). Originally, this deity must have been different from Yahweh, a god otherwise known as the Canaanite high god "El." The poetic parallelism of "El" and "Elyon" in the lines "the oracle of the one who hears the words of El,/and knows the knowledge of Elyon" (Num 24:16) also reflects the divine name El Elyon.

El Shaddai. Rare, but original form of the Hebrew name of the Lord of the Animals, with the meaning "god of the (uncultivated) fields" (see above, chapter 11). Contemporary scholarship rejects the traditional rendering "the Almighty," which is still retained by the NRSV. More common is the abbreviated form "Shaddai," frequently used in the book of Job (Job 40:2). "Yahweh appeared to Abram, and said to him, 'I am El Shaddai'" (Gen 17:1).

Eloah. Rare outside of the book of Job, this word means "God" (Job 3:4). Linguistically, it represents the singular of Elohim.

Elohê Yisra'el. The expression "the God of Israel" is occasionally used to define Yahweh (2 Sam 23:3; Isa 45:3).

Elohim. Used ca. 2,600 times, this is a stock term in the Bible's religious vocabulary. Three meanings can be distinguished. First, it may mean "gods, deities" in the plural. "You shall have no other gods [*elohim*] before me" (Deut 5:7). Second, when worshipers know only one deity or direct their attention to this deity, it means "the deity, a god, the god"—in the singular. "You cannot worship Yahweh, for he is a holy god [*elohim*]" (Josh 24:19). Third, where only one deity is recognized, it means simply "God," used as a personal name. "In the beginning, God [Elohim] created the heavens and the earth" (Gen 1:1).

Elohim of Heaven. See "God of Heaven."

Elyon. This Hebrew word means "upper"; as a divine name it is a short form of "El Elyon." Translations give "most High" (Deut 32:8, KJV) or "Most High" (NRSV). Although originally different from Yahweh, some texts explicitly identify the two; in Psalms we read: "Yahweh, the Most High [Elyon]" (Ps 7:17/Hebr. 7:18; 47:2). See "El Elyon."

Eternal, The. This rendition of "Yahweh" has a Christian and a Jewish story. On the Christian side, it was introduced by the reformer John Calvin (1509–64) in his later years, and was subsequently used in the French Bible of Geneva (1588), by the author Matthew Arnold (1822–88), and in the English Bible of James Moffatt (1870–1944). The first Jewish author to use it was the German philosopher and Bible translator Moses Mendelssohn (1729–86), and later it found its way into Jewish vernacular Bibles in French (1899) and German (the translation made under the direction of Leopold Zunz, 1794–1886).

God. The term functions in two ways: as a generic term (in expressions such as "the God [*elohim*] of your fathers" (Exod 3:13), or "he is a holy god [*elohim*]" (Josh 24:19)) and as a proper name designating the one God of monotheism. Conventionally, "God" is always spelled with a capital letter when Israel's deity is meant, whereas "god," without a capital letter, refers to a non-Israelite, polytheistic deity. The most common underlying Hebrew word is Elohim, but one can also find Eloah, El, and, though rarely, Yahweh (on the matter of Yahweh generally printed in small capital letters as GOD, see "Adonai Yahweh").

God of Abraham, God of Isaac, and God of Jacob. This solemn expression, which lists a series of ancestors, occurs only in Exod 3:6, 15; 4:5. The word for God is *elohim*. For the meaning, see "God of the Father(s)."

God Almighty. The traditional translation of "El Shaddai" (Exod 6:3, KJV, NRSV). Contemporary scholarship prefers to leave the name untranslated or to render it as "God of the (uncultivated) fields." See "Almighty."

God of the Ancestors, The. Used by the New Revised Standard Version (Exod 3:15) for "God of the Fathers."

God of the Father(s), The. In Genesis and Exodus, one repeatedly finds expressions such as "the God [*elohim*] of my father" (Gen 31:5, with the father being Isaac; Exod 15:2, without specific reference to a name) and "the God [*elohim*] of their fathers" (Exod 4:5, with the fathers being Abraham, Isaac, and Jacob). The reference is to the "personal god" who creates and protects the individual, and whose veneration is transmitted within the family (see above, chapter 14).

God of Heaven. The expressions "Yahweh, the God [*elohim*] of Heaven" (Ezra 1:2) or simply "God of Heaven" (Neh 1:4) tend to occur in "late" (post-586 B.C.E.) biblical texts. They highlight universal sovereignty and rulership, as is evident from the following expanded expressions: "Yahweh, the God of heaven and earth" (Gen 24:3); "Yahweh, the God of heaven, who made the sea and the dry land" (Jonah 1:9).

God of the Hebrews. This epithet of Yahweh is used only in the Exodus narrative. "The God [*elohim*] of the Hebrews has revealed himself to us" (Exod 5:3).

God of Israel, The. See "Elohê Yisra'el."

God Most High. See El Elyon.

Holy One of Israel, The. Most occurrences are in Isaiah. "They have despised the Holy One of Israel" (Isa 1:4). Since the "holy ones" are angels or subordinate deities of the polytheistic pantheon, the Isaianic expression reflects polytheism: the deity thus designated is one of the many "holy ones."

Jehovah. This reading of YHWH appears first among Christian scholars of the late Middle Ages. It is occasionally used for "Yahweh" in the KJV (Exod 6:3), but is now considered a misreading of YHWH (the correct consonants mixed with the vowels of the Hebrew word *Adonai*). Abandoned by contemporary scholarship; see "Yahweh" and "YHWH." In English poetry, the name "Jehovah" is well established: "Great are Thy works, Jehovah, infinite Thy power" (John Milton, *Paradise Lost* 7: 602–3).

Kyrios. Greek for "lord." This is how the ancient Greek version of the Hebrew Bible renders the divine names "Yahweh" and "Adonai." In the New Testament, *kyrios* is also used as a title for Jesus: "Jesus Christ, our *kyrios*" (Rom 1:4).

Lord. English equivalent of "Yahweh" and "Adonai" as well as of Greek "*kyrios.*" Following a suggestion first made by William Tyndale in 1530,

some Bibles print LORD in small capital letters to indicate that the underlying Hebrew is Yahweh rather than Adonai. The rule is Yahweh = LORD and
Adonai = Lord. "The LORD [Yahweh] appeared to him" (Gen 18:1). "Let me
take it upon myself to speak to the Lord (Adonai), I who am but dust and
ashes" (Gen 18:27).

Lord God. One of two different Hebrew expressions may underlie this rendering: Yahweh Elohim and Adonai Yahweh. The expression "Yahweh
Elohim" is rare and possibly meant to identify Elohim (the Creator) with
Yahweh (God of Israel). "In the day the LORD God [Yahweh Elohim] made
the earth . . ." (Gen 2:4, NRSV). "You shall say to them, Thus says the Lord
GOD [Adonai Yahweh]" (Ezek 2:4). Note the difference between Lord GOD
and LORD God; it is always the equivalent of the divine name Yahweh that is
written with small capital letters.

Lord of Hosts. See "Yahweh *tseva'ot.*"

Lord of Sabaoth. This expression is used twice in the New Testament (Rom
9:29; Jas 5:4, KJV). For the meaning, see "Yahweh *tseva'ot.*"

Most High. See "Elyon" and "El Elyon."

Shaddai. Abbreviated form of "El Shaddai."

Yah. This short form of Yahu or Yahweh is occasionally used as an independent name ("I will sing to Yah" [Exod 15:2]), but most often in the formu-
laic "hallelujah," which means "praise Yah" (Ps 146:1; KJV, NRSV: "praise
the LORD") and has become a word used in the Christian liturgy, for it is mentioned in the book of Revelation (Rev 19:1).

Yahu. An alternative spelling and pronunciation of Yahweh, found on an ostra-
con of Kuntillet Ajrud (YHW, ca. 800 B.C.E.) and in the documents written
by Aramaic-speaking fifth-century B.C.E. Jews living in Elephantine in Egypt
(YHW, YHH). The form "Yahu" also seems to underlie biblical names such
as Yeho-natan (Jonathan: Judg 18:30) and Yesha-yahu (the prophet Isaiah).
Most scholars take Yahu to be a short form of Yahweh, but the possibility
that it is actually an earlier form of the divine name cannot be ruled out
(L. Delekat).

Yahweh. More than 6,700 times the Hebrew God is called "Yahweh" in the
Bible, but this is concealed from the modern reader by the fact that virtually
all standard translations follow Jewish custom in rendering it as "the Lord"
(often printed as LORD) or "the Eternal." The only passage in which some
modern versions retain "Yahweh" (or, in the KJV, "Jehovah") is that in which
God reveals this name to Moses (Exod 6:2). Right from the time of early
Judaism, Jews have treated the name of their God with great reverence.[4] The
essential idea was to restrict its use to the two central institutions that defined
Jewish identity: the sacred scriptures and the temple of Jerusalem. In writing,
the name was used primarily in biblical manuscripts and, later, in the print-
ing of biblical texts. The name was declared too sacred to be spoken fre-

quently, and so its use was restricted to priests during worship at the Jerusalem temple; after the Romans had destroyed the temple in 70 C.E., Jews ceased to speak this name altogether. Even the original pronunciation of the name is now lost, and "Yahweh" represents no more than a modern conjecture based on linguistic considerations, first suggested by Gilbert Génébrard (1537–97), professor of Hebrew at the Collège Royal in Paris (today's prestigious Collège de France). We do not know when the divine name Yahweh was introduced into Hebrew religion. The name appears in the Moabite inscription of King Mesha (ca. 850–830 B.C.E.), the Khirbet el-Qôm burial inscription (eighth century B.C.E.), and the Kuntillet Ajrud inscriptions (ca. 800 B.C.E.). Arguing that biblical names generally have a discernible meaning, scholars have often tried to find that of Yahweh. There are two methods for establishing this meaning. The first is etymology, i.e. the idea that "Yahweh" is derived from a verb the meaning of which can be found; however, none of the scholarly suggestions—such as "He Is" (which can be said of any deity), "He Causes to Be" (said of the Creator), or "he blows" (a reference to the storm-god)—has won general acceptance. The second, more promising method involves analyzing the context in which the name occurs. Consider the following passage: "I am going to teach them my power and my might, and they shall know that my name is Yahweh" (Jer 16:21). Here "Yahweh" clearly carries the connotation "the Mighty One," and this meaning fits indeed many biblical texts (Exod 7:5; 1 Kgs 20:13, etc.). "The Mighty One" is what the ancients associated with the name, and this is why they rendered it, in Greek, as "*ho kyrios*" = "the Lord." The close association between "Yahweh" and "the Mighty One, the Lord" can be seen as reflecting the ancient Semitic trend of substituting divine names by words that signify "lord"; thus the weather-god, whose proper name is Hadad or Adad, is generally called Baal ("Lord"), and Marduk, the Babylonian state god, is known as Bêl ("Lord"). Appropriately, Yahweh can also be called "Adonai Yahweh," an expression that translates as "Lord Yahweh."

Yahweh Elohim. See "Lord God".

Yahweh tseva'ot. "Holy, holy, holy is Yahweh *tseva'ot*" (Isa 6:3), generally rendered as "Holy, holy, holy is the LORD of hosts" (KJV, NRSV). Yahweh *tseva'ot* (206 times in the Old Testament) is a short form of "Yahweh *elohê tseva'ot*" (Ps 89:8/Hebr. 89:9), i.e. "Yahweh, god of *tseva'ot*" (thirty-six times), with the *tseva'ot* being the members of the heavenly council and possibly also the numerous angelic servants who surround Yahweh as he sits on his heavenly throne governing his people (as described in Ps 89:5–8/Hebr. 89:6–9 and Isa 14:24–27).

YHWH. In ancient times, the Hebrew scribes wrote only consonants and no vowels, and so "Yahweh" was written with the four letters "YHWH" (sometimes referred to as the tetragrammaton or the tetragram, the four-letter word). YHWH is used as the philological transcription of Yahweh. Some scholars follow Jewish tradition and refrain from pronouncing the divine name out of religious respect and so prefer to write "YHWH" rather than "Yahweh."

Appendix II
The Ancient Near East, ca. 3400–500 B.C.E.:
A Brief Guide to Its Cultural History

For the benefit of the nonspecialist, a few names, dates, and facts of cultural history are here listed and explained. Only items mentioned in and immediately relevant to the present book have been included. All dates are B.C.E. Political dates before ca. 1500 are particularly conjectural and subject to scholarly controversy. Rarely can literary works be dated with any amount of accuracy, for they were transmitted and revised over long periods of time and often only "late," Iron Age versions of Bronze Age texts are known.

Nineteenth-century scholarship has devised an easy system for dividing the past into segments based on technological factors. Stone, bronze, and iron followed each other as the basis of technology. This progression was adopted as a historical classification system by Christian Jürgensen Thomsen in the 1820s; working in the Danish National Museum of Copenhagen, he used the idea as the basis for arranging its collections of ancient artifacts. In the Near East, the Bronze Age sets in around 3400 B.C.E., the Iron Age ca. 1200 B.C.E. This three-age system has all the weaknesses and advantages of another three-age system familiar to us: antiquity, Middle Ages, and modern times. While specialists insist that three-age systems obscure a certain amount of continuity between the various periods and often need subdivisions, these classifications do provide a means of orientation and help us to date artifacts.

Chart of elementary periodization

Stone Age	
Bronze Age	3400 B.C.E.
Iron Age	1200 B.C.E.
Antiquity	500 B.C.E.
Middle Ages	800 C.E.
Modern Times	1500 C.E.

As for the civilizations of the biblical world, we can broadly distinguish between those of the Bronze Age (ca. 3400–1200) and those of the Iron Age (ca. 1200–500). The Bronze Age saw the emergence of cities, states, early empires, and, above all, of intellectual activity, culminating in the creation first of writing and eventually of literature. Largely dependent upon the Bronze Age in its intellectual culture, the Iron Age witnessed the last flourishing of the ancient

Near Eastern civilizations and is the classic period of biblical (Old Testament) history. So a springtime of cultural invention and extraordinary creativity was followed by a more quiet harvest time.

A Springtime of Creativity: The Bronze Age

The term Bronze Age, applied to the civilizations here considered, is actually misleading, for it is not bronze objects (which did exist) but the invention of writing that epitomizes the achievements of this period. Traditionally, Bronze Age bureaucrats are referred to as "scribes" because literacy was their most conspicuous qualification. We owe to them the following cultural accomplishments:

— The development of usable systems of writing, including, eventually, the alphabet.
— The institution of schools for the training of "scribes," i.e. future bureaucrats, senior clerks, and high-ranking administrators.
— The transmission of specialized knowledge in intellectually sophisticated disciplines such as architecture and time-reckoning (which includes astronomy).
— The setting-up of a bureaucracy with a written memory—i.e. the founding of state archives for the storage of letters, contracts, directories, codes of law, and the like. Record-keeping came to be one of the most important tasks of the scribes.
— The creation of an impressive literature consisting of school exercise texts, collections of ritual texts, prayers, omens, and mythological and historical narratives.

In what follows, the most important cultural areas and centers are mentioned.

Egypt, in the land of the Nile, boasted a powerful Bronze Age culture, the most visible traces of which remain the pyramids. King Narmer (ca. 3050) inaugurated kingship as a permanent institution. Around 3000, hieroglyphic writing was invented. Thutmose III (1490–1436) is noteworthy for permanently establishing political control over Palestine and Syria, Amenophis IV (also known as Akhenaten, 1364–1347) for his short-lived promotion of the monotheistic worship of the sun-god, Aten. A victory poem of King Merneptah lists "Israel" among the peoples defeated in a military campaign of ca. 1208, but this is the period in which Egypt lost control over Syria and Palestine. Israel's sojourn and eventual flight out of Egypt (the "exodus") is never mentioned in Egyptian sources, and is today considered by most critics as a legend, with some possible roots in the collapse of Egypt as an empire, ca. 1200. The most famous piece of literature Egyptian scribes produced is the Tale of Sinuhe (ca. 1950), a kind of biographical adventure novella. It tells of the life of a high-ranking bureaucrat who left Egypt because of political difficulties, made a career among the tribes of Palestine, and returned to his homeland in old age. Inserted into the narrative is the letter by which the king of Egypt calls his former employee back, followed by Sinuhe's overjoyed reply; these letters highlight the scribal rather than popular background of the work. Of Egypt's poetry Akhenaten's enthusiastic hymns to the sun-god deserve to be singled out. The literature that tells us most about Egyptian ideals (from the point of view of the scribal elite) consists of books of ethical instruction; among these well-phrased epigrammatic writings are the Teaching for King Merikare (after 1900), the Instruction of Kheti (1900–1800), and the Instruction of Amenemope (twelfth century, famous for its personal piety and its later reception by Israelite scribes).

Western Asia. Unlike Egypt, Western Asia remained politically fragmented throughout the Bronze Age and never achieved political unity, for there was no central power. The general picture is one of contentious tribes interspersed with city-states led by dynasties of princes. Major cities include Lagash and Ur in southern, Akkad and Babylon in central, and Ashur and Mari in northern Mesopotamia. Mention must also be made of Hattusa in central Anatolia (Asia Minor) and Ugarit in Syria. Some of these city-states were intent on and succeeded in enlarging their territory so as to dominate the surrounding territory and sometimes even a whole empire. Particularly successful empire-builders were, in chronological order: the Semitic king Naram-Sin of Akkad (2260–2223), the Sumerian king Shulgi of Ur (2094–2047), and the Semitic kings Shamshi-Adad I of Ashur (1813–1781), Hammurabi of Babylon (1792–1750), and Ashur-uballit I of Ashur (1365–1245). In what follows, we will comment briefly on the cultural contributions made by some of these city-state civilizations.

Sumer. Sumerian culture flourished in southern Mesopotamia between 3200 and 2000. The Sumerians, a non-Semitic people with possible links to India, can be credited with the invention of cuneiform writing that spread to the Semites and proved to be the very foundation of Bronze Age culture throughout the Near East. Among the rulers of Sumerian cities stand out Eanatum of Lagash (ca. 2400), Gudea of Lagash (twenty-second century), and Shulgi of Ur (2094–2047). A noteworthy literature extolls these kings and their military achievements. The Sumerian language became part of the curriculum of the Babylonian scribes.

Babylonia. Between 1800 and the end of the first millennium, Babylonia was the foremost cultural force in Western Asia. Operating from the city of Babel (the Babylon of the Greeks) in central Mesopotamia, King Hammurabi (1792–1750) founded the Babylonian Empire which included most of

Mesopotamia. Even before the time of Hammurabi, Assyria, Babylonia's neighbor in northern Mesopotamia, had emerged as another superpower in the Near East, rivaling Babylonia and limiting its political influence. Culturally, however, Babylonia's leadership remained unchallenged; for many centuries, it functioned as the brain of Western Asia. Among the rich literature produced by Babylonian scribes, two works stand out as exemplary: Hammurabi's law code (ca. 1750) for its sophistication in legal matters, and the Epic of Gilgamesh for its unique narrative and poetic quality. The Epic of Gilgamesh, with the standard version dating from ca. 1200, relates the adventures of the eponymous hero, who with his friend kills a dangerous giant living in the mountains. Upon the death of his friend, Gilgamesh roams the earth in futile search of his lost companion; beyond the waters that surround the earth he meets a man who has never died because the gods have admitted him to their world. This man is the Mesopotamian equivalent of the biblical Noah—the hero who survived the deluge. Much insight into the religious mentality of the Babylonians comes from the Atrahasis Epic, the myth of Adapa, and the poem "I Will Praise the Lord of Wisdom," all dating from the second millennium. The Atrahasis Epic includes a deluge story comparable to that of the Bible and hints at the institution of temporary monolatry, i.e. the temporary concentration of all ritual attention on just one deity whose help is implored by the community. The Adapa myth tells of the heavenly journey of a human person, the scribe Adapa, whom the gods honor before sending him back to earth. "I Will Praise the Lord of Wisdom" is a significant discussion of the individual righteous sufferer who has not deserved his fate.

The Hittites. The Hittite Empire, with its core in central Anatolia (Asia Minor), flourished between 1400 and 1200. The Hittites adopted and adapted cuneiform writing from Mesopotamia to set down their own, Indo-European language. One of the Hittite myths recounts the conflict between the ultimately victorious storm-god and the serpent-shaped water demon Illuyanka (fourteenth century).

Ugarit. The city of Ugarit, situated on the Mediterranean in Syria (not far from modern Latakia), was an important city-state that flourished between 1500 and 1200. In modern times, its cuneiform archives have come to light. Their discovery in 1929 was sensational in that it shed light on the origins of the alphabet: the scribes of Ugarit used Mesopotamian-style cuneiform signs, but devised an alphabet of thirty letters (rather than the six hundred-odd signs used in Mesopotamia). Ugaritic is a Semitic language that looks very much like an ancestor of the Hebrew language of the Bible. In Ugarit's mythological texts, which date from ca. 1380, figure characters such as the god El, head of the pantheon; the young god Baal, weather-god and patron deity of Ugarit; and Yam, who, representing the impetuous Mediterranean, is Baal's opponent.

Time of a Rich Harvest: The Iron Age

The history of Western Asia during this period can be described as consisting of a succession of powers holding unrivaled political and cultural hegemony: first came the Assyrians (to 612), then the Babylonians (to 539), and finally the Persians. Of the Bronze Age civilizations, not only Assyria and Babylonia but also Egypt remained solid forces, and the weakened Hittite kingdom gradually reemerged. Ugarit disappeared, but other small powers made their appearance, notably the Hebrews with their two kingdoms: Israel in northern and Judah in southern Palestine. In order to understand Hebrew history, some knowledge about its setting within the empire established by the Assyrians is indispensable. Culturally, the Bronze Age heritage was preserved and, in Israel, adapted to new religious sensibilities.

The Assyrian Empire. Between the tenth and the mid-eighth centuries, the Assyrian territorial state in northern Mesopotamia gradually developed into an imperial power. It then dominated all of Western Asia until 612. At first, Assyria consolidated its control over Mesopotamia and some adjacent areas. Beginning with Tiglath-pileser III (744–727), Assyrian leadership was asserted by frequent and aggressive military campaigns and by the deportation and resettlement of defeated populations. Assyria also developed diplomatic activity to hold the empire together by a web of vassal treaties, of which the so-called Succession Treaty of King Esarhaddon (672) is the best-preserved example. No doubt the kingdom of Judah was bound by this treaty, which sought to obtain loyalty not only to Esarhaddon, but also to his son Ashurbanipal (669–630). Under Ashurbanipal, the Assyrian Empire was at its height and for some time also included Egypt and thus the entire Near East. The Assyrians are remembered as military experts, empire-builders, and shrewd diplomats. Apart from battle reports and annals of royal achievements in warfare, royal hunting, and building, they did not produce an independent literature; instead, they acknowledged Babylonian superiority, created libraries to store the Babylonian treasures that their scribes edited and copied, and worshiped Nabu, patron deity of the scribal arts. The Assyrians did not shrink from looting libraries during raids against their Babylonian neighbor, whom they either managed to control or, alternatively, sought to respect as an independent power. The largest library found in modern times is that of the palace of Nineveh.

Once it had been established, the Assyrian Empire never really came to an end, for it never disintegrated. Only its leaders changed—first the Babylonians (in control from 612) and then the Persians (from 539), in both cases with a relatively quiet transfer of power to the new rulers. Persian hegemony meant the introduction of fresh cultural elements into a realm heretofore dominated by Mesopotamian ideas. The Achaemenid kings, founders of the Persian Empire, were Indo-Europeans and followers of a monotheistic religion. Like much of Iron Age culture, this religion originated in the Bronze Age; its prophet, Zoroaster (Zarathustra), lived at an unknown date between 1400 and 1200.

The Hebrews. From ca. 900 on, the Bible and extrabiblical sources provide enough evidence to allow us to construct a reliable, albeit incomplete, picture of the two Hebrew states, the kingdom of Judah in southern Palestine and the kingdom of Israel in northern Palestine. The tenth-century beginnings of Hebrew statehood (associated with kings Saul, David, and Solomon, all familiar characters from the Bible) are shrouded in legend, as are its earlier, patriarchal periods and such historically elusive figures as Abraham, Jacob, and Moses. The northern kingdom was wealthy and politically more successful than its poor relative in the south, but both flourished during much of the eighth century, the golden age of both states under King Jeroboam II (782–747) in the north and King Uzziah (767–739) in the south. Subsequently, both kingdoms came under the authority of the Assyrians whom they had to serve as vassals. Reacting to Israelite disobedience, the Assyrians destroyed the northern kingdom and its capital city, Samaria, in 722. The southern kingdom survived the downfall of Assyrian rule in 612, but when it reacted against its new Babylonian overlord, Nebuchadnezzar did not hesitate to destroy it (586). In 597 and 586, many members of the Judean elite were deported and resettled in Babylonia (the "Babylonian exile" or "Babylonian captivity"). Some of the Jews, as they are now called by scholarly convention, returned home in Persian times, while others preferred to live outside of Palestine in the "Diaspora."

Literary activity leading to the formation of the Bible is the hallmark of Hebrew culture. Part of the book of Proverbs (Prov 1–9) and the book of Amos seem to represent the earliest extant examples of Hebrew literature (eighth century), though other works such as the Psalms may include earlier items. The first larger collection of literature was apparently compiled by Hilkiah, a priest in Jerusalem under King Josiah, whom he won over to a radical religious reform based on the exclusive worship of the state god Yahweh (622). This collection survives as the books of Deuteronomy, Joshua, Judges, Samuel, and Kings; presenting the partisan view of a minority, the Yahweh-alone movement, this "Deuteronomistic History" suppresses evidence for traditional Hebrew polytheism. Subsequently, it was enlarged by the addition of several other books (Genesis, Exodus, Leviticus, Numbers), of which, chronologically, the book of Genesis came last, presumably around 500. To this date can also be assigned the book of Job, which deals with an already venerable subject (reminiscent of Bronze Age Babylonian literature) in a series of powerful poems: the undeserved suffering of the righteous individual.

By the end of the Iron Age, much of the Hebrew Bible had been compiled to form the literary archive of those committed to the exclusive worship of

Yahweh. It also formed the storehouse into which the rich harvest of ancient Near Eastern culture was brought. The early urban centers with their palaces, fortresses, and temples decayed or were transformed, but their cultural and spiritual legacy survives in the Jewish scriptures.

Abbreviations

AEL	*Ancient Egyptian Literature*. M. Lichtheim
ÄHG	*Ägyptische Hymnen und Gebete*. 2d ed. J. Assmann
ANF	*Ante-Nicene Fathers*
COS	*The Context of Scripture*. Edited by W.W. Hallo
DDD²	*Dictionary of Deities and Demons in the Bible*. 2d ed. Edited by K. van der Toorn et al.
HAE	*Handbuch der althebräischen Epigraphik*. J. Renz and W. Röllig
JE	*The Jewish Encyclopedia*. Edited by I. Singer
KJV	King James Version of the Bible
LÄ	*Lexikon der Ägyptologie*. Edited by Wolfgang Helck et al.
LIMC	*Lexicon iconographicum mythologiae classicae*. Edited by J. Boardman et al.
NBL	*Neues Bibel-Lexikon*. Edited by M. Görg and B. Lang
NEB	The New English Bible
NERT	*Near Eastern Religious Texts Relating to the Old Testament*. Edited by W. Beyerlin
NPNF	*Nicene and Post-Nicene Fathers*
NRSV	New Revised Standard Version of the Bible
OTP	*Old Testament Pseudepigrapha*. Edited by J.H. Charlesworth
REB	Revised English Bible
RIMA	*The Royal Inscriptions of Mesopotamia. Assyrian Periods*
RLA	*Reallexikon der Assyriologie*. Edited by E. Ebeling et al.
SAA	State Archives of Assyria
Schneemelcher	Schneemelcher, W., ed., *New Testament Apocrypha*. Rev. ed.
ThWAT	*Theologisches Wörterbuch zum Alten Testament*. Edited by J.G. Botterweck et al.
TUAT	*Texte aus der Umwelt des Alten Testaments*. Edited by O. Kaiser
WA	"Weimarer Ausgabe" of the works of Martin Luther
WAOB	*Die Welt der altorientalischen Bildsymbolik und das Alte Testament*. O. Keel

Notes

Preface

1. M. Smith, *Palestinian Parties and Politics*, 21.
2. Keel, *Das Böcklein*, 10.
3. Kemp, *Ancient Egypt*, 320.
4. Nietzsche, *The Gay Science*, 205 (aphorism no. 189).
5. J.Z. Smith, *Drudgery Divine*, 52.
6. Dahrendorf, *Essays in the Theory of Society*, 22.

Introduction. Lord of Three Gifts: A New Approach to the Hebrew God

1. Indo-Europeanists study the languages, cultural institutions, religions, and folklore of a great number of peoples who form a homogeneous group speaking closely related languages and who can be traced to common origins and a homeland in prehistoric times, perhaps the fourth millennium B.C.E. or earlier. To the Indo-Europeans belong e.g. the Germanic peoples, Celts, Scandinavians, Greeks and Romans, Hittites, Persians, and Indo-Aryans. Their original homeland is thought to have been somewhere between eastern Europe and the Near East: scholarly suggestions include the highlands of modern Turkey, the steppes of southern Russia, the region between the Hungarian plain and the Baltic, and the area immediately north of modern Iraq.

2. Lincoln, *Myth, Cosmos, and Society*, 141–45.
3. Dumézil, *Mythe et épopée* 3:338–61, 365, and *La Courtisane et les seigneurs colorés*, 239–43.
4. Dumézil, *Archaic Roman Religion* 1:162.
5. Dumézil, *La Courtisane et les seigneurs colorés*, 243.
6. Wyatt, "Near Eastern Echoes of Aryan Tradition." Relevant statistics on Indo-European names can be found in Zadok, "A Prosopographic and Ethno-Linguistic Characterization."
7. Gordon, *A Scholar's Odyssey*, 110.
8. Gamkrelidze and Ivanov, *Indo-European and the Indo-Europeans*. Shared vocabulary is also studied by Levin, *Semitic and Indo-European*, who thinks more in terms of a common culture than of borrowing. For a recent assessment of the evidence, see Rubio, "On the Alleged Pre-Sumerian Substratum."
9. See Dubuisson, "Le roi indo-européen et la synthèse des trois fonctions."
10. Dumézil, *Rituels indo-européens à Rome*, 7.
11. "Only anthropologists could discover that social phenomena obey structural principles. The reason is evident, for structural patterns become visible only through observation from outside." Lévi-Strauss, "Les limites de la notion de structure," 44.
12. Atrahasis Epic (Dalley, *Myths from Mesopotamia*, 9–35). For an analysis, see Baumgart, *Die Umkehr des Schöpfergottes*, 419–94.

13. Kramer and Maier, *Myths of Enki*, 5.
14. 1 Kgs 10:21.
15. Van der Toorn, "The Babylonian New Year Festival," 332–35. The royal induction (or royal ritual) is studied in Halpern, *The Constitution of the Monarchy in Israel*, 125–48; Keel, WAOB 234–47.
16. This is the interpretation of Fletcher-Louis, "The High Priest as Divine Mediator," 182.
17. For the possibility that the Jerusalem temple included a divine image (which was later removed or whose existence was negated), see Niehr, "In Search of YHWH's Cult Statue."
18. See below, chapter 8.
19. Ps 21:4/Hebr. 5; 1 Kgs 3:9.
20. Dumézil, *La Courtisane et les seigneurs colorés*, 239–43.
21. 2 Sam 6:19. On the king as patron, see Lemche, "From Patronage Society to Patronage Society."
22. Dumézil, *Archaic Roman Religion* 1:169.
23. *Ibid.*, 170.
24. *Ibid.*, 252.
25. Pound, *Literary Essays*, 4.

The First Image:
Lord of Wisdom

1. Assyrian list of experts at court (SAA 7:4–5).
2. Pongratz-Leisten, *Herrschaftswissen in Mesopotamien*, 286–320, defines this knowledge as "Herrschaftswissen," a body of knowledge that ultimately legitimates claims to political authority. As a term, *Herrschaftswissen* is problematic, however, for, in Max Scheler's sociology of knowledge, it designates the scientist's empirical knowledge and his manipulative know-how.
3. Inscription of Ashurbanipal (Sweet, "The Sage in Akkadian Literature," 55).
4. Isa 47:13; Dan 5:11–12.
5. 2 Kgs 21:6; Jer 27:9.

6. 1 Sam 28:9.
7. Wis 7:17–21.
8. 1 Kgs 4:32–33/Hebr. 5:12–13; Josephus, *Jewish Antiquities* 8.45.
9. 1 Kgs 4:2.
10. Ezek 28.
11. Isa 14.
12. In the first poem (Ezek 28), the nationality of the king is in dispute. One expert suggests that the poem's original version was not about a king of the neighboring city-state of Tyre, but actually about a Judean monarch, and he marshals convincing evidence (Bogaert, "Montagne sainte, jardin d'Eden"). The second poem (Isa 14) deals with the king of Babylon, although the king of Assyria (presumably Sargon II, 721–705 B.C.E.) would fit the context better.
13. On a cultic image of Yahweh, see above, Introduction, n. 17.
14. Exod 34:29–35.
15. Ezekiel the Tragedian (OTP 2:811–12); see also van der Horst, "Moses' Throne Vision."
16. Myth of Etana (Dalley, *Myths from Mesopotamia*, 189–202). See the interpretations by Kirk, *Myth*, 125–31; Parpola, "The Assyrian Tree of Life," 195–99; Haul, *Das Etana–Epos*, 70–74.
17. Text in Lambert, "Enmeduranki," 132; interpretation in Widengren, *The Ascension of the Apostle*, 7–8.
18. The relevant passages from the Baal Cycle and the Story of King Keret (Wyatt, *Religious Texts from Ugarit*, 132, 198–99) are discussed by Wyatt, "Degrees of Divinity," 856–60.
19. Isa 6.
20. Zech 3.
21. Testaments of the Twelve Patriarchs/Levi 5:1–2 (OTP 1:789–90).
22. Myth of Adapa (Dalley, *Myths from Mesopotamia*, 182–88). Izre'el, *Adapa and the South Wind*, 137–49, elucidates the myth with reference to shamanistic initiation. See also the interpretations by Kirk, *Myth*, 122–25, and S. Parpola, SAA 10:xix.
23. Barker, *The Older Testament*.

24. Handy, *Among the Host of Heaven*, 65–95.
25. Baal Cycle (Wyatt, *Religious Texts from Ugarit*, 87, repeated 100).
26. Pseudo-Lucian, *De dea Syria* 35 (Attridge and Oden, *The Syrian Goddess*, 47).
27. Lang, *Wisdom and the Book of Proverbs*; Lang, DDD² 900–5.
28. Delekat, "Yáho-Yahwáe und die alttestamentlichen Gottesnamenkorrekturen," 48–51.
29. Adopting the marginal reading of NRSV: "little child" (v. 30).
30. 1 Kgs 4:32–33/Hebr. 5:12–13.
31. Deut 32:8–9 as discussed above, p. 29.
32. Barker, *The Great Angel*, 38: Yahweh; Collins, *Daniel*, 310: Michael; Fletcher-Louis, "The High Priest as Divine Mediator": high priest.
33. Law of Hammurabi, prologue (Roth, *Law Collections from Mesopotamia*, 78, 79).
34. Teaching for King Merikare 41 (Parkinson, *The Tale of Sinuhe and Other Ancient Egyptian Poems*, 225).
35. Relevant ancient sources are translated in Wälchli, *Der weise König Salomo*, 236–50 (with discussion 129–63).
36. Wilcke, *Wer las und schrieb in Babylonien und Assyrien*.
37. Law of Hammurabi § 128 (Roth, *Law Collections from Mesopotamia*, 105).
38. 2 Sam 8:15–18; 20:23–26; 1 Kgs 4:1–19.
39. According to Lipiński ("The King's Arbitration"), the Indian versions derive ultimately from the Bible.
40. Cohn, *Cosmos, Chaos and the World to Come*, 35.
41. Law of Hammurabi, prologue (Roth, *Law Collections from Mesopotamia*, 76–77).
42. Law of Hammurabi, prologue (Roth, *Law Collections from Mesopotamia*, 77).
43. This tradition can also be found in Exod 20:12; 34:1.
44. Frazer, *Folk-Lore in the Old Testament*, 1:134.
45. See the references in Otto, *Das Deuteronomium*, 73, 81–82, 85.
46. See below, chapter 17, p. 160.
47. Deut 1:1.
48. Deut 1–3.
49. Deut 12–26; see also 4:1–2; 5:1.
50. Deut 27:8; 31:9–13.
51. See Deut 32:1, the invocation of the heavens.
52. Deut 27–28.
53. Esarhaddon's Succession Treaty §§ 17, 25 (Parpola and Watanabe, *Neo-Assyrian Treaties*, 36, 41).
54. Ps 139:16.
55. F.-L. Hossfeld and E. Reuter, ThWAT 5:942–43.
56. Dan 10:21.
57. Cicero, *Ad familiares* 2:15,5.
58. F. Weber, *Jüdische Theologie*, 25.
59. Boswell, *Life of Johnson*, 751 (April 26, 1776).
60. This distinction was first recognized by Andrae, *Das Gotteshaus und die Urformen des Bauens*.
61. Deut 12:5; 1 Kgs 9:3.
62. Exod 29:43–45. The two temple theologies are explained in von Rad, *Gesammelte Studien* 2:127–32.
63. Deut 4:11–14.
64. Deut 34:10.
65. According to the ancient Near Eastern worldview, heaven is situated beyond the ocean that encircles the earth; see the illustration in Grelot, "La géographie mythique," 46.
66. Epic of Gilgamesh, Yale tablet (George, *The Epic of Gilgamesh*, 110).
67. Herrmann, *Gesammelte Studien*, 163, 175.
68. *Ibid.*, 175.
69. Dumézil, *Les Dieux souverains*, 55–85; Dumézil, *The Destiny of the Warrior*, 55–57.

The Second Image: Lord of War

1. Translated in Cooper, *Reconstructing History*, 45–48.
2. Mann, *Divine Presence*, 27; see also 2 Sam 5:24 and Judg 4:14.
3. Cooper, *Reconstructing History*, 13.

4. Stela of the Vultures (Cooper, *Reconstructing History*, 47).

5. Weippert, "Heiliger Krieg in Israel und Assyrien"; Kang, *Divine War in the Old Testament and in the Ancient Near East*.

6. Judg 18:17–18, 27.

7. 1 Sam 21:10; 31:10.

8. A. Schenker and B. Lang, NBL 3:492.

9. Josh 4:20–5:12.

10. Josh 4:20ff.

11. Josh 5:15.

12. Gen 28:10ff; 35:1–7, 9–15.

13. For references, see Dumézil, *Horace et les Curiaces*, 11–33.

14. Ammianus Marcellinus, *Res gestae* 31:9.5.

15. Saxo Grammaticus, *Gesta Danorum* 2 (Saxo Grammaticus, *The History of the Danes* 1:40–41).

16. Judg 14:19.

17. Mari letter A 1968 (Wyatt, "Arms and the King," 842; Malamat, *Mari and the Bible*, 152–53; Heintz, "Des textes sémitiques," 137).

18. Tacitus, *Germania* 13.

19. Lincoln, *Priests, Warriors, and Cattle*, 128.

20. Keen, *Chivalry*, 64–77; Le Jan, "Frankish Giving of Arms and Rituals of Power."

21. Adam, *Der königliche Held*, 86–93.

22. Inscription no. 1 of Tiglath-pileser I (RIMA 2:13; ca. 1100 B.C.E.).

23. Inscription no. 1 of Tiglath-pileser I (RIMA 2:25).

24. A Hebrew seal found in Jerusalem shows a similar scene: the king tends bow and arrows to a man standing on the framed inscription "governor of the city" (Avigad, *Hebrew Bullae from the Time of Jeremiah*, 30–33; ca. 650 B.C.E.).

25. For an interesting parallel, see Testaments of the Twelve Patriarchs/Testament of Levi 5:3 (OTP 1:790), where Levi is given a shield and a sword by an angel.

26. Further examples of this iconography as well as textual evidence can be found in Keel, *Wirkmächtige Siegeszeichen*, 178–80, figs. 34–37; Keel, "Powerful Symbols of Victory," 211–14.

27. Victory Stela of Merneptah (TUAT 1:545, "Israel Stela").

28. Rosetta Stone (Simpson, "The Demotic Text of the Memphis Decree," 200a).

29. Baal and Yam (Wyatt, *Religious Texts from Ugarit*, 69).

30. Matt 8:26.

31. Casson, *Travel in the Ancient World*, 150.

32. Gese, "Die Religionen Altsyriens," 65.

33. Baal and Yam (Wyatt, *Religious Texts from Ugarit*, 65).

34. Wyatt, "Arms and the King."

35. Eusebius, *Life of Constantine* 3:3 (NPNF 2/I:520).

36. Ps 77:15–20/Hebr. 16–21.

37. Ps 74, as discussed above, p. 59.

38. Köhler, *Der hebräische Mensch*, 114.

39. Fuchs, *Mythos und Hiobdichtung*, 62.

40. Eliade, *The Myth of the Eternal Return*; Hornung, "Geschichte als Fest."

41. NRSV modified. There is no "rider" mentioned here, but horse and "driver" of the chariot, as correctly rendered in Exod 15:19.

42. Batto, "The Reed Sea."

43. Drews, *The End of the Bronze Age*, 212–13; Caquot, "Cantique de la mer et miracle de la mer."

44. Victory Stela of Merneptah (COS 2:41—"Israel Stela," 1208 B.C.E.).

45. Ezek 38–39; Zech 14.

46. Dan 10–11.

47. Apparently, Dan 12:1a must be read twice: first, as a conclusion to chapter 11, and second, as an integral part of 12:1–3.

48. Mark 13, the "Markan Apocalypse."

49. On the minimization and eventual elimination of human warriordom see von Rad, *Holy War in Ancient Israel*. Von Rad compares early biblical battle accounts with their retelling by Jewish authors of the late biblical period. The retold versions highlight the element

of divine intervention at the expense of human fighting.

50. Van der Toorn, "Mesopotamian Prophecy between Immanence and Transcendence," 84–86.

51. Goethe, "Vier Jahreszeiten," no. 78. I owe the translation to John Williams.

52. According to Parpola, "the popular notion of Assyria as a primitive and crude military power" should be abandoned (SAA 2:xiv). Oppenheim, "The City of Assur in 714 B.C.," points out that Assyrian merchants, who engaged in foreign trade, transcended the imperialistic attitude toward other people.

53. As an example, one may refer to the two leaders of the Hasmonean revolt: Simeon, the wise counselor, and Judas Maccabeus, the warrior (1 Macc 2:65–66). Caquot, "Israelite Perceptions of Wisdom and Strength."

54. Teaching for King Merikare (AEL 1:99).

55. Dan 7.

56. Dan 12:1–3.

57. 1 En. 104 and Jub. 23 (OTP 1:85–86; 2:101–2), see Nickelsburg, *Resurrection, Immortality, and Eternal Life*, 11–42, 112–30.

58. Jub. 23:30–31 (OTP 2:102, modified).

59. It is all too obvious that this judgment apocalypse is based on a fairytale plot. A king, disguised as a beggar, traveled through his kingdom. Some of his subjects welcomed him into their homes, while others despised him, telling him to go away. The royal identity of the biblical judge clearly echoes the story's folktale model.

60. Dan 7:3.

61. 1 Kgs 22:19–23.

62. Testament of Isaac 5:32 (OTP 1:909).

63. Apocalypse of Peter, Rainer fragment (Schneemelcher 2:637–38 n. 43).

64. It seems that the angelic intercessor resorts to the heavenly treasure to get a ransom and thus bring about the accused person's acquittal. This is how

Oeming, "Ich habe ein Lösegeld gefunden!," reads Job 33:23–24.

65. Brunner-Traut, "Aspective," 430.

66. An early source for the Zoroastrian notion of the final overthrow of evil and the ensuing transformation of the world is Plutarch, *De Iside et Osiride* 46–47; the passage is translated and discussed in Widengren, "Leitende Ideen und Quellen der iranischen Apokalyptik," 127–33. For the influence of Zoroastrian eschatology, see Cohn, *Cosmos, Chaos and the World to Come*, 114–15, 220–31.

The Third Image:
Lord of the Animals

1. Pettazzoni, *The All-Knowing God*, 320–22, 441–55.

2. Von der Osten-Sacken, *Der Ziegen-"Dämon*," 205, lists a stamp seal dating from the "Ubaid 3" period, now dated 5000–4300 B.C.E.

3. *Ibid.*, 215–16, 253.

4. Horace, *Ars poetica* 393. For further sources, see M.-X. Garezou, LIMC 7/1:102–4.

5. Kemp, *Ancient Egypt*, 48.

6. Jacobsen, *The Treasures of Darkness*, 104–10.

7. Day, "Anat: Ugarit's Mistress of Animals"; Cornelius, "Anat and Qudshu as the 'Mistress of Animals'."

8. Babylonian inscription (Jacobsen, *The Treasures of Darkness*, 108).

9. Gen 1:28.

10. Keel, *Jahwes Entgegnung an Ijob*, 86–125.

11. Hymn to Amen-Re ("Papyrus Boulaq 17"; J.L. Foster, *Hymns, Prayers, and Songs*, 62).

12. The REB gives the passage an exquisite poetic flow: "The cow and the bear will be friends, and their young will lie down together; and the lion will eat straw like cattle. The infant will play over the cobra's hole, and the young child dance over the viper's nest."

13. Arrian, *Anabasis* 7:20.3–4.

14. Pseudo-Lucian, *De dea Syria* 41 (Attridge and Oden, *The Syrian Goddess*, 51). See also Kötting, "Tier und Heiligtum."

15. Drijvers, "Sanctuaries and Social Safety."

16. On the lion as the attribute animal of the goddess, see Hörig, *Dea Syria* 93–128.

17. Aramaic inscription from Palmyra (Hillers and Cussini, *Palmyrene Aramaic Texts*, no. 1122).

18. Apparently under Tiberius (14–37 C.E.), Palmyra was eventually incorporated into the Roman state.

19. Von Fürer-Haimendorf, *The Chenchus*, 9.

20. *Ibid.*, 181.

21. Von Fürer-Haimendorf explains the dual character of Garela-Maisama in terms of acculturation. Originally, he believes, this deity was a male sylvan god. But under the impact of the surrounding Hindu culture with its preponderance of female deities, the sylvan deity adopted female features (von Fürer-Haimendorf, *The Chenchus*, 184). The above reinterpretation of the evidence takes a different view, based on the economic duality of hunting and food-collecting.

22. Dequeker, "Green Herbage and Trees Bearing Fruit."

23. Weippert, "Tier und Mensch in einer menschenarmen Welt."

24. Lang, "Ein babylonisches Motiv in Israels Schöpfungsmythologie."

25. Gen 10:9; 27:20.

26. For Old Testament times, see Jer 5:26.

27. Amos 3:5 (Septuagint). On bird traps, see Dalman, *Arbeit und Sitte in Palästina* 6:338–39; Paul, *Amos*, 110–11.

28. Deut 12:15, 20.

29. While ritual killing is never explicitly explained in terms of the divine ownership of the animals, an echo of this idea can be discerned in the book of Psalms' critique of sacrifice. One of the psalmists prefers moral behavior to ritual acts, arguing that God owns all animals and does not depend on being fed with offerings of meat (Ps 50:8–15).

30. Ingold, "Hunting, Sacrifice and the Domestication of Animals."

31. Groß, *Studien zur Priesterschrift*, 11–36.

32. Epic of Gilgamesh (Dalley, *Myths from Mesopotamia*, 53).

33. Pausanias, *Description of Greece* 9:17.7.

34. Pseudo-Lucian, *De dea Syria* 12 (Attridge and Oden, *The Syrian Goddess*, 19–21).

35. Brueggemann, "The Kerygma of the Priestly Writers."

36. Lohfink, *Studien zum Pentateuch*, 227–42, 279, and *Theology of the Pentateuch*, 149–63, 195–210, writes perceptively on the Priestly Code (a dominant literary layer of Genesis) as lacking an interest in warfare and as transforming history into myth.

37. Job 41:19/Hebr. 41:11.

38. Job 40:15–41:26/Hebr. 40:15–41:34.

39. E.-A. Knauf, DDD[2] 749–53.

40. G.A. Smith, *The Historical Geography of the Holy Land*, 72.

41. Hopkins, *The Highlands of Canaan*, 112.

42. Loukianoff, "Le dieu Ched"; Berlandini, "Bès en aurige."

43. Metternich Stela 115–19, 125 (Borghouts, *Ancient Egyptian Magical Texts*, 84, modified).

44. Metternich Stela 168–251 (Borghouts, *Ancient Egyptian Magical Texts*, 62–69).

45. Quaegebeur, "Divinités égyptiennes sur des animaux dangereux."

46. Liber de ortu beatae Mariae 18 (Schneemelcher 1:462—Gospel of Pseudo-Matthew).

47. Liber de ortu beatae Mariae 19 (Schneemelcher 1:462).

48. The story of magical and human control of wild animals in Egypt does not end at this point; see Mayeur-Jaouen, "Crocodiles et saints du Nil." Some comparative material is

collected in Lutterbach, "Tiere—In allem gehorsam wie Mönche."

The Fourth Image: Lord of the Individual—the "Personal God"

1. Starbuck, *The Psychology of Religion*, 327.
2. *Ibid.*
3. *Ibid.*, 332.
4. *Ibid.*, 327.
5. James, *Varieties of Religious Experience*, 29 (lecture II). For John Wesley (1703–91), "personal religion" has to do with individual "communion with God"; see Wesley, *Works* 8:290.
6. James, *Varieties of Religious Experience*, 30 (lecture II).
7. Breasted, *Development*, 348–49.
8. Skinner, *Prophecy and Religion*, 16.
9. *Ibid.*, 219.
10. Fosdick, *A Guide to Understanding the Bible*, 66.
11. Fosdick, *The Modern Use of the Bible*, 21.
12. Marty, *Modern American Religion* 3:313.
13. Jacobsen, *The Treasures of Darkness*, 150.
14. Durkheim, *The Elementary Forms of Religious Life*, 39.
15. Albertz, *Persönliche Frömmigkeit und offizielle Religion*; van der Toorn, *Family Religion in Babylonia, Syria and Israel*; Sadek, *Popular Religion in Egypt*.
16. Van der Toorn, *Family Religion*, 147; H. Brunner, LÄ 4:951.
17. Blumenthal, "Sinuhes persönliche Frömmigkeit."
18. The "ear" motif is fairly common on ancient Egyptian monuments; see Sadek, *Popular Religion in Egypt*, 245–67 (with plates).
19. Assmann, "Weisheit, Loyalismus und Frömmigkeit," 12–15; Römheld, *Wege der Weisheit*, 131–50.
20. Votive stela of Neb-Re (NERT, 33).
21. Votive stela of Neferabu (AEL 2:109).

22. Inscription on a wooden statue found in tomb no. 265 in Thebes (ÄHG, no. 169, 1–3).
23. Assmann, *Herrschaft und Heil*, 122–26.
24. Prayer to Amen (AEL 2:112; "papyrus Anastasi II").
25. Inscription in tomb no. 409 in Thebes (NERT, 39).
26. Römheld, *Wege der Weisheit*, 151–81.
27. Instruction of Amenemope (NERT, 49–62—Hellmut Brunner).
28. Middleton, *Lugbara Religion*, 39.
29. Freud, *Gesammelte Werke* 7:139.
30. McKane, *Proverbs*, 11–12.
31. Brunner-Traut, *Frühformen des Erkennens*, 80.
32. Geertz, "Common Sense as a Cultural System," 90.
33. A typical expression with a strong Egyptian background is "the path of life" which means "behavior leading to success, wellbeing, and happiness" (Prov 10:17; 15:24; see Couroyer, "Le chemin de vie"; Vittmann, *Altägyptische Wegmetaphorik*, 31–49). The reference to "justice" as the "foundation of the throne" (Prov 16:12) echoes the Egyptian word for "truth, justice" [*ma'at*], which, in hieroglyphic writing, is represented as the pedestal of the royal throne (Brunner, "Gerechtigkeit als Fundament des Thrones").
34. According to the Septuagint. The traditional Hebrew text uses the divine name ("hands of Yahweh") to give the saying an Israelite flavor, but the original reading has been preserved by the Septuagint.
35. Blumenthal, "Sinuhes persönliche Frömmigkeit," 225.
36. Instruction of Amenemope 7:1ff (NERT 53).
37. Schipper, *Israel und Ägypten in der Königszeit*, 239.
38. Prov 20:9 has a close parallel in 1 Kgs 8:46, another "Solomonic" text presumably dating from the days of Josiah; see Knoppers, "Prayer and Propaganda."

39. Kämmerer, "Die Stellung des Menschen zu seinen Göttern."
40. Jacobsen, *The Treasures of Darkness*, 147.
41. Oppenheim, *Ancient Mesopotamia*, 199–200.
42. B.R. Foster, *Before the Muses*, 36. For a relevant source, see Vorländer, *Mein Gott*, 73.
43. Sumerian Shulgi Hymn (Jacobsen, *The Treasures of Darkness*, 158–59).
44. "Man and His God" (COS 1:574a).
45. Ashurbanipal's hymn to the Ishtars of Nineveh and Arbela (SAA 3:13).
46. Nebuchadnezzar II, inscription no. 9 (Langdon, *Die neubabylonischen Königsinschriften*, 89).
47. Nebuchadnezzar's cylinder inscription (TUAT 2:782).
48. Formula of prayer (Jüngling, "Was anders ist Gott," 372).
49. Babylonian "Dialogue between a Man and His God" (COS 1:485b).
50. Vorländer, *Mein Gott*, 46–47; van der Toorn, *Family Religion*, 75.
51. Plutarch, *Moralia/Advice to Bride and Groom* 19 (140D).
52. D. Bonhoeffer, "Von guten Mächten," poem.
53. Hymns of Thanksgiving 17:30–36 (García Martínez, *The Dead Sea Scrolls Translated*, 349–50, modified).
54. "I Will Praise the Lord of Wisdom," tablet I (TUAT 3:115–16, Wolfram von Soden).
55. Keel, *Das Böcklein*, 46–144.
56. Dialogue between Ashurbanipal and Nabu (SAA 3:34).
57. Prophecy for Crown Prince Ashurbanipal (SAA 9:39).
58. For *nephesh* in the sense of "mouth," see Isa 5:14.
59. Freud, *Gesammelte Werke* 11:324 ("Introductory Lectures on Psychoanalysis," lecture 20).
60. Andreas-Salomé, "Vom frühen Gottesdienst," 465–66.
61. Admonitions of Ipuwer 8:5–7 (AEL 1:157).
62. Epic of Gilgamesh, "Meissner fragment" from Sippar (George, *The Epic of Gilgamesh*, 124).
63. Tale of Sinuhe (AEL 1:227).
64. Feucht, *Das Kind im alten Ägypten*, 149–50.
65. Boudhiba, "The Child and the Mother," 133.
66. S. Aalen, ThWAT 1:174.
67. Odes of Solomon 1:1 (OTP 2:735).
68. For *il rêshîja*, "the god at my head," see Vorländer, *Mein Gott*, 21–22; van der Toorn, *Family Religion*, 76–77.
69. Old Babylonian letter (Albertz, *Persönliche Frömmigkeit*, 115).
70. See the parallel expressions "my god" and "the god of my father" in Exod 15:2.
71. See Ps 3:9; 7:7b, 8; 18:32, 44, 48; 22:4–6, 28–32, and other passages.

The Fifth Image: Lord of the Harvest

1. Breasted, *Ancient Times*, 101.
2. Zohary and Hopf, *Domestication of Plants in the Old World*, 37.
3. Tale of Sinuhe (AEL 1:226–27).
4. Isa 7:18–25. See Levine, "The Land of Milk and Honey."
5. G.A. Smith, *The Historical Geography of the Holy Land*, 72–75. Detailed information on the ancient Palestinian peasant's agrarian environment can be found in Hopkins, *The Highlands of Canaan*.
6. Jeremias, *The Parables of Jesus*, 12.
7. Gen 2:5.
8. Atrahasis Epic, tablet 2 (Dalley, *Myths from Mesopotamia*, 20–21).
9. Aramaic inscription from Fekheriye (COS 2:153).
10. Also Jer 25:30, 32.
11. Hittite Myth of Illuyanka (COS 1:150).
12. Ashbel, *Die Niederschlagsverhältnisse im südlichen Libanon*, 24; Wirth, *Syrien*, 79.
13. Lebanon has twenty to thirty days of thunderstorms annually, Palestine only five to ten days. Taha et al., "The Climate of the Near East," 207, 215.
14. Frankfort et al., *Before Philosophy*, 33–34.

15. Mishnah, Sukkah 4:9.
16. Zech 14:17.
17. Mishnah, Rosh ha-Shanah 1:2.
18. Ps 104. See the interpretation of Dion, "YHWH as Storm-God and Sun-God."
19. Aramaic inscription from Fekheriye (COS 2:153).
20. Inscription accompanying the Milna Mergi rock relief of Tiglath-pileser III (Tadmor, *The Inscriptions of Tiglath-pileser III*, 112–13).
21. Inscription of Shalmaneser III, no. 12 (RIMA 3:59).
22. Story of King Keret (Wyatt, *Religious Texts from Ugarit*, 231–32—"KTU 1.16 iii, 14–16").
23. Sahin, "Neue Beobachtungen zum Felsrelief."
24. Lebrun, "L'Anatolie et le monde phénicien," 28.
25. P. Collart, LIMC 3/1:76 (no. 2).
26. Hittite prayer (Haas, *Geschichte der hethitischen Religion*, 325).
27. Luwian inscription, Stela of Sultanhan (Haas, *Geschichte der hethitischen Religion*, 328).
28. Porton, "Grape-Clusters in Jewish Literature and Art."
29. Josephus, *Jewish War* 5:210.
30. Castriota, *The Ara Pacis Augustae and the Imagery of Abundance* (index under "grapevine").
31. Ps 104:20–29; see Dion, "YHWH as Storm-God and Sun-God," 58–62.
32. The underlying idea, that the blessing initiates the development of new life, can be seen in the one instance where the Hebrew idiom has entered the language of Christianity. Christians often quote the words with which the angel addressed the Virgin Mary: "Hail Mary, full of grace, the Lord is with thee. Blessed art thou among women, and blessed is the fruit of thy womb, Jesus" (*Ave Maria, gratia plena, Dominus tecum. Benedicta tu in mulieribus, et benedictus fructus ventris tui, Jesus*; based on Luke 1:28, 42). The blessing impregnates the Virgin, and the child she will give birth to is already growing within her womb;

this, and nothing else, is intended by the idiom. According to tradition, the very moment of the angelic salutation is the moment of the Virgin's impregnation, and this is why the scene figures so prominently in Christian art.

33. Westermann, *Elements of Old Testament Theology*, 103.
34. Spina, "The 'Ground' for Cain's Rejection."
35. Redfield, *Peasant Society and Culture*, 60–79.
36. Lutfiyya, *Baytîn*, 106.
37. Among the factors that diminish Syrian peasants' enthusiasm for agriculture are also the burden of taxation and the nostalgic memory of the freedom of Bedouin life; see Batatu, *Syria's Peasantry*, 11.
38. Lutfiyya, *Baytîn*, 113.
39. Dalman, *Arbeit und Sitte in Palästina* 4:311.
40. See the fig tree in Gen 3:7.
41. Gospel of Philip 15 (Schneemelcher 1:189–90).
42. Evans-Pritchard, *The Nuer*, 16–21, 76–85.
43. Judg 21:19.
44. The celebration takes place after the gathering of "the produce from the threshing floor and the wine press" (Deut 16:13). Since the cereal harvest is much earlier than the Feast of Tabernacles, the phrase may designate the totality of what is grown. No emphasis on the cereal harvest is intended.
45. Plutarch, *Moralia/Nine Books of Table-Talk* 4:6.2 (671 D).
46. 2 Kgs 15:29, Summary Inscription no. 4 of Tiglath-pileser III (COS 2:288).
47. On the Assyrian idea of the state and the contrasting Hebrew notion, see Block, *The Gods of the Nations*.
48. The deportees were not considered slaves, but were somehow owned by the Assyrian king; they were generally settled on crown land, see Oded, *Mass Deportations*, 40, 91–99.
49. Hebrew inscription from Khirbet Beit Lei (COS 2:180; translation modified).

50. Hosea's expression "land of Yahweh" corresponds to the term "land of Ashur" (Isa 7:18; Micah 5:6/Hebr. 5:5). In their own language, the Assyrians called their country "land of Ashur," frequently spelled with the divine determinative as "land of (the god) Ashur" (*mât dAshur*); see Tadmor, *The Inscriptions of Tiglath-pileser III*, 214; RLA 1:195; Parpola, *Neo-Assyrian Toponyms*, 50.
51. Ezek 36:17.
52. Hopkins, *The Highlands of Canaan*, 194–95; Otto, "Der Ackerbau in Juda," 232–33.
53. Reported by Mosca, "Ugarit and Daniel 7," 507 n. 49.
54. Bickerman, "The Babylonian Captivity," 346–47.
55. Herodotus, *Histories* 1:193 (Walter Blanco).
56. K. Butz, RLA 6:472.
57. On Ea as a creator, see Tsumura, *The Earth and the Waters*, 145–52.
58. Hopkins, *The Highlands of Canaan*, 186–87.
59. Martin, *The Temples that Jerusalem Forgot*, 288–321.
60. Gen 2:10–14.
61. Ezek 47:9–10.
62. G.A. Smith, *Jerusalem* 1:88–89.
63. A. Guttmacher, JE 6:230.
64. Plato, *Theaetetus* 186 D.
65. Gorssen, "La cohérence de la conception de Dieu," 321.
66. Sundén, *Die Religion und die Rollen*, 100, 106–7.
67. James, *Varieties of Religious Experience*, 122–23 (lectures IV–V).

Epilogue. The Hebrew God: Fragments of a History

1. The nucleus would be Gen 28:11–12, 16–19 (hierophany account), expanded first by the addition of vv. 10, 20–22 (epiphany account) and then by vv. 13–15 (theophany account). See B. Lang, NBL 3:415–16.
2. For recent statements of this theory,

see Karel van der Toorn, DDD² 911–12; Ernst Axel Knauf, NBL 3:608.
3. Renz, HAE 1:64; COS 2:172.
4. For Teman = Edom, see Jer 49:7.
5. Exod 3:8, 17; 13:5; Num 13:27.
6. Josh 10:28–39.
7. Geller, "The God of the Covenant," 285.
8. Gen 12:10ff.; 26:1ff.
9. Job 1:14–15, 17. For raiding pastoralists, see Evans-Pritchard, *The Nuer*, 49, 125.
10. Schmid, *Erzväter und Exodus*; Moberly, *The Old Testament of the Old Testament*; B. Lang, NBL 3:1009–13.
11. Lang, *Monotheism and the Prophetic Minority*. The scholarly debate is summarized in Gnuse, "The Emergence of Monotheism."
12. See e.g. Ps 20:6/Hebr. 7; John F. Sawyer, ThWAT 3:1051–52.
13. Atrahasis Epic (Dalley, *Myths from Mesopotamia*, 20–21). See also van Selms, "Temporary Henotheism."
14. Much of the relevant literature is summarized in Gnuse, "The Emergence of Monotheism"; recent titles include Albani, *Der eine Gott und die himmlischen Heerscharen*; Keel and Uehlinger, "Jahwe und die Sonnengottheit"; Otto, *Das Deuteronomium*, 74–75; Propp, "Monotheism and 'Moses.'"
15. Compare Ps 104 with the great hymn to Aten (COS 1:45–46). See also Dion, "YHWH as Storm-God and Sun-God"; Knigge, "Überlegungen zum Verhältnis von altägyptischer Hymnik und alttestamentlicher Psalmendichtung."
16. Nebuchadnezzar's cylinder inscription (TUAT 2:782). See also Lang, "Ein babylonisches Motiv in Israels Schöpfungsmythologie."
17. Matt 4:1–11; Luke 4:1–13. For the fasting of visionaries and the visionary nature of the event, see Dan 10:2–3 and Witherington, *Jesus the Seer*, 279–80.
18. Both the legend of the three tempta-

tions of Buddha and the story of the three temptations of Zoroaster are amenable to tripartite explanation. For Buddha, see Dumézil, *La courtisane et les seigneurs colorés*, 40–43, for Zoroaster, see Baldick, *Animal and Shaman*, 165.

19. Mark 8:1–9.
20. Deutsch, *Guardians of the Gate*, 151–57.
21. An interesting aspect of this role of Christ is discussed in Cancik, "Christus Imperator."
22. Ps 91:13 (90:13 Vulgate). Fischer, "Conculcabis leonem et draconem."
23. Vorländer, "Christus als persönlicher Gott."
24. Finney, *The Invisible God*, 116–45.
25. Tertullian, *De pudicitia / On Modesty* 7 (ANF 4:80), ca. 210.
26. Martyrdom of Perpetua and Felicity 4 (ANF 3:700).
27. Aberkios (Abercius) inscription, ca. 192–212 (Johnson, *Early-Christian Epitaphs from Anatolia*, 64).
28. 2 Cor 12:2–4.
29. Qumran text 4 Q 491, fragment 11 (Wise, "A Study of 4Q491c," 183). Ever since Morton Smith (*Studies in the Cult of Yahweh* 2:76–77) argued that this text implies the idea of mystical ascent and transformation into an angelic being, it has received much scholarly attention.
30. M. Smith, *Studies in the Cult of Yahweh* 2:47–86; Barker, *The Risen Lord*; Craffert, "Jesus and the Shamanic Complex."
31. Mark 1:9–11.
32. Bühner, *Der Gesandte und sein Weg im vierten Evangelium*, to be supplemented by DeConick, *Voices of the Mystics*. While Bühner explores the traces of pre-Johannine visionary mysticism, DeConick studies Johannine opposition to mysticism.
33. On this difficult passage, see O'Neill, "Who Is Comparable to Me in My Glory?," 28–33.
34. Gospel of Philip 21 (Schneemelcher 1:190).
35. Mark 1:9–11.
36. Pilch, "The Transfiguration of Jesus."
37. Luke 9:32.
38. M. Smith, *Studies in the Cult of Yahweh* 2:67.
39. Barker, *The Great Angel*. See above, chapter 4, p. 32.

Appendix I

1. Luther, WA 20:569.
2. Delekat, "Yáho-Yahwáe und die alttestamentlichen Gottesnamenkorrekturen."
3. Rösel, *Adonaj*, 182.
4. The ancient sources are discussed by McDonough, *YHWH at Patmos*, 58–122.

Illustration Credits and Museum Locations

1. Small bronze statuette; from Ugarit. National Museum of Damascus, no. 23394. Source: WAOB, no. 284.
2. Ugaritic metal statuette and Egyptian wall painting, used in the author's visualization of Hebrew polytheism.
3. Two Ugaritic metal statuettes, used in the author's visualization of Hebrew polytheism.
4. Detail of diorite stela of Hammurabi; found in Susa, Iran. Louvre, Paris. Source: WAOB, no. 390.
5. Stela of the Vultures, fragment; from Tello (ancient Girsu). Louvre, Paris. Source: Elizabeth Simpson in I.J. Winter, "After the Battle Is Over," 13.
6. Stela of the Vultures, fragment; found in Tello. Louvre, Paris. Source: Elizabeth Simpson in I.J. Winter, "After the Battle Is Over," 16.
7. Bronze statuette; from Megiddo, Israel. Rockefeller Archaeological Museum, Jerusalem, no. 1078. Source: NBL 1:879.
8. Gold pendant; from Urartu (eastern Turkey). Archäologische Staatssammlung, Munich, no. 1980, 6100. Source: Kellner, "Ein neues Goldmedaillon," 83.
9. Relief from Merneptah's "Israel Stela." Egyptian Museum, Cairo, no. 599. Source: Matthews and Benjamin, *Old Testament Parallels*, 92.
10. Stamp seal (left); found in Tepe Gawra, Iraq. University Museum of the University of Pennsylvania, Philadelphia, no. 37-16-357. Stamp seal (right); provenance unknown. Louvre, Paris, AO 21.392. Source: Amiet, *La Glyptique mésopotamienne archaïque*, plates 2 and 118.
11. Decorated vessel; from Warka, Mesopotamia. British Museum, London, WA 118465. Source: RLA 4:295.
12. "Two-Dogs Palette"; from Hierakonpolis, Egypt. Ashmolean Museum, Oxford, E 3924. Source: Kemp, *Ancient Egypt*, 48.
13. Marble relief; found in Intercisa, Hungary. Apparently lost. Source: LIMC 7/1:95 (no. 145a).
14. Lid of a small ivory pyxis; found in a tomb in Minet el-Beida, the sea port of Ugarit in Syria. Louvre, Paris, AO 11601. Source: *Journal of Near Eastern Studies* 51 (1992): 187.
15. Scaraboid (left); found in Tell es-Safi, Israel. Rockefeller Museum, Jerusalem, IAA J. 378. Seal impression (right); found in Wadi ed-Daliyeh, Israel. Rockefeller Museum, Jerusalem, IAA J. 748. Source: Uehlinger, "Powerful Persianisms," 144.
16. Hittite stone relief; from Carchemish, near the Euphrates in northern Syria. Archaeological Museum, Ankara. Source: Keel, *Jahwes Entgegnung an Ijob*, 124.
17. Limestone orthostat, 3.60 m high; found in Palmyra, Syria, in 1977. Now restored in the front garden of the museum of Palmyra/Tadmur, Syria. Original drawing by Manfred List.
18. Detail of the "Metternich stela"; from Alexandria. Metropolitan Museum, New York, Fletcher Fund, 1950 (50.85). Source: Budge, *The Gods of the Egyptians* 2:271.
19. Egyptian plaque. Rijksmuseum van Oudheden, Leiden, Netherlands, AED 311. Source: Budge, *From Fetish to God*, 132.

20. Egyptian cosmetic vessel in the form of a deity. Ägyptisches Museum, Berlin, no. 17882. Drawing: Duncan Stewart.
21. Egyptian stela with inscription; presumably from Der el-Medina. British Museum, London, EA 374. Source: Bierbrier, *Hieroglyphic Texts*, plate 51.
22. Egyptian stela with inscription; from Deir el-Medineh (ancient Thebes). Egyptian Museum, Berlin, no. 7354. Source: WAOB, no. 263.
23. Ivory plaque; found in Nimrud. Baghdad Museum, Iraq. Source: Keel, *Das Böcklein*, 135.
24. Stone relief; temple of the goddess Hathor in Deir el-Bahri, Egypt. Inscription: Assmann, "Die Zeugung des Sohnes," 37. Source: Keel, *Das Böcklein*, 79.
25. Ivory plaque; found in the royal residence of Ugarit, reconstructed from fragments. National Museum of Damascus. Source: U. Winter, *Frau und Göttin*, figure 409.
26. Map of the Middle East, indicating the "Fertile Crescent." Source: Breasted, *The Oriental Institute*, appendix.
27. Map of the Middle East, indicating the water resources. Source: Baly, *Geographical Companion*, 19.
28. Limestone stela with "Baal au foudre" relief; from Ugarit. Louvre, Paris, AO 15775. Source: NBL 1:224.
29. Assyrian cylinder seal. University of Fribourg, Switzerland, museum of the Institut biblique, no. 156a. Source: Keel, *Das Recht der Bilder*, 193.
30. Hittite rock relief in Ivriz near Konya, southeastern Anatolia, Turkey. Source: WAOB, no. 293.
31. Reconstruction of a detail of the Herodian temple of Jerusalem. Source: Busink, *Der Tempel von Jerusalem* 2:1119.
32. Detail of Assyrian monolithic water basin, reconstructed from fragments found in Ashur. Vorderasiatisches Museum, Berlin. Drawing by Manfred List.
33. Rubin's vase.
34. Giotto, *The Last Judgment*. Fresco in the Arena Chapel, Padua, Italy. Source: Wetzel, *Dante Alighieri*, 106.
35. Stuttgart Psalter. Württembergische Landesbibliothek, Stuttgart, Manuscript Biblia folio 23, fol. 107 verso. Source: Saxl, "The Ruthwell Cross," 11.
36. Terracotta lamp; from Italy. Museum für spätantike und byzantinische Kunst, Berlin, "Wulff 1224." Source: Koch, *Frühchristliche Kunst*, 137.
37. Title page of the English edition of John Paul II, *Catechism of the Catholic Church*.

Bibliography

Ancient Sources

Amiet, Pierre. *La Glyptique mésopotamienne archaïque.* 2d ed. Paris: Editions du Centre national de la recherche scientifique, 1980.

Assmann, Jan. *Ägyptische Hymnen und Gebete.* 2d ed. Fribourg: Universitätsverlag, 1999.

Attridge, Harold W., and Robert A. Oden. *The Syrian Goddess (De Dea Syria), Attributed to Lucian.* Missoula, Mont.: Scholars Press, 1976.

Avigad, Nahman. *Hebrew Bullae from the Time of Jeremiah.* Jerusalem: Israel Exploration Society, 1986.

Beyerlin, Walter, ed. *Near Eastern Religious Texts Relating to the Old Testament.* Translated by John Bowden. London: SCM Press, 1978.

Bierbrier, Morris L. *Hieroglyphic Texts from Egyptian Stelae.* Vol. 12. London: British Museum Press, 1993.

Borghouts, J.F. *Ancient Egyptian Magical Texts.* Leiden: Brill, 1978.

Charlesworth, James H., ed. *The Old Testament Pseudepigrapha.* 2 vols. London: Darton, Longman & Todd, 1983–85.

Cooper, Jerrold S. *Reconstructing History from Ancient Inscriptions: The Lagash-Umma Border Conflict.* Malibu, Calif.: Undena Publications, 1983. Pages 45–48: "Stela of the Vultures."

Dalley, Stephanie. *Myths from Mesopotamia.* Oxford: Oxford University Press, 1989.

Fales, Frederick M., and J. Nicholas Postgate. *Imperial Administrative Records, Part I.* SAA 7. Helsinki: Helsinki University Press, 1992.

Foster, Benjamin R. *Before the Muses: An Anthology of Akkadian Literature.* 2 vols. Bethesda, Md.: CDL Press, 1993.

Foster, John L. *Hymns, Prayers, and Songs: An Anthology of Ancient Egyptian Poetry.* Atlanta, Ga.: Scholars Press, 1995.

García Martínez, Florentino. *The Dead Sea Scrolls Translated.* Translated by Wilfred G.E. Watson. Leiden: Brill, 1994.

George, Andrew. *The Epic of Gilgamesh.* London: Penguin, 1999.

Grayson, Albert K. *Assyrian Rulers of the Early First Millennium B.C. I: 1114–859.* RIMA 2. Toronto: University of Toronto Press, 1991.

———. *Assyrian Rulers of the Early First Millennium B.C. II: 858–745.* RIMA 3. Toronto: University of Toronto Press, 1996.

Hallo, William W., ed. *The Context of Scripture.* 3 vols. Leiden: Brill, 1997–2002.

Haul, Michael. *Das Etana-Epos: Ein Mythos von der Himmelfahrt des Königs von Kisch.* Göttingen: Seminar für Keilschriftforschung, 2000.

Herodotus. *The Histories.* Translated by Walter Blanco. New York: Norton, 1992.

Hillers, Delbert R., and Eleonora Cussini. *Palmyrene Aramaic Texts.* Baltimore, Md.: Johns Hopkins University Press, 1996.

Izre'el, Shlomo. *Adapa and the South Wind.* Winona Lake, Ind.: Eisenbrauns, 2001.

Johnson, Gary J. *Early-Christian Epitaphs from Anatolia.* Atlanta, Ga.: Scholars Press, 1995.

Kaiser, Otto, ed. *Texte aus der Umwelt des Alten Testaments.* 3 vols. Gütersloh: Gütersloher Verlagshaus, 1981–97.

Keel, Othmar. *Die Welt der altorientalischen Bildsymbolik und das Alte Testament.* 2d ed. Zurich: Benziger, 1977.

Lambert, Wilfred G. "Enmeduranki and Related Matters." *Journal of Cuneiform Studies* 21 (1967): 126–38.

Langdon, Stephen. *Die neubabylonischen Königsinschriften*. Leipzig: Hinrichs, 1912.

Lichtheim, Miriam. *Ancient Egyptian Literature*. 3 vols. Berkeley: University of California Press, 1973–80.

Livingstone, Alasdair. *Court Poetry and Literary Miscellanea*. SAA 3. Helsinki: Helsinki University Press, 1989.

Matthews, Victor H., and Don C. Benjamin. *Old Testament Parallels*. 2d ed. New York: Paulist Press, 1997.

Parkinson, Richard B. *The Tale of Sinuhe and Other Ancient Egyptian Poems, 1940–1640 BC*. Oxford: Oxford University Press, 1998.

Parpola, Simo. *Letters from Assyrian and Babylonian Scholars*. SAA 10. Helsinki: Helsinki University Press, 1993.

————. *Assyrian Prophecies*. SAA 9. Helsinki: Helsinki University Press, 1997.

————, and Kazuko Watanabe. *Neo-Assyrian Treaties and Loyalty Oaths*. SAA 2. Helsinki: Helsinki University Press, 1989.

Renz, Johannes. *Die althebräischen Inschriften*. HAE 1. Darmstadt: Wissenschaftliche Buchgesellschaft, 1995.

Roth, Martha T. *Law Collections from Mesopotamia and Asia Minor*. Atlanta, Ga.: Scholars Press, 1995.

Saxo Grammaticus. *The History of the Danes: Books I–IX*. Translated by Peter Fisher. 2 vols. Cambridge: Brewer, 1979–80.

Schneemelcher, Wilhelm, ed. *New Testament Apocrypha*. 2 vols. Rev. ed. Translated by R. McL. Wilson. Cambridge: Clarke, 1991–92.

Simpson, R.S. "The Demotic Text of the Memphis Decree on the Rosetta Stone." Pages 198–200 in Richard Parkinson, *Cracking Codes: The Rosetta Stone and Decipherment*. London: British Museum Press, 1999.

Tadmor, Hayim. *The Inscriptions of Tiglath-pileser III, King of Assyria*. Jerusalem: The Israel Academy of Sciences and Humanities, 1994.

Wise, Michael O. "A Study of 4Q491c, 4Q471b, 4Q427 7 and 1QH^a 25:35–26:10." *Dead Sea Discoveries* 7 (2000): 173–219.

Wyatt, Nicolas. *Religious Texts from Ugarit*. Sheffield: Sheffield Academic Press, 1998.

Encyclopedias

Boardman, John, et al., eds. *Lexicon Iconographicum Mythologiae Classicae*. 8 vols. Zurich: Artemis, 1981–97.

Botterweck, G. Johannes, et al., eds. *Theologisches Wörterbuch zum Alten Testament*. 8 vols. Stuttgart: Kohlhammer, 1973–95.

Ebeling, Erich, et al., eds. *Reallexikon der Assyriologie*. Vol. 1– . Berlin: de Gruyter, 1932– .

Görg, Manfred, and Bernhard Lang, eds. *Neues Bibel-Lexikon*. 3 vols. Zurich: Benziger, 1991–2001.

Helck, Wolfgang, et al., eds. *Lexikon der Ägyptologie*. 7 vols. Wiesbaden: Harrassowitz, 1975–92.

Singer, Isidore, ed. *The Jewish Encyclopedia*. 12 vols. New York: Funk & Wagnalls, 1901–5.

Toorn, Karel van der, et al., eds. *Dictionary of Deities and Demons in the Bible*. 2d ed. Leiden: Brill, 1999.

Modern Works

Adam, Klaus-Peter. *Der königliche Held: Die Entsprechung von kämpfendem Gott und kämpfendem König in Psalm 18*. Neukirchen-Vluyn: Neukirchener Verlag, 2001.

Albani, Matthias. *Der eine Gott und die himmlischen Heerscharen.* Leipzig: Evangelische Verlagsanstalt, 2000.

Albertz, Rainer. *Persönliche Frömmigkeit und offizielle Religion.* Stuttgart: Calwer Verlag, 1978.

Andrae, Walter. *Das Gotteshaus und die Urformen des Bauens im alten Orient.* Berlin: Schoetz, 1930.

Andreas-Salomé, Lou. "Vom frühen Gottesdienst." *Imago* 2 (1913): 457–67.

Ashbel, D. *Die Niederschlagsverhältnisse im südlichen Libanon, in Palästina und im nördlichen Sinai.* Berlin: Viktoria, 1930.

Assmann, Jan. "Weisheit, Loyalismus und Frömmigkeit." Pages 11–72 in *Studien zu altägyptischen Lebenslehren.* Edited by Erik Hornung et al. Fribourg: Universitätsverlag, 1979.

———. "Die Zeugung des Sohnes." Pages 13–61 in Jan Assmann et al., *Funktionen und Leistungen des Mythos.* Fribourg: Universitätsverlag, 1982.

———. *Herrschaft und Heil: Politische Theologie in Altägypten, Israel und Europa.* Munich: Hanser, 2000.

Baldick, Julian. *Animal and Shaman: Ancient Religions of Central Asia.* New York: New York University Press, 2000.

Baly, Denis. *Geographical Companion to the Bible.* London: Lutterworth Press, 1963.

Barker, Margaret. *The Older Testament.* London: SPCK, 1987.

———. *The Great Angel: A Study of Israel's Second God.* London: SPCK, 1992.

———. *The Risen Lord.* Edinburgh: Clark, 1996.

Batatu, Hanna. *Syria's Peasantry, the Descendants of Its Lesser Rural Notables, and Their Politics.* Princeton, NJ: Princeton University Press, 1999.

Batto, Bernard F. "The Reed Sea: Requiescat in Pace." *Journal of Biblical Literature* 102 (1983): 27–35.

Baumgart, Norbert C. *Die Umkehr des Schöpfergottes.* Freiburg: Herder, 1999.

Berlandini, Jocelyne. "Bès en aurige dans le char du dieu-sauveur." Pages 31–55 in *Egyptian Religion: The Last Thousand Years.* Edited by Willy Clarysse et al. Leuwen: Peeters, 1998.

Bickerman, Elias J. "The Babylonian Captivity." Pages 1:342–58 in *The Cambridge History of Judaism.* Edited by W.D. Davies et al. Vol. 1– . Cambridge: Cambridge University Press, 1984– .

Block, Daniel I. *The Gods of the Nations: Studies in Ancient Near Eastern National Theology.* 2d ed. Grand Rapids, Mich.: Baker Book House, 2000.

Blumenthal, Elke. "Sinuhes persönliche Frömmigkeit." Pages 213–31 in *Jerusalem Studies in Egyptology.* Edited by Irene Shirun-Grumach. Wiesbaden: Harrassowitz, 1998.

Bogaert, Pierre-Maurice. "Montagne sainte, jardin d'Eden et sanctuaire (hiérosolymitain) dans un oracle d'Ezéchiel contre le prince de Tyr." Pages 131–53 in *Le Mythe, son langage et son message.* Edited by Henri Limet. Louvain-la-Neuve: Centre d'histoire des religions, 1983.

Boswell, James. *Life of Johnson.* Edited by R.W. Chapman. New ed. Oxford: Oxford University Press, 1970.

Boudhiba, Abdelwahab. "The Child and the Mother in Arab-Muslim Society." Pages 126–41 in *Psychological Dimensions of Near Eastern Studies.* Edited by L. Carl Brown and Norman Itzkowitz. Princeton, NJ: Darwin Press, 1977.

Breasted, James Henry. *Development of Religion and Thought in Ancient Egypt.* London: Hodder & Stoughton, 1912.

———. *Ancient Times: A History of the Early World.* Boston: Ginn, 1916.

———. *The Oriental Institute.* Chicago: University of Chicago Press, 1933.

Brueggemann, Walter. "The Kerygma of the Priestly Writers." *Zeitschrift für die alttestamentliche Wissenschaft* 84 (1972): 397–414.

Brunner, Hellmut. "Gerechtigkeit als Fundament des Thrones." *Vetus Testamentum* 8 (1958): 426–28.

Brunner-Traut, Emma. "Aspective." Pages 421–48 in Heinrich Schäfer, *Principles of Egyptian Art.* Translated by John Baines. Oxford: Clarendon Press, 1974.

————. *Frühformen des Erkennens: Aspektive im alten Ägypten.* 3d ed. Darmstadt: Wissenschaftliche Buchgesellschaft, 1996.

Budge, Ernest A. Wallis. *The Gods of the Egyptians.* 2 vols. London: Methuen, 1904.

————. *From Fetish to God in Ancient Egypt.* London: Oxford University Press, 1934.

Bühner, Jan-Adolf. *Der Gesandte und sein Weg im vierten Evangelium.* Tübingen: Mohr, 1977.

Busink, Theodor A. *Der Tempel von Jerusalem: Von Salomo bis Herodes.* 2 vols. Leiden: Brill, 1970–80.

Cancik, Hubert. "Christus Imperator: Zum Gebrauch militärischer Titulaturen im römischen Herrscherkult und im Christentum." Pages 112–30 in *Der Name Gottes.* Edited by Heinrich von Stietencron. Düsseldorf: Patmos, 1975.

Caquot, André. "Israelite Perceptions of Wisdom and Strength in the Light of the Ras Shamra Texts." Pages 25–33 in *Israelite Wisdom.* Edited by John G. Gammie et al. Missoula, Mont.: Scholars Press, 1978.

————. "Cantique de la mer et miracle de la mer." Pages 67–85 in *La protohistoire d'Israël.* Edited by Ernest-Marie Laperrousaz. Paris: Le Cerf, 1990.

Casson, Lionel. *Travel in the Ancient World.* Baltimore, Md.: Johns Hopkins University Press, 1994.

Castriota, David. *The Ara Pacis Augustae and the Imagery of Abundance in Later Greek and Early Roman Imperial Art.* Princeton, NJ: Princeton University Press, 1995.

Cohn, Norman. *Cosmos, Chaos and the World to Come.* 2d ed. New Haven, Conn.: Yale University Press, 2001.

Collins, John J. *Daniel.* Hermeneia. Minneapolis: Fortress Press, 1993.

Cornelius, Izak. "Anat and Qudshu as the 'Mistress of Animals': Aspects of the Iconography of the Canaanite Goddesses." *Studi epigrafi e linguistici sul Vicino Oriente antico* 10 (1993): 21–45.

Couroyer, Bernard. "Le chemin de vie en Egypte et en Israël." *Revue biblique* 56 (1949): 412–32.

Craffert, Pieter F. "Jesus and the Shamanic Complex." *Neotestamentica* 33 (1999): 321–42.

Dahrendorf, Ralf. *Essays in the Theory of Society.* Stanford, Calif.: Stanford University Press, 1968.

Dalman, Gustaf. *Arbeit und Sitte in Palästina.* 7 vols. Repr., Hildesheim: Olms, 1964.

Day, Peggy L. "Anat: Ugarit's Mistress of Animals." *Journal of Near Eastern Studies* 51 (1992): 181–90.

DeConick, April D. *Voices of the Mystics: Early Christian Discourse in the Gospels of John and Thomas and Other Ancient Christian Literature.* Sheffield: Sheffield Academic Press, 2001.

Delekat, Lienhard. "Yáho-Yahwáe und die alttestamentlichen Gottesnamenkorrekturen." Pages 23–75 in *Tradition und Glaube.* Edited by Gert Jeremias et al. Göttingen: Vandenhoeck & Ruprecht, 1971.

Dequeker, Luc. "Green Herbage and Trees Bearing Fruit (Gen 1, 28–30; 9, 1–3): Vegetarianism or Predominance of Man over the Animals?", *Bijdragen* 38 (1977): 118–27.

Deutsch, Nathaniel. *Guardians of the Gate: Angelic Vice-Regency in Late Antiquity.* Leiden: Brill, 1999. Pages 151–57: "Jesus."

Dion, Paul E. "YHWH as Storm-God and Sun-God: The Double Legacy of Egypt and Canaan as Reflected in Psalm 104." *Zeitschrift für die alttestaentliche Wissenschaft* 103 (1991): 43–71.

Drews, Robert. *The End of the Bronze Age: Changes in Warfare and the Catastrophe ca. 1200 B.C.* Princeton: Princeton University Press, 1993.

Drijvers, Han J.W. "Sanctuaries and Social Safety: The Iconography of Divine Peace in Hellenistic Syria." Pages 65–75 in *Visible Religion.* Vol. 1. Edited by Hans G. Kippenberg et al. Leiden: Brill, 1982.

Dubuisson, Daniel. "Le roi indo-européen et la synthèse des trois fonctions." *Annales économies sociétés civilisations* 33 (1978): 21–34.

Dumézil, Georges. *Horace et les Curiaces.* Paris: Gallimard, 1942. Pages 11–33: "Furor."

————. *Rituels indo-européens à Rome.* Paris: Klincksieck, 1954.

————. *Archaic Roman Religion*. 2 vols. Translated by Philip Krapp. Chicago: University of Chicago Press, 1970.

————. *The Destiny of the Warrior*. Translated by Alf Hiltebeitel. Chicago: University of Chicago Press, 1970.

————. *Les Dieux souverains des Indo-Européens*. Paris: Gallimard, 1977. Pages 55–85: "Mitra—Varuna."

————. *Mythe et épopée*. Vol. 3. 3d ed. Paris: Gallimard, 1981. Pages 338–61: "L'idéologie trifonctionelle des Indo-Européens et la Bible."

————. *La Courtisane et les seigneurs colorés*. Paris: Gallimard, 1983. Pages 239–43: "Les titres messianiques d'Isaïe IX,5."

————. *Mythe et épopée*. Vol. 1. 2d ed. Paris: Gallimard, 1986.

Durkheim, Emile. *The Elementary Forms of Religious Life*. Translated by Karen E. Fields. New York: Free Press, 1995.

Eliade, Mircea. *The Myth of the Eternal Return*. Translated by Willard R. Trask. 2d ed. Princeton, NJ: Princeton University Press, 1965.

Evans-Pritchard, Edward E. *The Nuer: A Description of the Modes of Livelihood and Political Institutions of a Nilotic People*. Oxford: Oxford University Press, 1940.

Feucht, Erika. *Das Kind im alten Ägypten*. Frankfurt: Campus, 1995.

Finney, Paul Corby. *The Invisible God: The Earliest Christians on Art*. New York: Oxford University Press, 1994.

Fischer, Balthasar. "Conculcabis leonem et draconem: Eine deutungsgeschichtliche Studie zur Verwendung von Psalm 90 in der Quadragesima." *Zeitschrift für katholische Theologie* 80 (1958): 421–29.

Fletcher-Louis, Crispin H.T. "The High Priest as Divine Mediator in the Hebrew Bible." *Society of Biblical Literature Seminar Papers Series* 36 (1997): 161–93.

Fosdick, Harry Emerson. *A Guide to Understanding the Bible*. New York: Harper, 1938.

————. *The Modern Use of the Bible*. New York: Macmillan, 1961.

Frankfort, Henri, et al. *Before Philosophy: The Intellectual Adventure of Ancient Man*. Harmondsworth: Penguin, 1951.

Frazer, James George. *Folk-Lore in the Old Testament*. 3 vols. London: Macmillan, 1918.

Freud, Sigmund. *Gesammelte Werke: Chronologisch geordnet*. Edited by Anna Freud. 17 vols. London: Imago, 1940–52.

Fuchs, Gisela. *Mythos und Hiobdichtung*. Stuttgart: Kohlhammer, 1993.

Fürer-Haimendorf, Christoph von. *The Chenchus: Jungle Folk of the Deccan*. London: Macmillan, 1943.

Gamkrelidze, T.V., and V.V. Ivanov. *Indo-European and the Indo-Europeans*. Berlin: de Gruyter, 1995.

Geertz, Clifford. *Local Knowledge*. New York: Basic Books, 1983. Pages 73–93: "Common Sense as a Cultural System."

Geller, Stephen A. "The God of the Covenant." Pages 273–319 in *One God or Many? Concepts of Divinity in the Ancient World*. Edited by Barbara N. Porter. Bethesda, Md.: CDL Press, 2000.

Gese, Hartmut. "Die Religionen Altsyriens." Pages 1–232 in *Religionen Altsyriens, Altarabiens und der Mandäer*. Edited by Hartmut Gese et al. Stuttgart: Kohlhammer, 1970.

Gnuse, Robert. "The Emergence of Monotheism in Ancient Israel: A Survey of Recent Scholarship." *Religion* 29 (1999): 315–36.

Gordon, Cyrus H. *A Scholar's Odyssey*. Atlanta, Ga.: Society of Biblical Literature, 2000.

Gorssen, Leo. "La cohérence de la conception de Dieu dans l'Ecclésiaste." *Ephemerides theologiae Lovanienses* 46 (1970): 282–324.

Grelot, Pierre. "La géographie mythique d'Hénoch et ses sources orientales." *Revue biblique* 65 (1958): 33–69.

Groß, Walter. *Studien zur Priesterschrift und zu alttestamentlichen Gottesbildern*. Stuttgart: Katholisches Bibelwerk, 1999.

Haas, Volkert. *Geschichte der hethitischen Religion.* Handbuch der Orientalistik. Leiden: Brill, 1994.

Habel, Norman C. *The Land Is Mine: Six Biblical Land Ideologies.* Minneapolis: Fortress Press, 1995.

Halpern, Baruch. *The Constitution of the Monarchy in Israel.* Chico, Calif.: Scholars Press, 1981.

Handy, Lowell K. *Among the Host of Heaven: The Syro-Palestinian Pantheon as Bureaucracy.* Winona Lake, Ind.: Eisenbrauns, 1994.

Heintz, Jean-Georges. "Des textes sémitiques à la bible hébraïque." Pages 127–56 in *Le comparatisme en histoire des religions.* Edited by François Boespflug et al. Paris: Le Cerf, 1997.

Herrmann, Siegfried. *Gesammelte Studien zur Geschichte und Theologie des Alten Testaments.* Munich: Kaiser, 1986.

Hopkins, David C. *The Highlands of Canaan: Agricultural Life in the Early Iron Age.* Sheffield: Almond Press, 1985.

Hörig, Monika. *Dea Syria: Studien zur religiösen Tradition der Fruchtbarkeitsgöttin in Vorderasien.* Kevelaer: Butzon & Bercker, 1979.

Hornung, Erik. *Geist der Pharaonenzeit.* 2d ed. Zurich: Artemis & Winkler, 1999. Pages 147–63: "Geschichte als Fest."

Horst, Pieter W. van der. "Moses' Throne Vision in Ezekiel the Dramatist." *Journal of Jewish Studies* 34 (1983): 21–29.

Ingold, Tim. *The Appropriation of Nature: Essays on Human Ecology and Social Relations.* Manchester: Manchester University Press, 1986. Pages 243–76: "Hunting, Sacrifice and the Domestication of Animals."

Jacobsen, Thorkild. "Mesopotamia: The Good Life." Pages 217–34 in *Before Philosophy: The Intellectual Adventure of Ancient Man.* Edited by Henri Frankfort et al. Harmondsworth: Penguin, 1951.

———. *The Treasures of Darkness: A History of Mesopotamian Religion.* New Haven, Conn.: Yale University Press, 1976.

James, William. *The Varieties of Religious Experience.* Edited by Martin E. Marty. Harmondsworth: Penguin, 1982.

Jeremias, Joachim. *The Parables of Jesus.* 3d ed. London: SCM Press, 1972.

John Paul II, ed. *Catechism of the Catholic Church.* 2d ed. Vatican City: Libreria Editrice Vaticana, 2000.

Jüngling, Hans-Winfried. "Was anders ist Gott für den Menschen, wenn nicht sein Vater und seine Mutter? Zu einer Doppelmetapher der religiösen Sprache." Pages 365–86 in *Ein Gott allein?* Edited by Walter Dietrich et al. Fribourg: Universitätsverlag, 1994.

Kämmerer, Thomas R. "Die Stellung der Menschen zu seinen Göttern: Vom sumerischen Kollektivismus zum babylonischen Individualismus." Pages 37–44 in *Religionen in einer sich ändernden Welt.* Edited by Manfried Dietrich. Münster: Ugarit-Verlag, 1999.

Kang, Sa-Moon. *Divine War in the Old Testament and in the Ancient Near East.* Berlin: de Gruyter, 1989.

Keel, Othmar. *Wirkmächtige Siegeszeichen im Alten Testament.* Fribourg: Universitätsverlag, 1974.

———. *Jahwes Entgegnung an Ijob.* Göttingen: Vandenhoeck & Ruprecht, 1978.

———. *Das Böcklein in der Milch seiner Mutter und Verwandtes.* Fribourg: Universitätsverlag, 1980.

———. *Das Recht der Bilder, gesehen zu werden.* Fribourg: Universitätsverlag, 1992.

———. "Powerful Symbols of Victory." *Journal of Northwest Semitic Languages* 25 (1999): 205–40.

———, and Christoph Uehlinger. "Jahwe und die Sonnengottheit von Jerusalem." Pages 269–306 in *Ein Gott allein?* Edited by Walter Dietrich and Martin A. Klopfenstein. Fribourg: Universitätsverlag, 1994.

Keen, Maurice. *Chivalry.* New Haven, Conn.: Yale University Press, 1984.

Kellner, Hans-Jörg. "Ein neues Goldmedaillon aus Urartu." *Archäologische Mitteilungen aus Iran* 13 (1980): 83–89.

Kemp, Barry J. *Ancient Egypt*. London: Routledge, 1989.

Kirk, G.S. *Myth: Its Meaning and Functions in Ancient and Other Cultures*. 2d ed. Cambridge: Cambridge University Press, 1971.

Knigge, Carsten. "Überlegungen zum Verhältnis von altägyptischer Hymnik und alttestamentlicher Psalmendichtung," *Protokolle zur Bibel* 9 (2000): 93–122.

Knoppers, Gary N. "Prayer and Propaganda: Solomon's Dedication of the Temple and the Deuteronomist's Program." *Catholic Biblical Quarterly* 57 (1995): 229–54.

Koch, Guntram. *Frühchristliche Kunst*. Stuttgart: Kohlhammer, 1995.

Köhler, Ludwig. *Der hebräische Mensch*. Tübingen: Mohr, 1953.

Kötting, Bernhard. "Tier und Heiligtum." *Jahrbuch für Antike und Christentum. Ergänzungsband* 1 (1964): 209–14.

Kramer, Samuel S., and John Maier. *Myths of Enki, the Crafty God*. New York: Oxford University Press, 1989.

Lang, Bernhard. "Ein babylonisches Motiv in Israels Schöpfungsmythologie." *Biblische Zeitschrift* 27 (1983): 236–37.

———. *Monotheism and the Prophetic Minority*. Sheffield: Almond, 1983.

———. *Wisdom and the Book of Proverbs: A Hebrew Goddess Redefined*. New York: Pilgrim Press, 1986.

Lebrun, R. "L'Anatolie et le monde phénicien du Xe au IVe siècle av. J.-C." *Studia Phoenicia* 5 (1985/87): 23–33.

Le Jan, Régine. "Frankish Giving of Arms and Rituals of Power." Pages 281–309 in *Rituals of Power*. Edited by Frans Theuws et al. Leiden: Brill, 2000.

Lemche, Niels P. "From Patronage Society to Patronage Society." Pages 106–20 in *The Origins of the Ancient Israelite States*. Edited by Volkmar Fritz et al. Sheffield: Sheffield Academic Press, 1996.

Lévi-Strauss, Claude. "Les limites de la notion de structure en ethnologie." Pages 40–45 in *Sens et usages du terme structure dans les sciences humaines et sociales*. Edited by Roger Bastide. The Hague: Mouton, 1962.

Levin, Saul. *Semitic and Indo-European: The Principal Etymologies*. Amsterdam: Benjamins, 1995.

Levine, Etan. "The Land of Milk and Honey." *Journal for the Study of the Old Testament* 87 (2000): 43–57.

Lincoln, Bruce. *Priests, Warriors, and Cattle*. Berkeley: University of California Press, 1981.

———. *Myth, Cosmos, and Society: Indo-European Themes of Creation and Destruction*. Cambridge, Mass.: Harvard University Press, 1986.

Lipiński, Edward. "The King's Arbitration in Ancient Near Eastern Folk-Tale." Pages 137–42 in *Keilschriftliche Literturen: Ausgewählte Vorträge der XXXII. Rencontre assyriologique internationale*. Edited by Karl Hecker and Walter Sommerfeld. Berlin: Reimer, 1986.

Lohfink, Norbert. *Studien zum Pentateuch*. Stuttgart: Katholisches Bibelwerk, 1988.

———. *Theology of the Pentateuch*. Translated by Linda M. Maloney. Edinburgh: Clark, 1994.

Loukianoff, Grégoire. "Le dieu Ched: l'évolution de son culte dans l'ancienne Egypte." *Bulletin de l'Institut d'Egypte* 13 (1931): 67–84.

Lutfiyya, Abulla M. *Baytîn: A Jordanian Village*. The Hague: Mouton, 1966.

Luther, Martin. *Werke. Kritische Gesamtausgabe*. Vols. 1– . Weimar: Böhlau, 1883– ("Weimarer Ausgabe").

Lutterbach, Hubertus. "Tiere—In allem gehorsam wie Mönche: Die Vorstellung vom kosmischen Frieden im Christentum." *Saeculum* 51 (2000): 294–331.

Malamat, Abraham. *Mari and the Bible*. Leiden: Brill, 1998.

Mann, Thomas W. *Divine Presence and Guidance in Israelite Traditions*. Baltimore, Md.: Johns Hopkins University Press, 1977.

Martin, Ernest L. *The Temples that Jerusalem Forgot*. Portland, Oreg.: Associates for Scriptural Knowledge, 2000.

Marty, Martin E. *Modern American Religion*. Vols. 1– . Chicago: University of Chicago Press, 1986– .

Mayeur-Jaouen, Catherine. "Crocodiles et saints du Nil: du talisman au miracle." *Revue de l'histoire des religions* 217 (2000): 733–60.

McDonough, Sean M. *YHWH at Patmos*. Tübingen: Mohr Siebeck, 1999.

McKane, William. *Proverbs: A New Approach*. London: SCM Press, 1970.

Middleton, John. *Lugbara Religion*. 2d ed. Washington, DC: Smithsonian Institution, 1987.

Moberly, R. Walter L. *The Old Testament of the Old Testament: Patriarchal Narratives and Mosaic Yahwism*. Minneapolis, Minn.: Fortress Press, 1992.

Mosca, Paul G. "Ugarit and Daniel 7: A Missing Link." *Biblica* 67 (1986): 496–517.

Nickelsburg, George W.E. *Resurrection, Immortality, and Eternal Life in Intertestamental Judaism*. Cambridge, Mass.: Harvard University Press, 1972.

Niehr, Herbert. "In Search of YHWH's Cult Statue in the First Temple." Pages 73–95 in *The Image and the Book*. Edited by Karel van der Toorn. Leuven: Peeters, 1997.

Nietzsche, Friedrich. *The Gay Science*. Trans. Walter Kaufmann. New York: Vintage Books, 1974.

Oded, Bustenay. *Mass Deportations and Deportees in the Neo-Assyrian Empire*. Wiesbaden: Reichert, 1979.

Oeming, Manfred. "Ich habe ein Lösegeld gefunden! (Hi 33,23)." Pages 89–101 in *Metapher und Wirklichkeit*. Edited by Reinhold Bernhardt et al. Göttingen: Vandenhoeck & Ruprecht, 1999.

O'Neill, John C. "Who Is Comparable to Me in My Glory? 4Q491 Fragment 11 (4Q491C) and the New Testament." *Novum Testamentum* 42 (2000): 24–38.

Oppenheim, A. Leo. "The City of Assur in 714 B.C." *Journal of Near Eastern Studies* 19 (1960): 133–47.

———. *Ancient Mesopotamia*. Rev. ed. Chicago: University of Chicago Press, 1977.

Osten-Sacken, Elisabeth von der. *Der Ziegen-"Dämon."* Kevelaer: Butzon & Bercker, 1992.

———. *Neo-Assyrian Toponyms*. Kevelaer: Butzon & Bercker, 1970.

Otto, Eckart. "Der Ackerbau in Juda im Spiegel der alttestamentlichen Rechtsüberlieferungen." Pages 229–36 in *Landwirtschaft im alten Orient: 41. Rencontre assyriologique internationale*. Edited by Horst Klengel et al. Berlin: Reimer, 1999.

———. *Das Deuteronomium: Politische Theologie und Rechtsreform in Juda und Assyrien*. Berlin: de Gruyter, 1999.

Parpola, Simo. "The Assyrian Tree of Life." *Journal of Near Eastern Studies* 52 (1993): 161–208.

———. *Neo-Assyrian Toponyms*. Kevelaer: Butzon & Bercker, 1970.

Paul, Shalom M. *Amos*. Hermeneia. Minneapolis, Minn.: Fortress Press, 1991.

Pettazzoni, Raffaele. *The All-Knowing God: Researches into Early Religion and Culture*. Translated by H.J. Rose. London: Methuen, 1956.

Pilch, John J. "The Transfiguration of Jesus." Pages 47–64 in *Modelling Early Christianity*. Edited by Philip F. Esler. London: Routledge, 1995.

Pongratz-Leisten, Beate. *Herrschaftswissen in Mesopotamien: Formen der Kommunikation zwischen Gott und König im 2. und 1. Jahrtausend v. Chr.* Helsinki: Neo-Assyrian Text Corpus Project, 1999.

Porton, Gary G. "Grape-Clusters in Jewish Literature and Art of Late Antiquity." *Journal of Jewish Studies* 27 (1976): 159–76.

Pound, Ezra. *Literary Essays*. Edited by T.S. Eliot. London: Faber & Faber, 1954.

Propp, William H.C. "Monotheism and 'Moses': The Problem of Early Israelite Religion." *Ugarit-Forschungen* 31 (1999): 537–75.

Quaegebeur, Jan. "Divinités égyptiennes sur des animaux dangereux." Pages 131–43 in *L'animal, l'homme, le dieu dans le Proche-Orient ancien*. Edited by Philippe Borgeaud et al. Leuven: Peeters, 1984.

Rad, Gerhard von. *Gesammelte Studien zum Alten Testament*. 2 vols. Munich: Kaiser, 1958–73.

————. *Holy War in Ancient Israel*. Translated by Marva J. Dawn. Grand Rapids, Mich.: Eerdmans, 1991.

Redfield, Robert. *Peasant Society and Culture*. Chicago: University of Chicago Press, 1956.

Römheld, Diethard. *Wege der Weisheit: Die Lehren Amenemopes und Proverbien 22,17–24, 22*. Berlin: de Gruyter, 1989.

Rose, Martin. "Entmilitarisierung des Krieges? Erwägungen zu den Patriarchen-Erzählungen der Genesis." *Biblische Zeitschrift* 20 (1976): 197–211.

Rösel, Martin. *Adonaj—warum Gott "Herr" genannt wird*. Tübingen: Mohr Siebeck, 2000.

Rubio, Gonzalo. "On the Alleged Pre-Sumerian Substratum." *Journal of Cuneiform Studies* 51 (1999): 1–16.

Sadek, Ashraf I. *Popular Religion in Egypt during the New Kingdom*. Hildesheim: Gerstenberg, 1987.

Sahin, Mustafa. "Neue Beobachtungen zum Felsrelief von Ivriz/Konya." *Anatolian Studies* 49 (1999): 165–76.

Saxl, Friedrich. "The Ruthwell Cross." *Journal of the Warburg and Courtauld Institutes* 6 (1943): 1–19.

Schipper, Berd Ulrich. *Israel und Ägypten in der Königszeit*. Fribourg: Universitätsverlag, 1999.

Schmid, Konrad. *Erzväter und Exodus: Untersuchungen zur doppelten Begründung der Ursprünge Israels*. Neukirchen-Vluyn: Neukirchener Verlag, 1999.

Selms, Adrian van. "Temporary Henotheism." Pages 341–48 in *Symbolae Biblicae et Mesopotamicae F.M.Th. de Liagre Böhl Dedicatae*. Edited by Martinus A. Beek et al. Leiden: Brill, 1973.

Skinner, John. *Prophecy and Religion*. Cambridge: Cambridge University Press, 1922.

Smith, George Adam. *Jerusalem: The Topography, Economics and History from the Earliest Times to A.D. 70*. 2 vols. London: Hodder & Stoughton, 1907–8.

————. *The Historical Geography of the Holy Land*. London: Collins, 1966.

Smith, Jonathan Z. *Drudgery Divine. On the Comparison of Early Christianity and the Religions of Late Antiquity*. London: School of Oriental and African Studies, 1990.

Smith, Morton. *Palestinian Parties and Politics that Shaped the Old Testament*. 2d ed. London: SCM Press, 1987.

————. *Studies in the Cult of Yahweh*. Edited by Shaye J.D. Cohen. 2 vols. Leiden: Brill, 1996.

Spina, Frank A. "The 'Ground' for Cain's Rejection (Gen 4)." *Zeitschrift für die alttestamentliche Wissenschaft* 104 (1992): 319–32.

Starbuck, Edwin D. *The Psychology of Religion*. London: Scott, 1899.

Sundén, Hjalmar. *Die Religion und die Rollen*. Berlin: Töpelmann, 1966.

Sweet, Ronald F.G. "The Sage in Akkadian Literature." Pages 45–65 in *The Sage in Israel and the Ancient Near East*. Edited by John G. Gammie et al. Winona Lake, Ind.: Eisenbrauns, 1990.

Taha, M.F., et al. "The Climate of the Near East." Pages 183–255 in *World Survey of Climatology*. Edited by H.E. Landsberg. Vol. 9. Amsterdam: Elsevier, 1981.

Toorn, Karel van der. "The Babylonian New Year Festival." Pages 331–44 in *Congress Volume Leuven 1989*. Edited by John A. Emerton. Leiden: Brill, 1991.

————. *Family Religion in Babylonia, Syria and Israel*. Leiden: Brill, 1996.

————. "Mesopotamian Prophecy between Immanence and Transcendence." Pages 71–87 in *Prophecy in Its Ancient Near Eastern Context*. Edited by Martti Nissinen. Atlanta, Ga.: Society of Biblical Literature, 2000.

Tsumura, David Toshio. *The Earth and the Waters in Genesis 1 and 2*. Sheffield: Sheffield Academic Press, 1989.

Uehlinger, Christoph. "Powerful Persianisms in Glyptic Iconography of Persian Period Palestine." Pages 134–82 in *The Crisis of Israelite Religion*. Edited by Bob Becking et al. Leiden: Brill, 1999.

Vittmann, Günter. *Altägyptische Wegmetaphorik*. Wien: Institut für Ägyptologie, 1999.

Vorländer, Hermann. "Christus als persönlicher Gott im Neuen Testament." *Kerygma und Dogma* 21 (1975): 120–46.

———. *Mein Gott: Die Vorstellung vom persönlichen Gott im Alten Orient und im Alten Testament*. Kevelaer: Butzon & Bercker, 1975.

Wälchli, Stefan. *Der weise König Salomo*. Stuttgart: Kohlhammer, 1999.

Weber, Ferdinand. *Jüdische Theologie auf Grund des Talmud und verwandter Schriften*. Leipzig: Dörffling & Franke, 1897.

Weber, Max. *Ancient Judaism*. Translated by Hans H. Gerth et al. Glencoe, Ill.: Free Press, 1952.

Weippert, Manfred. *Jahwe und die anderen Götter*. Tübingen: Mohr Siebeck, 1997. Pages 71–97: "Heiliger Krieg in Israel und Assyrien."

———. "Tier und Mensch in einer menschenarmen Welt." Pages 35–55 in *Ebenbild Gottes—Herrscher über die Welt*. Edited by Hans-Peter Mathys. Neukirchen-Vluyn: Neukirchener Verlag, 1998.

Wesley, John. *The Works. With a Life of the Author, by John Beecham*. 11th ed. 14 vols. London: Mason, 1856.

Westermann, Claus. *Elements of Old Testament Theology*. Translated by Douglas W. Stott. Atlanta, Ga.: John Knox Press, 1982.

Wetzel, Christoph. *Dante Alighieri*. Salzburg: Andreas & Andreas, 1979.

Widengren, Geo. *The Ascension of the Apostle and the Heavenly Book*. Uppsala Universitets Årsskrift 1950, no. 7. Uppsala: Lundequist, 1950.

———. *Kungar, Profeter och Harlekiner*. Stockholm: Aldis/Bonnier, 1961.

———. "Leitende Ideen und Quellen der iranischen Apokalyptik." Pages 77–162 in *Apocalypticism in the Mediterranean World and the Near East*. Edited by David Hellholm. Tübingen: Mohr, 1983.

Wilcke, Claus. *Wer las und schrieb in Babylonien und Assyrien: Überlegungen zur Literalität im alten Zweistromland*. Munich: Bayerische Akademie der Wissenschaften, 2000.

Winter, Irene J. "*After the Battle Is Over*: The Stele of the Vultures and the Beginning of Historical Narrative in the Art of the Ancient Near East." Pages 11–32 in *Pictorial Narrative in Antiquity and the Middle Ages*. Edited by Herbert L. Kessler et al. Washington: National Gallery of Art, 1985.

Winter, Urs. *Frau und Göttin: Exegetische und ikonographische Studien zum weiblichen Gottesbild*. Fribourg: Universitätsverlag, 1983.

Wirth, Eugen. *Syrien. Eine geographische Landeskunde*. Darmstadt: Wissenschaftliche Buchgesellschaft, 1971.

Witherington, Ben. *Jesus the Seer*. Peabody, Mass.: Hendrickson, 1999.

Wyatt, Nicolas. "Near Eastern Echoes of Aryan Tradition." *Studi e materiali di storia delle religioni* 55/NS 13 (1989): 5–29.

———. "David's Census and the Tripartite Theory." *Vetus Testamentum* 40 (1990): 352–60.

———. "Arms and the King: The Earliest Allusions to the Chaoskampf Motif and Their Implications for the Interpretation of the Ugaritic and Biblical Traditions." Pages 833–82 in *Und Mose schrieb dieses Lied auf: Studien zum Alten Testament und zum Alten Orient*. Edited by Manfried Dietrich et al. Münster: Ugarit-Verlag, 1998.

———. "Degrees of Divinity: Some Mythical and Ritual Aspects of West Semitic Kingship." *Ugarit-Forschungen* 31 (1999): 853–87.

Zadok, Ran. "A Prosopographic and Ethno–Linguistic Characterization of Southern Canaan in the Second Millennium B.C." Pages 97–145 in *Mutual Influences of Peoples and Cultures in the Ancient Near East*. Edited by Meir Malul. Haifa: The Reuben and Edith Hecht Museum, 1996.

Zohary, Michael, and Maria Hopf. *Domestication of Plants in the Old World*. 2d ed. Oxford: Oxford University Press, 1983.

Index

Aberkios inscription, 194
Adad
  as war-god, 54
  as weather-god, 56, 146, 151, 186–87
Adapa, myth of, 22–23, 212
agriculture
  in Fertile Crescent, 141, 143–44 (*see also* irrigation farming)
  Hebrew dislike for, 156–57
Allât (goddess), 88–89
Amenemope, Instruction of, 211
  influence of, on Bible, 118–19, 121, 123, 124
Amos, book of: God as Lord of the Harvest in, 162
Andreas-Salomé, Lou, 132
animals
  divine care for, 81–86
  domestic, 81, 83
  and Jesus, 107–8
  killing of, 91–98
  peace among, 79–80, 86–90
  royal rule over, 93
  See also Lord of the Animals
anthropological parallels
  Chenchus, 91–92, 94
  circumboreal peoples, 95–96
  hunter-gatherers, 77
  Lugbara, 122
  Nuer, 157–58
  peasant anthropology, 157, 163
  shamanism, 18–19
aphoristic thinking, 123
apocalypse
  of judgment, 68–72
  of war, 65–67, 71–72
Ara Pacis (temple in Rome), 153
ark, 50–51
Arrian, 88
ascent to heaven. *See* heavenly journey
Ashur (Assyrian god), 55, 160, 185, 187–88
Ashurbanipal (king of Assyria), 213
  diviners at court of, 17
  esoteric learning of, 17
  personal gods of, 128, 129–30
aspective thinking, 71, 123 (*see also* Brunner-Traut)

Aten (Egyptian god)
  associated with monotheism, 210
  influence on Israel of, 154, 187
Atrahasis Epic, 212
  deluge story in, 7–8
  temporary monolatry in, 186–87

Baal (god)
  and chaos battle, 57–58, 60–61
  iconography of, 147 (fig. 28)
  meaning of name of, 207
  weather-god, 146, 149–50, 207, 212
Barker, Margaret: on "Older Testament," 24
Bes (god), 106–7
blessing
  in Genesis, 83, 104, 181–82
  in Job, 102, 104
  notion of, explained, 13, 83, 155–56
Bonhoeffer, Dietrich, 128
book of life, 40
book religion, 41, 42
Book of the Virgin Mary's Birth, 107–8
Boudhiba, Abdelwahab, 133
Breasted, James Henry
  on Fertile Crescent, 141, 142 (fig. 26 map)
  on personal piety, 109, 112
Bronze Age, 17
  dating of, 209
  historical summary of, 210–12
Brunner-Traut, Emma: on aspective thought, 71, 123
Bühner, Jan, 196

Carlyle, Thomas: on hero-worship, 113
chaos battle (myth), 57–62
  related to politics, 60–61
Chenchus (Indian tribe), 91–92, 94
Christ. *See* Jesus Christ
Constantine (emperor), 61, 192
covenant: between God and Israel, 38–40, 41
Creator, creation, 24, 25, 27–28, 59, 83, 85
  called Elohim, 25, 200
  superior to Yahweh, 28–29, 202

Daniel (prophet)
  as diviner, 17